Territoriality in Christian Faith and Mission

American Society of Missiology Monograph Series

Chair of Series Editorial Committee, James R. Krabill

The ASM Monograph Series provides a forum for publishing quality dissertations and studies in the field of missiology. Collaborating with Pickwick Publications—a division of Wipf and Stock Publishers of Eugene, Oregon—the American Society of Missiology selects high quality dissertations and other monographic studies that offer research materials in mission studies for scholars, mission and church leaders, and the academic community at large. The ASM seeks scholarly work for publication in the series that throws light on issues confronting Christian world mission in its cultural, social, historical, biblical, and theological dimensions.

Missiology is an academic field that brings together scholars whose professional training ranges from doctoral-level preparation in areas such as Scripture, history and sociology of religions, anthropology, theology, international relations, interreligious interchange, mission history, inculturation, and church law. The American Society of Missiology, which sponsors this series, is an ecumenical body drawing members from Independent and Ecumenical Protestant, Catholic, Orthodox, and other traditions. Members of the ASM are united by their commitment to reflect on and do scholarly work relating to both mission history and the present-day mission of the church. The ASM Monograph Series aims to publish works of exceptional merit on specialized topics, with particular attention given to work by younger scholars, the dissemination and publication of which is difficult under the economic pressures of standard publishing models.

Persons seeking information about the ASM or the guidelines for having their dissertations considered for publication in the ASM Monograph Series should consult the Society's website—www.asmweb.org.

Members of the ASM Monograph Committee who approved this book are:

Recently Published in the ASM Monograph Series

George Shakwelele, *Explaining the Practice of Elevating an Ancestor for Veneration*

Peter T. Lee, *Hybridizing Mission: Intercultural Social Dynamics among Christian Workers on Multicultural Teams in North Africa*

Territoriality in Christian Faith and Mission

Esther M. Theonugraha

American Society of Missiology Monograph Series 77

PICKWICK *Publications* • Eugene, Oregon

TERRITORIALITY IN CHRISTIAN FAITH AND MISSION

American Society of Missiology Monograph Series 77

Pickwick Publications
An Imprint of Wipf and Stock Publishers
199 W. 8th Ave., Suite 3
Eugene, OR 97401

www.wipfandstock.com

PAPERBACK ISBN: 979-8-3852-5654-9
HARDCOVER ISBN: 979-8-3852-5655-6
EBOOK ISBN: 979-8-3852-5656-3

Cataloging-in-Publication data:

Names: Theonugraha, Esther M., author.

Title: Territoriality in Christian faith and mission / Esther M. Theonugraha.

Description: Eugene, OR: Pickwick Publications, 2026. | American Society of Missiology Monograph Series 77. | Includes bibliographical references.

Identifiers: ISBN: 979-8-3852-5654-9 (PAPERBACK). | ISBN: 979-8-3852-5655-6 (HARDCOVER). | ISBN: 979-8-3852-5656-3 (EBOOK).

Subjects: LCSH: Missions—Theory. | Human territoriality. | Human geography.

Classification: BV2061 T51 2026 (print). | BV2061 (epub).

VERSION NUMBER 03/13/26

To Isaiah and Nora.

How I enjoy exploring God's vast and exciting world through your eyes!

And to Felix, for all the places we may go, you will always be my home.

Contents

Illustrations

Acknowledgments

THE JOURNEY THAT LED to this work has been one of overflowing grace, and I am deeply grateful. I have been blessed to know scholars who are far wiser and more insightful than I will ever be. Among them are Don Grigorenko, Jeanette Hsieh, Paul Weston, Robert Priest, Craig Ott, Harold Netland, Robert Sack, Andrew Walls, Lamin Sanneh, and most of all, Tite Tiénou. I hope to not disappoint you too much. Along the way, thoughtful colleagues and conversation partners have influenced both my thinking and the formation of this project. Thank you to Ghada Talhammi, Alice Ott, Greg Carlson, Daniel Hartman, Yamil Acevedo, Zachs Gaiya, Rhonda Haynes, and David Greenlee.

I am deeply grateful for friends and family whose encouragement sustained me, whose humor lightened the work, and whose love made it possible to see it through. To name but a few, Marie Tiénou, Jana Holiday, Amanda Onapito, Roberta and Michael Lee, Valerie and Steve Spoelhof, Marcia Pratt, Kate Kraak, Sherrie Brower, Drew Ericks, Carrie VanDerKolk, Emily Hoeve and many other wonderful people of Faith Church in Zeeland.

Thank you also to James Krabill and the ASM Scholarly Monograph Series, and to the editorial staff at Wipf and Stock Publishers, including Matthew Wimer, Ian Creeger, and George Callihan. And to Sherrie Brower for helping to check references and offer suggestions.

To my parents, David and Kathy Fowler, thank you for everything you have done to help me become the person that I am today. For my children, Isaiah and Nora, I am so deeply grateful for who you are and the influence you have had on my life. Thank you both for taking this journey with me and listening to lectures in the living room. Thank you for grabbing books off the shelf and that one time, Isaiah, when you helped me find a reference. You are both treasures to me.

Finally, to my husband Felix, there are not enough words to describe how grateful I am for you in my life. I am deeply moved when I think of how you have encouraged me, protected me, served me, and loved me. To have a partner like you is such a rich and meaningful blessing. Thank you.

I have the privilege to serve a good God, and I am his daughter. He is most worthy of all praise. I hope that this work honors him.

1

Introduction

RESEARCH CONCERN

On April 9th, 2016, I met with Dr. Ghada Talhammi, D. K. Pearsons Professor of Politics, emerita Lake Forest College, at a restaurant outside Chicago. The meeting was for the purpose of discussing elements of the historical relationship between Christians and Muslims, particularly in the area of Jerusalem and from a Muslim perspective. Dr. Talhammi described how certain places and spaces were possessed and controlled by different groups of people and the arguments for who rightfully should possess the land. These arguments were advanced by some who claimed to be Jews, Christians, and Muslims. But as she spoke of the Christians actually living in Israel and Palestine, she paused reflectively stating, "they're not very territorial." Despite her own arguments, she offered this comment in a complimentary tone.

What was it about being "not very territorial," that Dr. Talhammi sought to commend? Her observation is particularly fascinating in light of the way that some assess Christians, Jews, and Muslims to be "equally unwilling to yield control" of Jerusalem.[1] These conflicting accounts exist because Christians have thought about the link between land, territory, and faith in different ways. A range of approaches can be found in the literature of Christian thinkers and historically various models have been operative among different Christian groups.

1. Johnson and Toft, "Grounds for War," 7.

Territoriality in Christian Faith and Mission

Two thinkers, Andrew Walls and Lamin Sanneh, have both argued that "Christianity is no longer territorial."[2] Walls states that "no longer does the word *Christianity* have a territorial connotation" and that "the idea of territorial Christianity, of geographically contiguous Christian states, lies irretrievably broken."[3] His understanding of Christianity as territorial is linked with Christendom. Whatever lingering territoriality remains is the residual effect of Christendom.

Sanneh also writes about the "loss of territoriality."[4] He asserts that, "whatever religion may mean to us, I maintain, it does not any longer imply territorial expression."[5] Similar to Walls, Sanneh connects non-territoriality with the end of Christendom. He describes the current state of the Christian faith as that of a "deterritorialized, post-Christendom Christianity."[6] At the same time, he addresses the "ambiguity of Christian non-territoriality."[7] While territoriality is said to have ended, he understands that there are those who would seek to reassert it.[8] He claims that "we continue to flounder in the cracks between a lost Christendom and the pressures of religious territoriality."[9] It is for this reason that Sanneh urges that this moment in history "requires critical reflection on the issue of religious territoriality."[10]

For Walls and Sanneh the end of Christendom and the end of territoriality are positive developments for at least two reasons. First, their understanding of Christian beliefs does not require the possession, maintenance, defense, or expansion of territory under the name of Christ. Second, they believe that God is impartial, no place is out of the reach of God and no place offers special access to the divine, as the reign of God extends equally over all the earth. Sanneh believes Christianity, from the beginning,

2. Walls, "The Significance of Christianity in Africa," 3.
3. Walls, *Missionary Movement in Christian History*, 237, 258.
4. Sanneh *Encountering the West*, 214.
5. Sanneh *Encountering the West*, 219.
6. Sanneh *Encountering the West*, 211.
7. Sanneh *Encountering the West*, 185.
8. Sanneh *Encountering the West*, 226.
9. Sanneh *Encountering the West*, 227.
10. Sanneh *Encountering the West*, 225. In February 2020 a conference which served to launch The Sanneh Institute for Research, Religion, & Society at the University of Ghana in Accra and co-sponsored by the Centre for Muslim-Christian Studies at Oxford was held in Accra on the theme of "Territoriality and Hospitality: Muslims and Christians Learning to Live Together." The choice of this conference theme indicates that some have acknowledged Sanneh's suggestion.

"was a religion destined for all time and for the whole world, and not just for one time, place, or people."[11] Likewise, Walls claims that "Christianity has always been global in principle, and for much of its history, global in practice."[12] Both Walls and Sanneh have marveled at the historical development that has grafted Christianity into places far from its origins. For them, the current geographic extent of those who claim to be Christians is set in contrast to "Christendom, the territorial conception of the Christian faith" which linked faith to one particular geographic region.[13]

Research Questions and Rationale

The central question of this work is *To what extent are Walls and Sanneh correct in their assertions that the end of Christendom means the end of territoriality?* The answer to this question requires consideration of the following: How can their assertions be evaluated? What is territoriality? By what means could instances of territoriality be assessed? Within the context of the Christian faith, how has territoriality been made manifest, have these manifestations changed in different places and time periods, and is there evidence of continued territoriality beyond Christendom?

In this book, I argue for a broader understanding of territoriality, an understanding that includes the territorial behavior present in Christendom but also extends beyond it. The thesis of this work is that even though Christendom has ended, territoriality continues and is relevant for understanding Christian faith and mission.

Neither Walls nor Sanneh offers a definition of territoriality. Geographer Robert Sack understands territoriality as a "powerful geographic strategy to control people and things by controlling area."[14] His broad approach to territoriality links the ideas of power and place, ranging from the interpersonal to the international. According to his theory, humans give order and meaning to a territory. Their classifications can lead to enforcement as a way to control the resources therein and as a device for influencing people and things.

Sack's definition leans into the descriptive aspects of territoriality which states facts related to human spatial behavior. This can give one the impression that territoriality is a neutral concept, but the ethical dimensions

11. Sanneh, *Disciples of All Nations*, 3.

12. Walls, *Crossing Cultural Frontiers*, 4.

13. Walls, *Missionary Movement in Christian History*, 81.

14. Sack, *Human Territoriality*, 5.

are never far from view. Territoriality has multiple purposes which one may judge to be motivated by good or bad intentions and achieving good or bad outcomes. Sack descriptive account aims to show how territoriality is a "pervasive element in our lives."[15] It is inescapable. Sack's theoretical approach to understanding territoriality provides a basis for exploring the complex connections of people, places, and power.

In Sack's perspective, Christianity is a particularly interesting case study on territoriality. Whether it is a broad geographical demarcation of religious territory, cities that operate as central points of a religion, or even places that are understood to be holy, territoriality plays a significant part in human and religious experience. The world operates under many unexamined geographical decisions, Sack believes his theory of territoriality can help analyze this spatial behavior.

The work of Walls and Sanneh is viewed as contributing to mission studies. In light of how their work is positioned within mission studies the question of territoriality is relevant for understanding Christian faith and mission. Furthermore, the geographical decisions of mission practitioners and missiologists are evident in the ways that they classify territory and when they articulate the extent of their work with references to geography. Geographic elements are present in the regular use of maps in education, planning, and recruitment by those engaging in or evaluating mission. The classification of certain lands or territories as *Christian* or *Non-Christian*, *reached* or *unreached* is a common practice that has implications for strategy, logistics, and the distribution of resources. Vision statements for mission initiatives are constructed with geographic terms, such as the language of latitude in the *10/40 Window*. Likewise, the *Back to Jerusalem* movement in China frames their vision in terms of an east to west movement of the gospel.[16] In all of these cases, geography plays a role in defining the outcomes of the initiative or organization.

PRECEDENT LITERATURE

Missiology, in the words of Ross Langmead, is an "interdisciplinary enterprise."[17] If the use of geography plays a role in the practice of mission, has there been any integration between the study of geography and mission? In a review of accessible, published research in the English language,

15. Sack, *Human Territoriality*, 1.
16. Park, "Chosen to Fulfill the Great Commission?," 166.
17. Langmead, "What Is Missiology?," 67.

there is limited engagement between missiology and geography, even less on the specific topic of territoriality. Four sources exemplify the available research. Richard Bauckham's work *Bible and Mission,* devotes a quarter of his brief work on the topic of Geography–Sacred and Symbolic. Bauckham's work bridges the gap between biblical references to geography and the history of mission activity to reflect theologically on both. He asserts that more work in this area is required, but does not look to any geographical theories or scholars.[18]

John Benson's, *Missionary Families Find a Sense of Place and Identity,* explores the experiences of multiple generations of missionaries in terms of place and belonging. Benson is a geographer who provides a good example of an integrative approach between geography and missiology. In a review of this work, David Greenlee states that "geography as a discipline seems to be overlooked in our missiological discussions, Benson's emphasis on 'place' is a helpful step toward correcting that oversight."[19] Greenlee's observation speaks to the need for geography to inform more of missiological research.

In the article "Maps Matter: the 10/40 Window and Missionary Geography," historians Hannah de Korte and David Onnekink consider the geographical assumptions that are behind the 10/40 Window.[20] Though the authors reference a theory of territoriality, it is not clear how the theory specifically influenced their analysis.

The final example is Ksenija Magda's *Paul's Territoriality and Mission Strategy.* Writing in the area of New Testament scholarship, her work investigates the logic behind Paul's mission strategy on his evangelistic travels. Magda's work will be discussed in the next chapter, but her use of territoriality is a misnomer. That said, Magda draws on geographical theory concerning the influence of place to understand Paul's missionary impulse. While this and the above references indicate that there are some examples of research that connects mission with ideas of geography and territoriality, there is room for more.

The limited research that bridges geography and missiology means that while missiologists and mission practitioners may incorporate elements of geography or geographic terms, they do so without the tools and reflection that the discipline itself provides. Without these, the opportunity

18. Bauckham, *Bible and Mission*, 55.

19. Greenlee, *Pastoral Care in the Early Church*, 272.

20. de Korte and Onnekink, "Maps Matter," 2020.

for deeper analysis and clarity is lost on issues ranging from proximity, propinquity, scale, distantiation, place, and space. One may be able to use a map, but the tools and theories of geography help one to perceive how maps themselves reveal or change one's view of the world. Greater missiological engagement with the discipline of geography could also help one to understand the significance of what it means to be territorial. Territoriality is just one piece of geographical analysis, but exploring it offers the opportunity to examine theoretical and practical dimensions of integrating geography with missiological research.

This work evaluates Walls and Sanneh's claims regarding Christianity and territoriality. The argument that I will advance is that even though the specific territorial structures related to Christendom have changed, this has not put an end to the use of territoriality by Christians. Understanding territoriality continues to be relevant for Christian faith and mission. The intent of this study is not to disagree with Walls and Sanneh, but to nuance and reframe their claims with the use of geographical theory. The loss of Christendom was significant, and it brought an end to some specific forms of territoriality, but to say in an unqualified way that "Christianity is no longer territorial" would be inaccurate. To do so may also inadvertently close the door on the subject of territoriality without appreciating how the conversation can move forward in helpful ways. Because territoriality continues to take new forms and exists on various scales, understanding it in greater depth offers another tool of analysis for Christians and missiologists.

RESEARCH SIGNIFICANCE

The significance of this study is to expand the missiological research that is informed by the discipline of geography. For both mission practitioners and missiologists this serves several concrete purposes. First, it helps mission practitioners to make informed decisions about how they construct their goals particularly when they do so in territorial terms. It helps them assess their own perspectives and behavior as to whether their use of territoriality is helping them to achieve their goals. Secondly, it helps missiologists evaluate instances of territoriality and territorial arrangements in mission history and current practice.

This study also highlights and extends the contributions of Andrew Walls and Lamin Sanneh. In particular it highlights the ways that they write about place and territoriality, the way that they view Christendom as not just a time period but a territory, and their belief that Christians today need to adjust their mental maps. It extends their contributions by grounding their ideas in geographical theory and reframing their statements of non-territoriality.

This study also advances the idea that mission is from everywhere to everywhere, rather than primarily an endeavor of geographical advancement from one location.

METHODOLOGY

This work is an interdisciplinary literature-based study incorporating research and theory from geography, and research from history and missiology. The methodology employed is library research. The writings of Robert Sack, Andrew Walls, and Lamin Sanneh are written in English. I read, analyzed, and critically evaluated the selected texts from each author. For each set of textual data, I identified patterns related to the concern of this study. In the work of Sack, I was particularly concerned with understanding, evaluating, and applying his theory of territoriality and his *geographic awareness paradigm*. In the work of Walls and Sanneh I was particularly attentive to references of geography, place, territory, territoriality, Christendom, land, location, local and other aspects of physical terrain. These references were then considered in light of Sack's work.

Robert Sack

I am using Robert Sack's theory of territoriality from his *Human Territoriality* and his *geographic awareness paradigm* from his *Homo Geographicus*. The theory will be used to identify instances of territoriality and understand the effects that flow out from it. Sack's *geographic awareness paradigm* will be applied to understand the perspectives, formed by one's place, that feed into territoriality. The combination of these two theoretical tools will be utilized to show how territoriality changes and how this is made manifest at different times and across different scales of territory.

Prior to being named Professor Emeritus, Robert D. Sack was the Clarence J. Glacken and John Bascomb Professor of Geography and Professor of Integrated Liberal Studies at University of Wisconsin, Madison. Sack's work is part of the tradition of human geography, which explores the interrelationships of places, people, and their environments. Sack has researched territoriality within the context of the Roman Catholic Church, but I could not find any stated Christian commitments. He explains that his theory of territoriality is not intended to be "used to predict human actions" but is rather "an interrelated group of characteristics which can be used to explain or make sense of behavior."[21] He uses spatial, historical, and social analysis to uncover the reasons people may make use of territoriality and the results that often follow. Sack's approach is not to give an exhaustive account of all examples of territoriality, but to stimulate further research on the topic. His *geographic awareness paradigm* is used here to further develop how the classifications of territoriality are influenced by one's perspectives and their place.

In a review of the English texts that look at both territoriality and either mission, religion, theology, or biblical studies, there are those that write about territoriality without reference to any particular theory or geographer. But for those that do, Sack's work is most often the theoretical base.[22] Some articles do not cite Sack directly, but their references eventually lead to Sack.[23] I could find no other author that has produced a work that has so thoroughly and systematically expounded upon the subject of territoriality.

While Sack's work is several decades old, geographers tend to hold his work in high esteem.[24] In a review that looks back at significant works that have contributed to the research of human geography, John Agnew and Anssi Paasi describe it as a seminal work.[25] They see the value of Sack's

21. Sack, *Human Territoriality*, 3.

22. Malina, "'Apocalyptic' and Territoriality"; Scott, *Paul and the Nations*; Bernabé Ubieta, "'Neither Xenoi Nor Paroikoi, Sympolitai and Oikeioi Tou Theou' (Eph 2:19)"; Jones, "Whose Homeland?"; Shilhav, "Jewish Territoriality Between Land and State."; Magda, *Paul's Territoriality*; de Korte and Onnekink, "Maps Matter."

23. Derrick, "Containing the Umma?," cites Penrose, "Nations, States and Homelands," who cites Sack; and Roudometof, "Greek Orthodoxy, Territoriality, and Globality," cites Held et al., *Global Transformations*, who cites Rosenau, *Along the Domestic-Foreign Frontier*, who cites Ruggie, "Territoriality and Beyond," who cites Sack.

24. Reviews of Sack's *Human Territoriality* by historians Henry Bowden, "Human Territoriality" and Susan Reynolds, "Human Territoriality (Book Review)," were not as enthusiastic. While Reynolds is tentative, Bowden is dismissive in his assessment. He asserts that "the author introduces basic definitions in a helpful way but then plods rather tediously through multiple combinations of more rarified theories," Bowden, "Human Territoriality," 557. On one hand Bowden's criticism is not entirely off base. Sack's theories, particularly for those outside of geography, can be challenging to grasp and call for careful reading. Yet Bowden's review seems to be somewhat superficial. He mentions Sack's "abiding fascination" with, among other things "tables and equations," when no such equations can be found.

25. Agnew, "Classics in Human Geography Revisited," 92.

Human Territoriality in terms of originality, usefulness, and in the depth of its rigorous theoretical analysis. Agnew states, "it is one of those few books that push debate and research in a fundamentally new direction as a result of their publication."[26] Paasi writes that "Sack's book was widely cited after its publication and has been a 'must' for geographers and others dealing with problems of territory and territoriality on different spatial scales."[27] Agnew and Paasi both note gaps in his theory particularly in the area of the ethical issues related to territoriality. In response to this, Sack points to his *Homo Geographicus* as the development of his ethical ideas. There is a connection between the two works which is why understanding his theory of territoriality alone without the ideas presented in his *geographic awareness paradigm* would be insufficient. The ethical dimensions of territoriality will be addressed in chapter two and seven of this book.

Homo Geographicus has also earned praise from geographers. David Smith refers to it as a project of "breadth and complexity" claiming that "it should be essential reading for all who take geography seriously, and strongly recommended for those who do not."[28] Describing it as an ambitious work, Martin Kenzer states that "because this book is decidedly thick with meaning and was written strictly for the more philosophically minded among us, I doubt that most geographers will start, much less finish, reading such an arduous volume."[29] At least one geographer has used Sack's *geographic awareness paradigm* as it is the basis for Benson's understanding of place.

Despite its complexity, Ksenija Magda has also made use of Sack's work. She maintains that "Robert Sack is, to [her] knowledge, the first to attempt a holistic paradigm which shows how forces from different realms of experience gather around a person's geographical place."[30] While Magda writes on the Apostle Paul's territoriality, she makes more use of Sack's *Homo Geographicus* than his other text.

Sack's work is the theoretical basis for understanding territoriality, but the work of Walls and Sanneh provides much of the context for exploring the evidence pertaining to the continued relevance of territoriality.

26. Agnew, "Classics in Human Geography Revisited," 92.

27. Agnew, "Classics in Human Geography Revisited," 93.

28. Smith, "Book Review Article: Homo Geographicus," 609–10.

29. Kenzer, "Geographical Reviews: Homo Geographicus," 166.

30. Madga, *Paul's Territoriality*, 24.

Territoriality in Christian Faith and Mission

Andrew Walls and Lamin Sanneh

While this work makes use of other sources, the primary textual data for understanding the occurrences of territoriality will come from Walls and Sanneh. Doing so will show that the evidence of territoriality, while often organized and labeled differently in Walls's and Sanneh's work, is not inconsistent with their understanding of the historical record. There is much that Walls and Sanneh have said that needs to be thought about in light of spatial and territorial dynamics. This work seeks to highlight and extend what they have written.

Relying on Walls and Sanneh also helps to limit the scope of investigation. For example, much more could be said about the use of territoriality in Catholic missionary efforts, but this is not generally the focus of Walls's and Sanneh's work. Discussion of territoriality used by Catholic missionaries will be left to what is said in regard to the Spanish and Portuguese mission and the contrasting methods their two expressions represent. Likewise, more could be said about the use of territoriality by European states after Christendom. However, in keeping with Walls and Sanneh, unless the use of territoriality by state actors has an impact on missionary efforts, it will be treated as outside the scope of this investigation.

The work of both Walls and Sanneh is widely appreciated and often cited among Christian scholars. Andrew Walls has had teaching appointments at Fourah Bay College in Sierra Leone, University of Nigeria in Nigeria, University of Aberdeen and University of Edinburgh in Scotland, as well as at the Akrofi-Christaller Institute of Theology, Mission and Culture in Ghana. Walls has had an indelible influence on the studies of World Christianity. Many of his writings can be found in three collections of essays, *The Missionary Movement in Christian History: Studies in the Transmission of Faith*, *The Cross-Cultural Process in Christian History*, and *Crossing Cultural Frontiers*. Two other articles not included in these volumes will also be consulted, "The Significance of Christianity in Africa" and "The Ecumenical Missiology in Anabaptist Perspective."

Lamin Sanneh has had faculty appointments at the University of Ghana, the University of Aberdeen, and Harvard University. He was also a dually appointed Professor of History at Yale University and D. Willis James Professor of Mission and World Christianity at Yale Divinity School. Sanneh has also written many works. I will focus on *Encountering the West: Christianity and the Global Cultural Process*, *Disciples of All Nations: Pillars of World Christianity*, and *Summoned from the Margin: Homecoming of an African.*

Neither Walls and Sanneh have written at great length on the topic of territoriality or place. Sanneh includes several pages in *Encountering the West* on territoriality. For Walls, comments about "the territorial principle" are made in passing but never directly developed at length.[31] For both Walls and Sanneh the statement "every place" is often listed among "every culture" and "every language" to describe the Christian faith that extends beyond boundaries. But the idea of "every place" has not received the same amount of focus as the other two ideas. The purpose of this work is not to present a complete evaluation of the totality of their work but to highlight what Walls and Sanneh have written on territoriality and place and extend it further.

OVERVIEW

The chapters proceed in the following way. The next two chapters of this work explain the geographical theories that are used for understanding territoriality. Chapter 2 examines Sack's theory and argues for its usefulness in evaluating instances of territoriality. In his view, a definition must be broad enough to cover a variety of cases and yet rich enough to be useful for understanding the different effects. He states, "we need to know not only what territoriality is, but what it does. It is principally on helping to point to the important effects of a phenomenon that the value of a definition rests."[32] His definition of territoriality is provided and the descriptive characteristics and effects that flow from territoriality will be explored.

Chapter 3 continues to build the theoretical framework for understanding territoriality by looking deeper at classifications. Sack's *geographic awareness paradigm* is used to understand how classifications are derived from one's perspectives which are formed by one's place. This chapter establishes how one's ideas about constructing the world are not disconnected from the constructed world they live in. In other words, the way one seeks to change a place is influenced by the way they have been changed by the places that have influenced them. In this way, just as territoriality influences place, so too does place influence territoriality. The combination of chapters 2 and 3 provide a more holistic explanation of the perspectives that feed into territoriality and the effects that flow out of it. Chapter 3 closes with an example that ties the elements of place, perspective, classification, and

31. Walls, *Missionary Movement in Christian History*, 82.

32. Sack, *Human Territoriality*, 18.

territoriality together by considering the demarcation of the 38th parallel north latitude on the Korean peninsula.

Chapters 4, 5, and 6 consider how territoriality is made manifest in a selection of relevant moments in Christian and mission history ranging from the first Christians to the present day. In chapter 4 it is shown that territoriality developed within the structures of the church organization prior to Constantine and therefore prior to what many consider to be the early dating of Christendom. Sack's exploration of territoriality in the church is what initially drew me to his theory. In this chapter, Sack's insights serve as training wheels for applying his theory to particular situations. Initially the church developed with values that deemphasized the kind of spatial organization implied in territoriality, but smaller scale examples of territoriality emerged to meet the church's needs of discipline and leadership organization. Constantine only accelerated this process when he placed Christianity in the position of privileged status within the Roman world.

Chapter 5 begins with clarifying how Walls and Sanneh understand Christendom. It then proceeds to examine how territoriality within Christendom manifested itself in a variety of ways, representing a particularly powerful expression. But as the unity of Christendom began to fragment, expressions of territoriality continued. Innovative approaches to territoriality created new forms of expression and manifestation for engaging space and hierarchically organizing. The effects of territoriality related to the breakdown of Christendom are explored by considering Spanish colonization in the Americas and the Protestant Reformation.

To further show the continuation of territoriality after Christendom, chapter 6 gives four examples from Protestant missionary activity and reflects on contemporary expressions of territoriality. The first example looks at how Christians organized themselves into voluntary societies, separate from the formal church structures, to meet their evangelistic goals. The other three examples, mission stations, comity agreements, and the classifications of the 1910 missionary conference, show how the missionary strategies that were implemented indicate ongoing territoriality. The chapter closes by noting some contemporary expressions of territorial innovation that potentially could give rise to instances of territoriality.

Chapter 7 summarizes the overall argument and lays out how this study contributes to understanding the significance of geography, territoriality, and place for Christians and missiologists. The theory of territoriality is understood to be a useful tool for evaluating the ongoing instances of territoriality. Christianity is no longer territorial in the ways it once was, but this requires Christians to consider how understanding territoriality is still relevant today.

PRELIMINARY MATTERS

A few preliminary matters need to be addressed before moving to the main argument. These matters include clarifying some definitions, some delimitations, and then casting a larger vision for the value of integrating insights from the discipline of geography.

Definitions

Geographic versus Geographical

Considering the way that I will draw comparisons between the discipline of history and geography, the following note regarding language is made. There is a more distinct difference in meaning between the terms *historic* and *historical* which, as of yet, is not quite the case for the terms *geographic* and *geographical*. Some grammar commentators see little difference, where the one is just a variant spelling of the other. Joseph Spring offers some clarification while recognizing that many conclusions come down to stylistic preferences and whether one is using British or American English. Spring claims that *geographic* "is used to describe the geography of our Earth . . . your place is geographic, not geographical."[33] In this way the term is closely linked to the elements of the physical world. By contrast, he holds that geographical "is more holistic in terms of gathering all the different aspects of geography, not simply maps and physical systems."[34] He explains that "geographic factors are those such as altitude, aspect, wind-chill," while "geographical factors include those of conventional 'senior school geography' but also include social, political, economic, historical ones."[35] The term *geographical* aligns with the tradition of human geography and Sack's understanding of the discipline which seeks to integrate a variety of systems. I will follow Spring's recommended usage of the terms.

33. Spring, "Geographic vs. Geographical."
34. Spring, "Geographic vs. Geographical."
35. Spring, "Geographic vs. Geographical."

The Early Church

Particularly relevant in chapter 5, *the early church* is defined as the period after the ascension of Jesus and prior to the influence of the Roman emperor Constantine. The reason for defining *the early church* in this way has to do with the concept and dating of Christendom that is central to the argument of this work. Regrettably, defining it in this way can obscure the reality of early Christianity in areas of Africa and Asia that were beyond the border of the Roman Empire and for whom the influence of Constantine was of much less significance.

Place, Space, and Territory

In this work, place is where the social, the mental, and the physical forces of life assemble. This is to say that "place is both physical and cultural" while alternatively, space is a physical property.[36] Place can constrain and enable one's actions, but one's actions can also "construct and maintain places."[37] Territoriality is one of the strategies for constructing and maintaining places.

A place can be described in terms of the concrete metrics of space, distance and measurement, longitude and latitude, and the substance of the physical material present. But because place is more than physical elements, it can also be described in ways less concrete and more abstract or idealistic. This approach to describing place can be marked by a nostalgia for a particular location often lamenting change that has been fostered by homogeneity or standardization.[38]

A place can be a territory, which tends to stress the notions of specificity and boundedness. Following Sack's usage, these terms, *place* and *territory*, will often be used somewhat interchangeably. Sack does not define territory, something that Stuart Elden points out. Elden states that for Sack "it is generally assumed that territory is self-evident in meaning, and that its particular manifestations—territorial disputes, the territory of specific countries, etc.—can be studied without theoretical reflection on territory itself."[39] Sack takes the concept of territory as a given and focuses his at-

36. Sack, *Homo Geographicus*, 33.
37. Sack, *Homo Geographicus*, 13.
38. O'Donovan, "The Loss of a Sense of Place"; and Kunstler, *Geography of Nowhere*.
39. Elden, *The Birth of Territory*, 3.

tention on the creation and maintenance of that territory through the concept of *territoriality*. Elden finds this approach problematic because *territory* itself is "a historical question: produced, mutable, and fluid . . . [and] profoundly uneven in its development."[40] Nonetheless, Elden believes that *territory* also "comprises the techniques" used in the controlling and management of terrain including the economic, strategic, legal, and technical.[41] In this way it can seem as if Sack and Elden are saying the same thing while using slightly different terms (in Elden terrain is to territory, as in Sack, territory is to territoriality). I will be following Sack's use of the terms.

There are other terms and ideas that are defined within this body of work including Christendom and territoriality.

Delimitations

The tendency of research in the areas of geography and missiology is to be highly integrative. As the case is made for the continuation of territoriality, this work touches on a variety of topics and themes that cannot be fully explored but are nonetheless germane to fully appreciating the significance of territoriality. These include, but are not limited to, Christian nationalism, modernity, autochthony, hybridity, ethics of power, and globalization. Given the thrust and focus of this work, for some of these issues only a passing reference can be made. For the concept of globalization, I address the topic by highlighting changes in technology and travel.

The third preliminary concern is a discussion on the discipline of geography, its relationship to culture, and the use of geography by Walls and Sanneh.

A Greater Vision for the Role of Geography

Sack's theory of territoriality and *geographic awareness paradigm* come from the discipline of geography. For a variety of reasons, there has been a tendency for the contributions of geography to be overlooked or diminished. Furthermore, historians have often filled this void with their own geographical reflections that have not always engaged, or have superficially engaged the geographical theories that are relevant to their discussions. Walls and Sanneh have both written about geographical ideas in their work,

40. Elden, *The Birth of Territory*, 330.

41. Elden, *The Birth of Territory*, 17, 330.

often making reference to the "geographic scope of missions."[42] Their writings focus attention on the dynamics of culture with geography playing a supporting role. What follows explores how geography may offer tools for missiological research.

All or Nothing

In 1948, Harvard eliminated its geography program. This act acquired more significance when then University President, James Conant, made a statement questioning "the appropriateness of geography as a university subject."[43] As Neil Smith explains, many geographers understood this to be "'a terrible blow . . . to American geography' and one from which 'it has never completely recovered.'"[44] Harvard's decision about geography did not happen in a vacuum. Questions about the purpose of the discipline had built over time.

In the late nineteenth century, the development of geography in the US aligned with the needs of a growing nation-state and economy. Pushing back the frontier required a geography that helped explain terrain, natural resources, and diverse physical environments. As a result, geography was closely aligned with geology.[45] Benjamin Sacks comments that "in 1900, nearly all major American colleges and universities maintained active (even thriving) geography departments."[46] Geography was then considered a major academic field.

By the mid-twentieth century the needs related to geographical understanding had changed. The "natural frontiers in the landscape were progressively replaced by social ones" and from this change emerged the idea of human geography.[47] One of the consequences of this shift was a lack of clarity about the focus of geographical research. Geography as a discipline "justified its existence by characterizing itself as the mother science, or science of sciences, with claims of inclusivity arrogating to itself the study of all facts relating to the earth's surface and human occupancy of it."[48] This

42. Walls, *The* Cross-Cultural Process in Christian History, 206.

43. Smith, "Academic War Over the Field of Geography," 156.

44. Smith, "Academic War Over the Field of Geography," 155.

45. Smith, "Academic War Over the Field of Geography," 168.

46. Sacks, "What Happened to the American Geography Department?"

47. Smith, "Academic War Over the Field of Geography," 168.

48. Glick, "In Search of Geography," 92. Glick writes, "An extravagant attempt

was an all or nothing approach that, at Harvard in 1948, proved to amount to nothing. According to Smith, geography was either "defined so broadly that it was virtually all-inclusive or so narrowly that it had little raison d'être as an independent pursuit."[49] Stuck between a myth of everything or "a grade school emphasis on topographical facts" it leaves one wondering, "what is the unique purview of geography?"[50]

Andrew Walls has noted that the same integrative tension exists within missiology. Walls remarks on how "missiologists are the magpies of the academic world; they invade the scholarly territory of their neighbors and steal their topics. Geographers, as anyone who has worked in a social science faculty knows, do the same."[51] Walls's observation may reflect his experience in the European educational system. In Benjamin Sacks' analysis the United Kingdom "continues to dominate geographic research and study," while "the situation is unfortunately vastly different in the United States."[52] Social scientists in the United States may not as easily be aware of the comparison Walls references; most never having worked alongside a geographer. It may also be true to say that Walls's approach to history makes regular integrative invasions into the field of geography.

The Use of Geography in the Work of Walls and Sanneh

Walls and Sanneh value a view of Christian history that is geographically broad. Evidence for this can be found in how Walls commends Latourette's work because his "ecumenical vision is as remarkable for this period as his geographic range."[53] If Walls points to Latourette's work as the ideal, Sanneh observes that the tendency among historians is to produce work with much less geographical range. He argues that "history was mainly the history of nations, so that when Hegel proposed to write a universal history it only

to institutionalize the unity myth was Wallace Atwood's creation in the 1920s of the Graduate School of Geography at Clark University, which involved phasing out doctoral programs in biology, chemistry, physics and mathematics, and folding the remaining graduate programs into his "great Geographical institute." See also Koelsch, William A, "Wallace Atwood's 'Great Geographical Institute.'"

49. Smith, "Academic War Over the Field of Geography," 168.

50. Glick, "In Search of Geography," 92.

51. Walls, *Crossing Cultural Frontiers*, 259.

52. Sacks, "What Happened to the American Geography Department?"

53. Walls, *The* Cross-Cultural *Process in Christian History*, 5.

culminated in the Prussian state."[54] Sanneh argues that the tendency among some historians is to write as if Christianity culminated in a European expression. Such approaches indicate why the Christian story in places of China, or Afghanistan, or India has been neglected for so long.[55]

The pattern of geographical advance and recession of the Christian faith is as formative to Walls's articulation of Christian history as it is for Latourette. The first of the "Tests of Christian Expansion" presented by Walls, considers the professions of faith in a particular geographic area.[56] He states, "the other tests themselves presuppose this one, the existence of a statistically identifiable, geographically locatable Christian community, however small."[57] Walls links the rise and fall pattern in Christian history to specific geographically situated cultural expressions of the gospel. For example, Walls connects the threat of the "removal of the candlestick" in Revelation 2:5 to a regional or geographic loss of the gospel.[58] He claims that "the Christian story is serial; its center moves from place to place. No one church or place or culture owns it. At different times, different peoples and places have become its heartlands, its chief representatives."[59] In Walls's work, time and place are drawn together to tell the story of the spread and decline of Christianity.

In his version of Christian history, Walls speaks of areas of land, movements of people, boundaries and frontiers, and locations that are the "center of gravity" for the Christian faith.[60] He writes regularly about the demographic and geographic shifts such as "the emergence of Africa as a continent of the Christian heartlands."[61] The northern continents are compared to the southern continents when Walls describes the "massive movement towards Christian faith in . . . sub-Saharan Africa, Latin America, certain parts of Asia, [and] the Pacific Islands."[62] Consider the knowledge of geography, past and present, that is required for one to fully appreciate remarks such as these. "It is clear that early Christianity saw northern

54. Sanneh, *Encountering the West*, 175.
55. Sanneh, *Disciples of All Nations*, 281.
56. Walls, *The Cross-Cultural Process in Christian History*, 7, 9.
57. Walls, *The* Cross-Cultural *Process in Christian History*, 10.
58. Walls, *The Cross-Cultural Process in Christian History*, 29.
59. Walls, *The Cross-cultural Process in Christian History*, 66.
60. Walls, *Missionary Movement in Christian History*, 68.
61. Walls, *The Cross-cultural Process in Christian History*, 58.
62. Walls, *Missionary Movement in Christian History*, 68.

Africa, Egypt, Ethiopia, and Nubia as part of a single Christian universe that extended also over the northern Mediterranean lands and the Middle East. No purely geographical factor finally divides Mediterranean Africa from tropical Africa. There are, and were, political and cultural factors to do so, but early Christianity transcended these."[63] One is inclined to read Walls with an atlas at hand.

Geographical thinking about Christian history is part of Sanneh's approach as well. He writes about Christianity embarking "on its world errand deeply conscious of its claim that it was a religion destined for all time and for the whole world, and not just for one time, place, or people."[64] Geography (and geographical assumptions) appear regularly in his writing. While the focus of Sanneh's study of human particularity is language and culture, he believes in a profound connection between place and people. At times he makes what amounts to passing comments in this regard, stating that "human geography was the way we were taught about climate, soil, terrain, and rivers" and his conviction that "terrain could shape one's attitude to the world and to people."[65]

If, for Walls and Sanneh, geography is essential to their understanding of Christian history, this may be problematic for some of their readers. According to studies by the National Geographic Society, people in the United States show disturbingly low geo-literacy.[66] The discipline of geography has had to actively defend itself against statements of its own demise.[67] Within some philosophical traditions the ideas of time and space are coupled. But Michel Foucault argues that a "devaluation of space . . . has prevailed for generations. Space was treated as the dead, the fixed, the undialectical, the immobile. Time, on the contrary, was richness, fecundity, life, dialectic."[68] This has led Edward Casey to argue that "the quintessential modernist view of the relation between place and self is that there is no such relation."[69] While space was relegated to a position of lesser importance, time seems ubiquitous.

63. Walls, *The Cross-cultural Process in Christian History*, 90.

64. Sanneh, *Disciples of All Nations*, 3.

65. Sanneh, *Summoned from the Margin*, 81, 114.

66. Trivedi, "Survey Reveals Geographic Illiteracy."

67. Morgan, "The Exaggerated Death of Geography."

68. Foucault, *Power/Knowledge*, 70.

69. Casey, "Between Geography and Philosophy," 684.

In an academic environment where the geographical perspective is diminished, other disciplines absorb the material that were once the focus of geography. No discipline has absorbed the diminishment of geography as much as history. Edward Soja states that, "the last decades of the nineteenth century, examined in retrospect, can be seen as an era of rising historicism and the parallel submergence of space in critical social thought."[70] It is thus not surprising that as historians, the writings of Andrew Walls and Lamin Sanneh address geographical ideas regularly. The challenge this creates is that when historians absorb the material that was once the purview of geographers, the geographical tools that would be helpful for analysis are not explored and ethical questions related to geography go unconsidered. It is time for missiology to more directly engage the theoretical tools of geography.

Reduction and Integration

This section explores the study of geography through the work of Robert Sack. His work provides a rationale for why geography has been ignored and why it is necessary for drawing together divergent aspects of one's lived experience. Writing within the tradition of human geography and focusing on spatial analysis, Sack offers a more robust view of geography than mere topological facts. While it will not be necessary for the reader to agree with Sack's vision of geography, the goal is to show how geography may offer tools for missiological research and to further clarify how Walls and Sanneh make use of geography, even if they do so in nonexplicit ways.

Specialization and Fragmentation

In the midst of questions about whether geography has a unique purview, Robert Sack sees the predisposition toward integration as a benefit. Other bodies of knowledge suffer from increasing specialization and fragmentation. In Sack's perspective, contemporary life has influenced a person's understanding and experience with spatial reality.[71] He speaks of the ten-

70. Soja, *Postmodern Geographies*, 4.

71. Sack, in *Homo Geographicus*, often references "modernity" to describe these dynamics, but does not offer a definition (3, 11, 27, 57, 103, 172). It seems that the way he refers to modernity is similar to the definition provided by Mark Elvin in "A Working Definition of 'Modernity'?" Elvin states, "let us therefore define 'modernity' as a complex

dency to perpetually assign "people and things to particular places," with ever increasing rules to codify the process.[72] This intense spatial organization results in a thinning out of the meaning of place. Places then become useful for only one thing. A person is healed here, works there, sleeps there. A place for everything and everything in its place. Sack describes how "the thinning out and segmentation of places make them less visible and lends to our actions the illusion of being dissociated from geography."[73] It is only when a place is disturbed, when something goes wrong, that it returns to the foreground of one's mind.

Sack sees specialization and fragmentation within academic fields as well. If contemporary life is marked by assigning and separating people and things to places, Sack argues that academics follow this pattern with ever increasing specializations of knowledge. The division of knowledge into greater and greater specialization is a move away from integration and synthesis. Sack argues that when many academic disciplines attempt to integrate, they tend to cluster around three main realms: The *natural realm*, which understands the world through nature in disciplines like biology, geology, chemistry, and genetics; the *social realm*, which explores how humans engage socially through the disciplines such as anthropology, economics, or sociology; and the *mental realm*, the way that minds make sense of the world, exemplified in psychology, theology, and philosophy. All these disciplines, with a multitude of their own subdivisions, lead to an overly specialized world. Sack argues that "when it comes to drawing connections among them, they fragment along the lines of different disciplines and subdisciplines."[74] Consequently, there is a need for synthesis that keeps humanity from continual fragmentation.

---

of more or less effectively realized concerns with power. The complex contains at least the following three components: 1) Power over other human beings, whether states, groups or individuals, according to the level of the system under consideration. 2) Practical power over nature in terms of the capacity for economic production. 3) Intellectual power over nature in the form of the capacity for prediction, and–more generally–of an accurate and compactly expressed understating" (210). The advantage of Elvin's definition is that it is not chronologically based and also allows for "seeing societies as varying combinations of 'modern' and 'non-modern' elements" (209). Finally, Elvin's definition does not rely on notions of increasing 'progress' or 'rationality.' While Sack seems to have some notions of chronology in mind (e.g., he contrasts 'modern' with 'pre-modern'), the focus on power, systems, and economic production aligns well with his understanding.

72. Sack, *Homo Geographicus*, 9.

73. Sack, *Homo Geographicus*, 9.

74. Sack, *Homo Geographicus*, 12.

> How, then, do we begin to gain a common understanding of our place in the world? The answer presents itself in the very concepts used to pose our questions: world, place, home, space. These are accessible concepts that we use in everyday life to describe our condition. They do not belong to any of the disciplines mentioned above but rather combine them: world, place, home, space draw together the natural, the social, and the intellectual. In fact, they are geographical concepts and indispensable for understanding our place in the world precisely because we are geographical beings.[75]

For Sack, it is geography that provides the foundation for assembling the different realms of our experience, the natural, the social, and the mental (with culture being a combination of the latter two).

This may seem an enormous task for geography. It could be argued that geography's potential overreach may only be tolerable because of its position of relative weakness. As an integrative discipline, geography is seemingly left with the threads at the boundaries and periphery of other disciplines. Geography may synthesize but for some it may never adequately specialize. Yet Sack's argument for how an emphasis on specialization has led to the proliferation of fragmentation is compelling and the outcomes are significant. He alleges, "Most of natural science does not consider human behavior; most of sociology and political science do not consider nature, and give only perfunctory attention to theories of the mind; those interested in psychology and intellectual history do not emphasize social relations or the natural world."[76] The tendency toward specialization results in active reduction of the significance of other disciplines. By contrast, "thinking of ourselves as geographical beings helps dissolve this deadlock."[77] Geography helps connect the threads of one's existence, bringing them together in a meaningful whole.

Perhaps Sack's case is overstated. There may be evidence that runs contrary to the accusations he levels at other disciplines, but in the broad strokes the argument has merit. It is worth examining how Sack sees this tendency play out among the three realms. He states, "reviewing the forces of nature, meaning, and social relations without geography means considering how they are conceived of by fields that ignore place, and for the

75. Sack, *Homo Geographicus*, 12.
76. Sack, *Homo Geographicus*, 35.
77. Sack, *Homo Geographicus*, 25.

most part ignore space, too."[78] The value in this discussion comes from the opportunity to consider the kinds of fragmentation that occur and the tendency of each realm to make use of geographical concepts by hiding them under their framework. This examination of Sack's argument proceeds by considering the natural, the social, the mental, and then the combination of the latter two in the idea of culture.

The Natural Realm's Reduction

The natural realm looks at life in terms of natural systems and processes. When human behavior is described by biologists or geneticists as "biological inheritance," Sack argues that these scientists "seem to be saying that areas of social relations and meaning can be explained by or reduced to biological forces."[79] Saying "it's all in the DNA" can become a deterministic approach to human life and activity. Humanity is understood to be merely part of a natural system, reduced to chemical and biological processes.[80] Additionally, one may look at the influence brought by the natural world beyond human DNA. They may seek to answer questions about how air quality, food resources, or climate impact humans. Either of these accounts of the role of nature can become an overarching assessment that obscures the interconnection with other realms.

The notion that land or climate influences one's character is not particularly prevalent today. Yet ideas that link blood and soil have a long history. The "classical Greek doctrine of elements and humors [were] a tradition of theories arguing that a people's culture and character are molded, if not determined, by its natural environments."[81] In the nineteenth century, Fredrick Jackson Turner's frontier thesis argued that the European settlers' experience with the frontier had a far-reaching influence on the character of the American people.[82] In Sack's words, Turner believed that "the frontier was a democratizing force. It stripped everyone of his culture and made him start from scratch."[83] Supposedly, their new culture was formed as a result of human encounter with nature. Turner's remarks speak to the

78. Sack, *Homo Geographicus*, 34.

79. Sack, *Homo Geographicus*, 36.

80. Sack, *Homo Geographicus*, 115.

81. Sack, *Homo Geographicus*, 105.

82. Turner, *The Significance of the Frontier in American History*.

83. Sack, *Homo Geographicus*, 109.

change that often occurs when people experience different places, but as Sack points out, Turner is underestimating the role of culture and its mobility. One's culture influences more than the particulars of, for example, dress and transportation. It influences how one views and understands ideas such as "the frontier." In Sack's perspective, Turner is diminishing the role of the social and intellectual realm. This affords Turner the opportunity to ignore his own cultural lens and how it might affect his perspectives of "the frontier." For example, Sack would argue that Turner's view of the frontier amounts to conceptually empty space (an effect related to territoriality which is covered in chapter 2). This perspective, that land is understood to be empty space, was culturally constructed. One may believe they are stripped of their European roots but in the process they could be just naturalizing their own culture as if it had somehow always belonged in this new place.[84] Or perhaps their culture has changed, as all cultures do whether tightly tethered to a place or in dispersion, but exaggerating that change is not helpful or accurate.

Another example can be found in Herbert Baxter Adam's germ theory, which argued that certain values originated in Germanic forests and "were planted in American soil by Englishmen."[85] The Nazis used similar ideas when they claimed that the landscape of Germany was for them "a natural region, which, just as a natural habitat does for animals in an ecosystem, provided the German people with their identity and character."[86] Just as in Adam's view of the United States, "the soil from this region was to course through German blood, uniting the one with the other."[87] Peter Geschiere summarizes this concept with the term *autochthony*. He is struck by autochthony's universal appeal despite that it is often built on little more than mythology and breeds a constant obsession with deciphering who really belongs.[88] The problem with myths of origin is how they are used to classify, categorize, divide, and exclude often based on a shaky relationship with the truth.

The physical boundaries of the Nazis' "natural" habitat were flexible enough to allow for a certain amount of territorial expansion.[89] The

84. Sack, *Homo Geographicus*, 81.

85. Sack, *Homo Geographicus*, 109.

86. Sack, *Homo Geographicus*, 112.

87. Sack, *Homo Geographicus*, 112.

88. Geschiere, *The Perils of* Belonging, 2 and 27.

89. Klinghoffer, *The Power of Projections*, 91.

geographical logic of natural habitat also became paired with ideas of 'race.' According to Klinghoffer, this approach to "biological and climatic linkages to race" is one of the reasons behavioral geography has fallen out of favor.[90] In what Sack sees as a continuation of the germ theory, ideas of inferior 'races' and 'contaminated gene pools' were seen as a threat to the greatness of German culture. Racialization did not have as much of the inherent geographical limitations as were present in the idea of the *natural habitat*.[91] In the long run racialization became the more well-known concept, but geographical connotations continued to comingle with racialization. "Races themselves were historically identified with places and were thought of as resulting from their different natural conditions and relative geographic isolation. A popular idea in the West was that each race had its place or continent, blacks in Africa, Asians in Asia, and Caucasians in Europe and later in America; and these were where they belonged. Place, then, is part of the history of race."[92] Racialization served to strengthen the link between people and land. These links give rise to a host of questions—'Do people have a place to which they genetically belong?', 'Am I permanently connected to a particular land?', 'Is there a natural habitat for my genetic makeup?' Given one's answers to these questions, they may begin asking questions of territoriality, "How does one keep people in a place where they belong and keep those who do not belong, out?"

Sack contends that when place brings nature and culture together it can "humanize nature. But it simultaneously naturalizes culture."[93] This is a significant observation for how people understand the relationship between culture and place. When "culture becomes intermeshed with the physical and biological content of a place" then culture is made concrete, tethered, and synonymous to a location.[94] This makes it difficult to imagine the possibility that culture can move, or even allowance for culture to change in that location. According to this view, the natural habitat is what truly determines the culture. "The line between nature and culture becomes blurred, as does the distinctiveness of self, when the place is personified as Motherland or Fatherland. Here the threads between people and place are drawn even more tightly. The intense and unconscious conflation occurs in part

90. Klinghoffer, *The Power of Projections*, 119.

91. Sack, *Homo Geographicus*, 112.

92. Sack, *Homo Geographicus*, 112–13.

93. Sack, *Homo Geographicus*, 81.

94. Sack, *Homo Geographicus*, 81.

because place is a convenient device for classifying and collecting elements, and because it can routinize practices so that we become unaware of them and of the place."[95] Land becomes an extension of one's understanding of their self (or their society). For example, Sack states "under patriotic fervor, an attack on the border of one's country is not simply a symbol of an attack on its people, but is such an attack; hence the place is the people, at least for the moment."[96] This conflation of place and people is also fundamental to nationalism.

The idea of place as a container for discrete people and culture can be effective, as long as humans remain where they are. Whatever one's attachment to land, viewing it as natural habitat fails to acknowledge the way that people move–tendencies which are well documented in the social realm.

The Social Realm's Reduction

If the realm of nature can reduce all things to a natural process, the realm of the social is just as capable of reduction. Sack contends that "most social scientists and humanists act as though their subject is spaceless."[97] This is implied in the way "the social sciences rarely consider explicitly how spatial relations affect the phenomena they investigate."[98] Those who emphasize the social realm reduce the importance of nature and place by ignoring the way that social relations happen in the context of space. Sack proceeds to give examples, "as when the rich move here, the poor stay there, or when one racial group is integrated with another."[99] Phenomena such as these are often considered by the social realm but not always with the intentional focus on the spatial realities and concerns. Class division, ethnic heritage, and the gendered experience are each a powerful force, but, "To argue from the start that self is not just affected by, but that it is nothing more than a racial, gender, ethnic, or some other construct, is to reduce it, and thereby deny it has any efficacy, even before the analysis begins. Disclosing the basic relationships between place and self in general will help form the foundations for a geographic approach to a gendered or racial self."[100] To ignore

95. Sack, *Homo Geographicus*, 136.
96. Sack, *Homo Geographicus*, 136.
97. Sack, *Homo Geographicus*, 34.
98. Sack, *Homo Geographicus*, 41.
99. Sack, *Homo Geographicus*, 93.
100. Sack, *Homo Geographicus*, 127.

place runs the risk of trivializing the context as being merely a point of application for the more significant universal principle.

Another kind of reduction that can come from the social realm is found in the perspective that "our ideas, values, and beliefs are molded by our social roles."[101] In this perspective, a conviction one might hold is not arrived at by some process of rational inquiry or the influence of one's physical location. The person, the process, and the access to knowledge are all dependent on social factors. To this "social construction of meaning" Sack points to the way that this theory is "offered as a truth transcending any particular social context, time, and place," thereby contradicting its premise.[102] If the theory is socially constructed, then consequently a different group of people may come to a divergent position based on their own social influences and there would be no means of mutually agreed upon adjudication. He holds that the most extreme forms of relativism present in some approaches of social science are completely unlivable. There is no ability to transcend one's socially determined perspective, and this inhibits the ability to engage others in critical dialogue. Sack rejects this kind of relativism.

The social realm can minimize the natural and the intellectual realms creating the impression that relationships exist in thin air and that one is unable to intellectually relate across social spheres. Consider F. LeRon Shults' observation that a "Western" ontological prioritization on substance led to a focus of humans as isolated individuals. He instead celebrates the "turn toward relationality," arguing that humans are not floating along unattached, they are in relationship.[103] But these relationships also happen within a context, not floating individually or collectively, but on the ground, in a place. Human relationships imply spatial interaction, and this too should be taken seriously.

The Mental Realm's Reduction

The mental realm, or the realm of meaning, consists of theories, traditions, stories, and worldviews. Ideas are powerful, influencing human thought and behavior. However, some can prioritize the significance of ideas as if they are the lone motivator of one's actions. Sack states, "the meanings we

101. Sack, *Homo Geographicus*, 42.

102. Sack, *Homo Geographicus*, 72.

103. Shultz, *Reforming Theological Anthropology*, 11.

give to the world are influenced by our own social situations, and also by such natural conditions as our genes; still, the realm of meaning asserts that the primary power lies in the mind's ability to structure the world."[104] In this view, ideas drive the realm of the social and they drive one's construction of the natural world. Sack presents this viewpoint in its various forms:

> Not only do our meanings possess power, they also contain structures that lead from one idea to another—the aprioris of Kant, the deep structures of transformational grammar, the generative structures of language, the oppositional structures of symbolic thought, the Freudian structure of our subconscious, the structure of learning curves, the structure of mythic forms and magical representations, the structure of scientific explanations, and the logic of mathematics. These are all examples of how types of meanings follow patterns and relationships that are as rigid, complex, powerful, and as difficult to escape as are social forces of bureaucracy, class, gender, supply and demand; or the natural forces of genetics chemical bonding, or even gravity.[105]

The mental realm is attentive to the metanarratives and worldviews that become the basic building blocks for understanding reality. Obviously, one's thoughts do not change natural laws. Gravity does not disappear because someone thought differently of it. But the mental realm can overstate the impact of ideas on the world and how humans engage them. As Lefebvre observes, "the mental realm comes to envelop the social and the physical one."[106]

As Sack explains his *geographic awareness paradigm*, he argues that one's perspectives are linked to their place (see chapter 3 of this work). Each place has a unique mixture of social, intellectual, and natural forces influencing how one sees the world. While at times it may be difficult to discern, Sack is distinguishing these ideological frameworks from merely one's individual perspectives. Thinking in terms of metanarratives, and how they influence the world, may helpfully clarify this distinction between the intellectual realm and one's individual perspectives. With this in mind, a reductive approach from the mental realm would argue that one's behavior, one's interactions, can be attributed to their religion or their philosophy or some other significant worldview or metanarrative.

104. Sack, *Homo Geographicus*, 45.

105. Sack, *Homo Geographicus*, 45.

106. Lefebvre, *The Production of Space*, 5.

One of the challenges with this type of reduction is that it can minimize particularity. The kind of particularity offered by place, as well as different social groups. For example, a perspective that over emphasizes the mental realm can assume that all Christians hold the same beliefs no matter where they live. This rendering makes Christianity the controlling ideology that stands as the most significant influencer. This is the kind of unhelpful reduction Sack seeks to avoid. He argues that these established ideologies, such as religious frameworks and economic philosophies, are insufficient to account for the complexity of human behavior on the earth.

Sack offers an example put forward by geographer Yi-Fu Tuan to bolster his point. Tuan considers the hypothesis that metanarratives which contain views about the natural world produce measurably different outcomes in human behavior with respect to land and resources. If one society believed that land and resources were to be dominated by humans (as some hold that Western cultures contend) and another believes in harmony with nature (as some contend a Chinese Taoist may hold), then it should follow that these societies engage their natural resources accordingly.[107] Tuan agrees with these broad ideological caricatures, but then considers how they translate into behavior. "Comparing the scale of environmental changes caused by both civilizations until the rise of the industrial revolution, Tuan is hard-pressed to find a difference: the transformation wrought in the two traditions is comparable."[108] The difference in worldviews did not translate into significantly different behavior. Worldviews matter, but there are other powerful forces that serve to construct the world. These can lead to behaving inconsistently with one's worldview. It is therefore not the power of metanarratives that Sack calls into question, it is the idea that this power is unlimited.

The Cultural Reduction

If the mental realm and the social realm individually have the potential to reduce the role of the natural realm, the combination of the two under the label of 'culture' can be quite effective. Because Sack understands place as the assemblage of the three realms in a location, when culture obscures the natural realm it in effect obscures the role of place. Throughout the

107. Tuan, "Discrepancies Between Environmental Attitude and Behavior."

108. Sack, *Homo Geographicus*, 47–48.

exploration of how culture can reduce the role of nature, it is presented in terms of culture and place.

One way reduction becomes noticeable is through language. Sack notes, for example, that "elements such as coal, oil, and natural gas [can] be represented by chemical symbols or as instances of energy," but under the social realm, these same elements could be understood as "raw materials, resources, or commodities in an economic system."[109] Such shifts illustrate how connecting the elements of the different realms can occur through reducing complexity to a more narrow term. Words and phrases are chosen to reframe the situation in a way that privileges one realm over others. The use of the word *culture* has this kind of reframing capacity.

Such shifts illustrate how connecting elements across realms often relies on compressing a complex process into a summary term—one that inevitably obscures important dimensions. In this reframing, certain realms are elevated while others recede from view. The term *culture* functions in this way, carrying the capacity to reorient interpretation toward one realm at the expense of others.

Culture can fold in the idea of place and nature in a way that helps to obscure, or at least overshadow, their significance. Culture becomes an all-inclusive container idea. Raffestin points out that "representations are like currency: they are subject to inflation and progressively lose their value."[110] Is it possible that the term *culture* is a representation that has become somewhat inflated? If so, this inflation of culture can create imprecision and ambiguity regarding issues of place and nature. As a result, culture can be understood as tightly tethered to a place in such ways that the distinction is blurred.[111]

Walls and Sanneh write about culture repeatedly. How do they use the term in relation to nature and place? Is the reductive tendency present in their usage of the term? In his *Encountering the West: Christianity and the Global Cultural Process*, Sanneh contemplates the relationship between culture and Christianity. As he considers notions of culture, Sanneh rejects the view that culture is mainly about "interior cultivation and contemplative discipline."[112] He argues that Kant broke culture away "from all local, mother tongue moorings," and consequently "established for culture its

109. Sack, *Homo Geographicus*, 115.

110. Raffestin, "Space, Territory, and Territoriality," 125.

111. Sack, *Homo Geographicus*, 136.

112. Sanneh, *Encountering the West*, 43.

own system of transcendentalism."[113] In this approach, culture became internalized and individualized, as when one has supposedly become "cultured." Sanneh sees this approach as presenting a significant problem. "When culture has been thus dissolved and distilled into Kantian ideals of 'universal pleasure', it leaves in place an elite corps of cultural arbiters whose sensibilities determine the course of evolutionary development from primitive forms to abstract conceptions."[114] The result is that some are more "cultured" than others based on a seemingly arbitrary system of evaluation. Setting the significant concerns of inequality aside, there is the question of whether this approach can actually be put into practice.[115] Can one strip away their cultural particularity, as Turner's frontier thesis assumed? No, they can only be successful at ignoring particularity in their search for some preferred universal ideals.

This transcendental view of culture is not as common today, but the view of culture as tightly tethered to "local, mother tongue moorings" is evident.[116] Sanneh has concerns with this approach as well. First, it does not reflect the reality of human movement in and out of place. Second, Sanneh argues that it can inhibit the development of individuals and the community. Sanneh proposes the following alternative:

> To recognize that the cultural project, in being spiritual and intellectual, is at heart a theological matter, that reason is only secondarily human and primarily divine, not the wear and tear of nature's exterior drapery but its sap and fibre. Culture, 'whether personal or communal, is not reducible to genetics or ethnicity because man is always capable of transcending his origins, that is, of ending his journey in a different and better place than he began it.'[117]

This quotation reveals Sanneh's own concerns of reductionism. He does not believe that culture can be reduced to one's ethnicity or genetic

113. Sanneh, *Encountering the West*, 40.

114. Sanneh, *Encountering the West*, 46.

115. Sanneh argues that this "mechanistic and materialist notion of culture . . .has obvious implications for the cultures of weaker nations, not to say anything of the disadvantaged classes in the West itself. The problem is actually made even more acute if we idealize language and empty it of all content, such as we find in Winckelmann's statement that culture, like beauty, 'should be like the purest water, which, the less taste it has, is regarded as the most healthful because it is free from foreign elements,'" in Sanneh, *Encountering the West*, 45–46.

116. Sanneh, *Encountering the West*, 40.

117. Sanneh, *Encountering the West*, 63.

makeup, as evidenced by the capability for one to transcend their origins. Sanneh may have meant this metaphorically, but the literal sense also holds true and migration easily comes to mind as Sanneh's own personal history can attest. Sanneh speaks to the cultural project as a spiritually and theologically integrative activity, somewhere between abstract elite concepts transcending above and rigidly anchored to the particularity below.

Sanneh addresses the complexity of how *culture* as a term is used and acknowledges the potential problem with too tightly conflating culture with place, genetics, or ethnicity. At the same time, Sanneh presents an expansive vision for culture that is often inclusive of place.

Walls and Sanneh both write about culture in a way that seems to imply or include elements of place and nature. One can see evidence of this when statements about spatial interaction, ideas of locality, or references to place, nation, or soil are summarized with the idea of culture. These may be found in metaphors or in more direct references to geographical terms and ideas. Both scholars write about culture while indirectly addressing issues of place and nature.

In their efforts to explain the relationship between language, culture, and the gospel, Walls and Sanneh make regular use of metaphors that evoke imagery of place—"soil," "springs," "seeds," "earthiness."[118] They are grounding the abstract ideas they want to convey in terms of physical place. When Walls talks about "Krio identity rooted in African soil," he speaks of culture deeply connected to a location."[119] When he describes the soil as responsive or fertile with respect to the gospel message, the soil stands for the people. When Sanneh speaks of translation work and says, "the mother tongue was fertile soil for the new religion," this is not inadvertent.[120] The

118. Just to give a few examples from both authors. From Sanneh in *Encountering the West*: the use of "field" (239), "cultural hinterland" (240), "drain the indigenous reservoir . . .with the Bible as a scarecrow in a barren meadow" (238). From *Disciples of All Nations*, "bound to sow the seeds" (217), "salvation was a stepping stone of civilization" (203), "muddied the water" (135). From *Summoned from the Margin*, "religious landscape" (231), "center of gravity" (231), "tide" (232), "local rivers" for cultural analogues, and "laboring in a stony meadow" (248). Walls, *Missionary Movement in Christian History*: "biblical images rooted in the soil" (29), "plastered cistern and the ever-flowing spring" (50), "kingdom of God is fermenting yeast." From *The Cross-cultural Process in Christian History* (14), "landmarks" (38), "cultural island" (89), "planting of Christianity in Africa" (89), and from *Crossing Cultural Frontiers*, "fertile soil for inter-Christian culture clashes" (13), and "Greek intellectual soil" (27).

119. Walls, *Missionary Movement in Christian History*, 214.

120. Sanneh, *Disciples of All Nations*, 177.

use of physical place stands as an analog to the other kinds of particularity Walls and Sanneh want to call attention to. All of these metaphors speak to the basic significance of earthly lived experience in a place, with its soil and land and references of particularity like "the mighty Zambezi."[121] When Walls and Sanneh want to talk about culture and language, the elements of nature and place are the nearest metaphor they can find to make sense of these ideas.

Beyond metaphor, there are other ways that demonstrate how culture is used by Walls and Sanneh as inclusive of the elements of place. Consider how Sanneh writes of his own cultural project as "a personal intellectual testament" of one "who was educated on four continents and who carries within him some of the formative strands of several distinct cultural traditions: the African, the Islamic, the Christian, and the modern West."[122] Notice how Sanneh uses "cultural traditions" as a broad container for ideas of the religious, the geographic, and the intellectual. Notice also the significance he gives to his experience of being "educated on four continents."

Words of remoteness or marginality also speak to spatial interaction. At a minimum they evoke a sense of nature and place. Note the way that Sanneh uses the language of spatial interaction to get at his theological conviction of the equality of cultures before God.

> The characteristic pattern of Christianity's engagement with the languages and cultures of the world has God at the *center* of the universe of cultures, implying equality among cultures and the necessarily relative status of cultures vis-à-vis the truth of God. No culture is so advanced and so superior that it can claim exclusive access or advantage to the truth of God, and none so *marginal and remote* that it can be excluded.[123]

Is it possible Sanneh wrote of culture this way because he understood culture as generally attached and inclusive of place? This spatial interaction language could be merely metaphorical. But if one were to substitute place for culture in the above quotation, it would read quite similarly. The idea of place is at least an analog to culture in what Sanneh is writing.

In other passages, Sanneh speaks of "the localization of Christianity" as a concrete grounding of the Christian faith rooted in a particular

121. Sanneh, *Encountering the West*, 177

122. Sanneh, *Encountering the West*, 24.

123. Sanneh, *Disciples of All Nations*, 25.

place.[124] He then continues, "it is precisely the historical concreteness of Christianity that makes cross-cultural mutuality possible."[125] Culture is the summarizing framework that makes sense of the particularity found in localization.

Walls writes about culture similarly to Sanneh. When he remarks on the "cultural variety that six continents can bring," one can see an intermixture of culture and place.[126] When Walls writes of "Christianity as it has entered and penetrated another culture," or when he refers to "things and people outside the culture," this is language of spatial interaction.[127] Can one literally enter a culture, or is it more accurate to say that humans experience culture in a place? Consider this statement by Walls. "Christ must rule in the minds of his people; which means extending his dominion over those corporate structures of thought that constitute a culture. The very act of doing so must sharpen the identity of those who share a culture. The faith of Christ is infinitely translatable, it creates 'a place to feel at home.' But it must not make a place where we are so much at home that no one else can live there. Here we have no abiding city."[128] In this statement culture is initially spoken of in the abstract terms of "corporate structures of thought." Then he leans into a metaphor, "a place to feel at home." But then the metaphor takes on a tone of reality, "but it must not make a place where we are so much at home that no one else can live there." Where do these corporate structures of thought assemble? They do not hang in the air, they live within people, who, for the most part, live on the ground, in a place.

Walls uses culture as a label for a variety of human realities. Humans "are conditioned by a particular time and place, by our family and group and society, by 'culture' in fact. In Christ God accepts us . . .with that cultural conditioning that makes us feel at home in one part of human society and less at home in another."[129] Recall that Sack argues that the use of words like *home* are geographical concepts, yet here culture is the dominant rubric.

In his writing, Walls regularly details how diaspora and migration influenced Christian history. Of their significance he states, "these developments make migration an essential theme of world Christian history, and

124. Sanneh, *Encountering the West*, 129.

125. Sanneh, *Encountering the West*, 129.

126. Walls, *Missionary Movement in Christian History*, xvii.

127. Walls, *Missionary Movement in Christian History*, 22 and 9.

128. Walls, *Missionary Movement in Christian History*, 25.

129. Walls, *Missionary Movement in Christian History*, 7.

the Great Reverse Migration is clearly a vital factor for the future of World Christianity."[130] Both ideas of diaspora and migration are easily understood as forms of spatial interaction, geographical realities. If they are central themes, so is the idea of place. Put another way, if the tendency has been to conflate place and culture, and if the ties that bind culture to place have been cut, then a clearer understanding of both is required.

Culture Uncontained

There may have been places where the manners, behaviors, beliefs, and artifacts of a group of people (give or take a few) were all contained within a particular location. This culture would be so tethered to a place that it would essentially eclipse the significance of the place. In such an instance where one place was understood to contain one culture, then speaking of culture as inclusive of place would be logical. But this kind of fixed arrangement was probably less often the case than one tends to assume. Humans have always been on the move. They do so for a host of reasons: war, famine, jobs, marriage, and adventure, just to name a few. These moving humans bring their culture with them, changing the places they go to and the places they leave behind. Culture moves and at much greater speed and frequency than place does (even if tectonic plates and changing rivers remind us that place is not completely static).

Humans also have peculiar ways of identifying their culture by means of geography, at times even referencing geographic space where they themselves have never inhabited. Labels with explicit geographical reference such as Chinese American–are common. The complexity further presents itself when one considers larger urban centers. If one were seeking to represent the culture of a place like Chicago, this would likely instigate the question–'Which culture?'. Chicago is a city where many cultures exist. Any answer to the question, 'What is the culture of Chicago,' requires a selection process that will diminish the role of some cultures and people compared to others. While culture is a necessary component of place, when one particular culture becomes preeminent in a place, other cultures can be excluded or simply made invisible. Is it possible that place analysis offers the opportunity to see this complexity in a way that cultural analysis does not? Using culture in the singular as the all-inclusive framework of understanding leads toward an approach that is probably not sufficient to

130. Walls, *Crossing Cultural Frontiers*, x.

represent reality. Not only does it reduce the importance of place, but it also obscures the variety of cultures that assemble in a location as if only the dominant culture matters.

For Sack, human action is "inescapably constrained and enabled by space and place," braiding together the natural and the cultural. Indeed "as geographical beings we incorporate and alter each of these in the particular places we occupy."[131] This is taken for granted and geography naturally becomes part of the human conception of culture. So much so that one wonders if it is possible to effectively disentangle them. But many of the things Walls and Sanneh describe in terms of culture, Sack would argue need to be properly understood in terms of geography–place and spatial interaction, even territoriality.

A focus on culture alone can reduce awareness of the natural realm. Place brings culture and the physical world together. An inflated approach to culture needs to be problematized so the important nuances of geography are not lost. But in this world, culture is becoming increasingly untethered. Not so much in the direction of the idealistic abstractions of Kant but untethered from place itself, and toward (at a minimum) the increased awareness of human mobility. If Kant unbound culture from the earth, perhaps the result is not getting lost in the transcendental clouds. But instead, one is free to roam the earth and carry their culture along with them, amassing increasing hybridity.[132] If culture is increasingly understood to be untethered, then place, along with the geographical tools for studying it, matters all the more.

The purpose of the above analysis was to show how different disciplines explain the world and how in the process they can reduce the contribution of other disciplines. The resulting fragmentation from these approaches segments life in ways that are often hard to recognize.

> Nature and culture, wilderness and city, seem geographically far apart; the thinned-out places of our lives spatially segment ordinary activities as well as intellectual pursuits: a genetic process is explored in this laboratory, a market force is examined in that department, and the structure of mythical thought in yet another. At the same time, this very same modern world makes it clear that actions and thoughts are completely interconnected from the local to the global level. As the dynamic quality of modernity increases,

131. Sack, *Homo Geographicus*, 25.

132. Burke, *Cultural Hybridity* and Kraidy, *Hybridity, Or the Cultural Logic of Globalization*.

> the problem of understanding these interconnections becomes ever more difficult.[133]

This presents a fascinating puzzle. The tendency of our world is towards increasing fragmentation while continually drawing attention to our need for meaningful synthesis.

Synthesis in Geography

In the 1990s, a mixture of factors had prognosticators declaring that the world was becoming borderless.[134] The importance of nation-states was understood to be diminished as transnational corporations and humanitarian aid organizations seemed to have an almost universal jurisdiction. Klinghoffer argues that "forms of globalization belie state sovereignty, reduce the salience of borders, and stress dynamic 'flows and networks.'"[135] The way in which technology and travel seem to compress time and space encourage people to view themselves as unbound to any particular location, keeping the focus away from place and instead on one's ability to move between places. These dynamics have given people the impression that humanity is moving toward an "increasingly deterritorialized" world, without borders and without roots.[136] According to Sack, in the midst of this 'borderless world' one needs to be even more attentive to the realities of territoriality.

> We would see ourselves more and more as potentially free and independent agents choosing our own locations, our own occupations, our own patterns of consumption. It is this heightened state of individualism and mobility in mass society that constitutes the significant context for examining the uses of territoriality.[137]

Humans are more interconnected and simultaneously disconnected than ever before, and at a much larger scale.

Invisibility of place encourages people to think of themselves as non-geographic. The challenge this invisibility poses is that an over emphasis on a borderless world can eschew the richness of the local experience that comes from "person-embodied, context-dependent, spatially sticky . . .

133. Sack, *Homo Geographicus*, 57.

134. See O'Brien, *Global Financial Integration.*

135. Klinghoffer, *The Power of Projections*, 127–28.

136. Schreiter, *The New Catholicity*, 26.

137. Sack, *Human Territoriality*, 155.

direct physical interaction."[138] Furthermore, "we run the risk of becoming geographically unaware at the very moment we have to be most aware, and this cannot help but shroud our conception of the world."[139] Contrary to the non-geographic borderless narrative, "it matters if I am born in Somalia or the United States; if I grow up in a ghetto or a suburb; if I attend one class or another. It matters even when society tries to make places alike."[140] The particularity of one's experience, their geographic story that combines all the mental, social, and natural influences of their life makes a fundamental difference in how they understand and conceptualize the world. This is true even if they can order the same Starbucks latte as someone else halfway around the world.

Terrorism, conflict, and war have dampened the optimism of the 1990s. More recently, scholars argue that the changes in territorial structuring are more complicated and unexpected than previously thought.[141] While the capabilities for interconnected autonomy may be present, they are often distributed unequally to the wealthy few. Sanneh argues that globalization is best understood as "the corralling of the world's resources by dominant powers, and traversing the globe for that purpose."[142] Sack too sees the economic connections with capitalism and traces this in terms of geographic mobility. Political entities become concerned with extending their own power for the purpose of securing "access to new markets, and raw materials, and to maintain reliable transportation and safe conduct within the domain."[143] Globalization has created winners and losers on a global scale and there is a great amount of power that upholds this dynamic.

While some have embraced the global interconnections of travel and technology, others have resisted the breakdown of borders. As the rise of nationalism demonstrates, walls are far from unfashionable. The push to "conform to common purpose" is countered with an isolationist approach that behaves as a kind of muscular defense for the particularity of place. This impulse of division and containment is a backlash to globalization, but it is as much of a force in contemporary life as the alternative. Some

138. Morgan, "The Exaggerated Death of Geography," 12.

139. Sack, *Homo Geographicus*, 257.

140. Sack, *Homo Geographicus*, 13.

141. Kahler, *Territoriality and Conflict in an Era of Globalization.*

142. Sanneh, *Disciples of All Nations*, 94.

143. Sack, *Human Territoriality*, 82.

Christians have considered strategies of withdrawal for similar purposes.[144] Sack recognizes the tendency toward separation but argues against it.

> Can we reverse the course of things by shutting ourselves off from the world? Can we restrict our connections and limit our contacts? Can we build walls around ourselves? To divide us into smaller and more self-contained units, perhaps even ethnic enclaves, could conceivably make our actions more manageable and the places we occupy thicker in meaning and shared experiences. But it would also narrow our sense of responsibility and caring for those beyond our borders, and hinder the spread of ideas; for if the ideas travel, they surely will set other things in motion.[145]

If Sack is right, that an isolationist approach hinders the spread of ideas, this surely has implications for Christian mission. There are unforeseen consequences to global agency, but Sack argues for the value of being a responsible global actor and not giving into the temptation of withdrawing.

Contrary to the idea of a borderless world, researchers are finding a continuing strong attachment to land for either economic resources or symbolic reasons.[146] The continuation of territorial conflict demonstrates that "globalization has produced changes in territoriality and the functions of borders, but it has eliminated neither."[147] The efforts of isolationists have shown an increasing interest in the particularity of place and the idea of territory.[148] The influence of modern-day travel and technology cast a vision for a limitless world filled with options, but human behavior demonstrates a strong tendency to restrict the freedom of oneself and others to particular places.

Humans make attempts to bring these threads together even as one's place or culture can act as an inhibiting force. Sack holds that "our knowledge that others have this difficulty, and that we live in an increasingly interconnected world, makes it all the more urgent to attempt such syntheses."[149] Sack believes that geography and understanding the significance of place helps to facilitate this need. As each of the different realms are combined and interrelate in a place, this "provides a nonreductionist means" of

144. Dreher, *The Benedict Option*.

145. Sack, *Homo Geographicus*, 11.

146. Lyons, "Diasporas and Homeland Conflict."

147. Lyons, "Diasporas and Homeland Conflict," 1.

148. Inge, *A Christian Theology of Place*.

149. Sack, *Homo Geographicus*, 175.

integration.[150] Attention to place allows the natural realm and the realms of culture (social and mental) to not overrule each other and encourages the integration of these various forces in one's life.

Recall earlier how Neil Smith described the dilemma for the field of geography as either all-inclusive or merely topological facts. It is clear that Sack's argument is this all-inclusive approach. This fits well with Smith's contention that most geographers articulate geography's uniqueness by "providing a bridge between the natural and social sciences." Smith agrees that the path forward for geography is a field working to unite "physical and human geography," but he has some doubts whether the clarity of the synthesizing approach is sufficient.[151] Sack has argued that it is the forces of contemporary life that have created an even more pressing need for synthesis. In this way, geography is once again attempting to respond to the changing needs of our world.

In this section, it has been argued that geography is a highly integrative discipline that can unite the different realms of human understanding without reducing their particular importance. While geography is often ignored or subsumed under other disciplines of study, it can play an important role in making sense of one's lived experience. For those who tend to focus on culture to the exclusion of the physical realm, spatial analysis offers opportunity for a better understanding of the world. Because Sack's understanding of place unites the natural and the cultural, the complexities related to the nature of place are similar to those of the nature of culture. In this way, some of the ideas of culture by Sanneh and Walls have similarities to that of Sack.

Sack's more robust view of geography opens opportunities for unexplored connections with missiology. While Sack is but one geographer, a close reading of his work gives an example of the benefits that can come from engaging with the theoretical tools the field of geography has to offer.

CONCLUSION

To what extent does the end of Christendom constitute the end of territoriality for Christianity? Is Christianity no longer territorial? What is territoriality and how has it been expressed in Christian and mission history? In this work, Sack's theory of territoriality and his *geographic awareness paradigm* are used to highlight and extend Walls's and Sanneh's insights on

150. Sack, *Homo Geographicus*, 116.

151. Smith, "Academic War Over the Field of Geography," 169.

territoriality and place. These tools come from the discipline of geography, which has been undervalued particularly in a US academic environment. Geographical analysis unites the realms of culture and nature to provide a more comprehensive understanding of life. In particular, Sack's theoretical tools will provide clarity for evaluating Walls's and Sanneh's claims of Christian non-territoriality and show the continued relevance of territoriality.

The preliminary matters of this introduction are a foundation for understanding place and the perspectives that feed into territoriality. We now move to look specifically at what territoriality is and the effects that flow from it.

2

The Theory of Territoriality

THE ARGUMENT

THE FIRST STEP IN arguing for the continued relevance of territoriality in Christian faith and mission begins with a clear understanding of territoriality. In this chapter it is argued that Robert Sack's theory of territoriality is a useful and substantive tool for understanding and evaluating instances of territoriality.

SACK'S THEORY OF TERRITORIALITY

In the Connecticut Western Reserve of the early nineteenth century, the establishment of fences and other orderly maintenance of physical space were an indication of morality in the eyes of missionaries.[1] Roughly a hundred years later, the antagonist in Robert Frost's poem, *Mending Wall* gives voice to this idea in the statement, "good fences make good neighbors." Frost critiques this colloquialism but he does not argue for the elimination of boundaries. Instead, he asks the reader to reflect on the consequences and

1. DeRogatis, *Moral Geography*, 4. DeRogatis writes, "the link between moral discourse and the physical landscape is prominent in Protestant frontier missionaries' letters and diaries . . .For example, one missionary lamented the Western Reserve settlers' disinterest in religious matters in a letter to the home society, stating that 'our fields + farms lie unfenced, untilled, unsaved.' Here is illustrated the direct relationship between uncultivated landscapes and souls, and the echoes of Puritan concern for using fences to manage the land properly and to maintain boundaries to enclose the community of believers," Quoting John Seward to Connecticut Missionary Society, October 19, 1812, John Seward Letters, Connecticut Missionary Society Papers.

necessity of such boundaries–"Before I built a wall I'd ask to know, What I was walling in or walling out, And to whom I was like to give offense."[2]

Forms of physical boundary, such as walls and fences, serve a purpose. Robert Sack states, "for the most part, people and their activities cannot find room in space, without forms of control over area–without territoriality."[3] The study of territoriality, among other things, is one way of considering the answers to Frost's questions. The purpose of understanding territoriality is not to eliminate boundaries, or to encourage their creation, but to discern clearly what is being walled in or walled out and the implications that flow from these actions.

How might Sack's theory of territoriality be useful for this goal? In this section, Sack's definition of territoriality, a description of the characteristics associated with it, ethical concerns related to it, and the effects that flow from it are explained.

Territoriality Defined

The relatively neglected role of geography in the United States, may go toward explaining why territoriality is not a familiar word. Sack even has reservations about the term, admitting "that it is not a pretty sounding word."[4] While territoriality may lack a euphonious quality, the advantage of an unfamiliar term is that it can prompt the curious to ask, "what does that mean?"

As stated in the introduction, Sack understands his theory to be situated within the tradition of human geography.[5] Territoriality is an essential fact of human spatial interaction, part of "how people use the land, how they organize themselves in space, and how they give meaning to place."[6] Sack's approach is different from theories of territoriality that are related to animals. Commonly, 'being territorial' is thought of in a way that stresses notions of competitiveness, where territoriality can make "humans appear

2. Frost, *North of Boston*, 12.

3. Sack, *Human Territoriality*, 25.

4. Sack, *Human Territoriality*, 2. Within the confines of the English language, Sack says he cannot find a better term–"sovereignty, property, and jurisdiction are too restrictive in scope to be suitable alternatives" to encompass the broad range and significance of "*a human strategy to affect, influence, and control.*"

5. Sack, *Human Territoriality*, 3.

6. Sack, *Human Territoriality*, 2.

animalistic."[7] It can be an accusation directed at someone for being overly, and perhaps illogically protective as if the behavior is instinctual. The use of the term "territorial" in this way links it to evolutionary biology, which was further developed in psychology.[8] In this way of thinking, territoriality is understood as a psychological need for dominance or security.[9] Sack disagrees with this approach. What makes human territoriality different is the capacity humans have to turn it on or off.[10] Territoriality is not an uncontrollable urge nor is it illogical but instead a willful and cognitively engaged action by human agents. This perspective is born out in his definition.

Sack defines territoriality as "*the attempt by an individual or group to affect, influence, or control people, phenomena, and relationships, by delimiting and asserting control over a geographic area*."[11] In his theory, territoriality is an expression of power which can range from the largest international scales to one's personal space. Territoriality is a strategy "to create and maintain much of the geographic context through which we experience the world and give it meaning."[12] His approach to territoriality suggests that it is pervasive in human behavior, particularly when considering the dynamics of power. At the same time, he recognizes that it has often gone unnoticed, receiving little attention even in the realm of geographical spatial analysis.[13] Sack believes the goal for geographers should be to draw attention to the broad idea of territoriality and to develop greater understanding of the familiar territorial aspects of one's life. It is to this end that Sack examines human territoriality and why his text has become foundational to the discussion of the topic.

Descriptive Characteristics

To expand upon Sack's definition several characteristics become important to developing a more complete description of territoriality. These characteristics include 1) the scale of the territory being controlled, 2) the span of control or the number of those affected, and 3) the intensity of force. Each

7. Klinghoffer, *The Power of Projections*, 199.
8. Raffestin, "Space, Territory, and Territoriality."
9. Altman and Haythorn, "The Ecology of Isolated Groups."
10. Sack, *Human Territoriality*, 24.
11. Sack, *Human Territoriality*, 19.
12. Sack, *Human Territoriality*, 219.
13. Sack, *Human Territoriality*, 25.

of these characteristics serve as a kind of metric for observing the extent of territoriality.

Territorial Scale

Territoriality is an expression of power over a geographical area. While power and control can be wielded in ways that do not require spatial form, doing so is a distinctive of territoriality. The geographical area of a territory can be spoken of on various scales.[14] The scale of one area can be small, such as a home or a room within that home. At a somewhat larger scale, one can find a church building, a campus, or the home office of a mission organization. The scale of territory can be still larger. Christians have often lived and worshiped within the context of a parish, or a diocese. These are smaller building blocks of what makes up an even larger territory. Scales increase in size from various forms of regional, to national, continental, and international territories.

The various territories of different scales often exist within the boundaries of other territories, creating nested and overlapping layers of territorial hierarchy. For example, a person's home could be simultaneously within the boundaries of a town, the limits of a school district, the jurisdiction of a particular political representative, within a particular parish, state, and country, all at the same time. Leadership on all of these territorial scales exert influence over the home. Some of these layers coordinate with each other, others are autonomous. This layering effect is why Sack describes territoriality as an expression of "geography's concern with multiple uses and conceptions of space as a complex framework in which individuals and groups are situated, through which they interact, and by which they make statements."[15]

The variety of scale is more complex than conversations of local and global. There is a tendency to speak of the diversity of these layers of scale as diametrical opposites–at the macro level, global, and at the micro level,

14. The term 'scale' can be understood in different ways. For example, Rankin in *After the Map* states that "*small scale* and *large scale* might mean two things when describing a map: either the size of the land area shown, or the size of the ratio between real-world lengths and lengths on a paper," (vii). Among cartographers and geographers, scale is often used in this second sense which counterintuitively sees scale as inversely proportionate to the size of the area. Sack uses scale in the first sense, where increasing in scale corresponds to increasing size. Throughout this work, I will also use scale in this way.

15. Sack, *Human Territoriality*, 25.

local. Peter Dicken points out in reference to "the *spatiality* of globalizing processes . . . [that] the non-geographical globalization literature" presents scale as "invariably dichotomized simplistically into 'global' and 'local.'"[16] Dicken urges those outside of the discipline of geography to appreciate the complexity beyond these two options of territorial scale.

Span of Control

In addition to the size of the territorial scale, another metric for determining the extent of territoriality would be the size of the population that is influenced. The importance of any particular act of territoriality "depends on who is controlling whom and for what purposes."[17] Territorial power can be exerted over individuals, groups, relationships, objects, or nature. We are concerned with territoriality in terms of power exerted over people. Span of control is used to refer to the quantity of those impacted by the territoriality.[18] The notion of span of control can also be thought of in terms of proportion related to a geographical area. This helps to give further texture to the quantitative notion of span of control. One's control may be over all the people in a territory, or it may be over particular people that are distributed across the territory who make up a lower proportion of the overall population.

Intensity of Force

The intensity of force is the third characteristic useful for understanding the extent of territoriality. As the "primary geographical expression of social power," territoriality has a range of intensity in which that power is expressed.[19] In his definition Sack lists "affect, influence, or control" to represent a spectrum of force that "is always used in conjunction with non-territorial spatial strategies."[20] Examples of power at one's disposal could range from the subtlety of influence or persuasion, to giving or withholding resources, to more visible acts of physical force and manipulation.

16. Dicken, "Geographers and Globalization," 8.
17. Sack, *Human Territoriality*, 55.
18. Sack, *Human Territoriality*, 44.
19. Sack, *Human Territoriality*, 5.
20. Sack, *Human Territoriality*, 52.

Territoriality is more obviously exhibited when a group or individual protects a territory, or when they forcefully expand the territory beyond the previously understood borders. By contrast, the more subtle forms of influence often escape notice.

There are entities that have the ability to assert control over an area with a greater intensity of force than others. To call attention to this difference, these entities will be referred to as primary territorialities and the others as secondary territorialities. Often, but not always, the primary territorial control rests with the government of a nation-state. They have the sovereign ability to wield significant power to achieve their goals with respect to an area. Their use of force can be coordinated, persistent, and legitimized under laws. Secondary territorialities would include other influential groups or organizations that function with various degrees of autonomy from the primary territoriality. They may attempt to take actions of significant enforcement, but they will ultimately have to answer to the primary controlling body of an area. The relationship between the primary territoriality and the secondary territoriality significantly shapes the function of the secondary territoriality. How this is the case will become clearer in chapter 6.

Degree of Territoriality

The characteristics of scale, span of control, and intensity of force are important for describing and distinguishing the variety of forms territoriality takes. A lessening of these characteristics can be thought of as lesser territoriality. As an example, within Christendom the territory under the leadership of the pope was large. It included multiple nested scales on which the hierarchy of the church was built. Furthermore, a high proportion of those in the territory fell under his purview. Because of the close association of the church with the governmental apparatus, the intensity of force available to the pope could include the entire range of control from influence, persuasion, giving, withholding, and physical force. The characteristics speak to the potential for a high degree of territoriality.

In the present day, the leader of a protestant denomination in the US would stand in contrast to a pope of Christendom as an example of one wielding a form of lesser territoriality. While the size of the territory may be large, the proportion of the population under the leader's purview would be more limited. He or she would not be allowed to use more intense elements of force without consequence. The characteristics speak to the potential for a lesser degree of territoriality. The three characteristics help one to understand the extent of specific instances of territoriality. If one only sees territorial behavior in large area land grabs, they will have missed the subtle ways in which it influences the world today. It also draws attention to the way that forms of territoriality can change over time.

Ethical Concerns

The power dynamics in territoriality, particularly evident in the use of force, raise ethical questions. Yet Sack leaves the ethical aspects underdeveloped. He acknowledges that "the theory itself will not present procedures by which one can judge whether an action is, on its own merits, good or bad.[21] In his later work, *Homo Geographicus*, Sack's ethics with respect to place become more important. While principles from *Homo Geographicus* apply to evaluating territoriality, the specific ethical concerns related to the use of this strategy are not thoroughly addressed.

Sack's underdeveloped ethical framework does provide a general comparison between a more protective or custodial role of territoriality versus something more malicious. For instance, a mother may limit access to a garage with various sharp tools so that her small children are not harmed. The mother is using territoriality to protect her children. She exercises her power for a custodial purpose. There are other non-spatial or spatial options available to her. If the mother were to explain to her children which tools are dangerous and why they may not be touched, this would address her concerns in a non-spatial way. She could also remove the dangerous tools from the garage. That would be an example of a spatial strategy, but only territoriality limits access to the area.[22] Territoriality provides an efficient means for the mother to keep her children safe.

By contrast, "when differential access through territoriality benefits those exercising territoriality at the expense of those being controlled" this is deemed malevolent.[23] It should be noted that territoriality may begin with a more custodial function, at least ostensibly, but then over time it is either revealed to be, or simply becomes, more malevolent.

Determining whether a particular instance of territoriality would fall in one category or another is also complicated by the fact that different

21. Sack, *Human Territoriality*, 31.

22. Sack, *Human Territoriality*, 16.

23. Sack, *Human Territoriality*, 31.

people experience territoriality differently. Some who are influenced by territoriality may perceive the experience as beneficial, while others feel it is not. Whose assessment is valid and who gets to determine validity can be problematic. Small children may not fully appreciate the custodial actions of their parents, from their perspective they are being kept from that which would benefit them. Most would judge that parents know better. Yet outside of the parent and small child relationship, this justification is often disputed. When a group exerts territoriality, be it governmental or organizational, and claims to know better, this knowledge is often contested based on differential experiences or wider frames of reference. For example, the state may use territoriality to limit travel or activity during a pandemic. Some may see this as a custodial action by the government, a territoriality introduced to benefit the health and wellbeing of the community. They will judge the territoriality to be good. Others may see such actions as malevolent, detrimental to their economic wellbeing or even sneaky attempts to influence the political realm. They will judge the territoriality to be bad.

There are other ways to assess territoriality that are not centered on the question of morality but instead on the issue of effectiveness. Continuing with the example of the pandemic, one could question whether the territoriality that is being used by the government is the right kind of territoriality. They may be in full agreement with the intent and goals of the government, but may be concerned with how well the particular territoriality is able to accomplish these goals. Are the factors being influenced or controlled, the right factors to achieve the government's goal of suppressing the pandemic? Were the classifications made by the territoriality the most useful classifications? Was the territoriality communicated effectively and enforced appropriately? The answers to these questions may border on issues of morality, but the principal concern is related to the effectiveness of achieving a goal held in common. The effectiveness of a territoriality is considered good while the lack of success is considered bad.

While Sack's theory of territoriality does not provide sufficient means for determining whether a territoriality is custodial or malevolent, he does provide more tools for assessing effectiveness. Instead of reflecting on the ethical concerns of motive and intent, the definition and theory of territoriality emphasizes action and outcomes. Past instances of territoriality become a guide for one to understand more current examples of territoriality. Learning from past territorialities helps one to predict potential pitfalls and guard against ineffective forms. His descriptions of the characteristics related to territoriality, and his detailed account of the causes and effects that flow from it, all contribute to evaluating its effectiveness.

THE EFFECTS OF TERRITORIALITY

Sack wants to push past merely saying what territoriality is to explain what it can do and under what circumstances it is most often used. Sack argues that "it is principally on helping to point to the important effects of a phenomenon that the value of a definition rests."[24] To this end, Sack provides a list of causes and effects that flow from instances of territoriality.[25] His goal is to articulate a theory of territoriality that was broad enough to explain a variety of forms, and yet detailed enough to explore the nuances of particular instances.[26]

Sack lays out ten tendencies and an additional fourteen combinations under different names which are related to territoriality's possible outcomes. Some of the effects include the establishment of hierarchy, the construction of impersonal relationships, viewing space as emptiable containers, obscuring or exhibiting power, and creating differential access to resources. These effects are also linked to each other in ways that one might stimulate the occurrence of another. I have chosen to highlight only those that are relevant for this particular study. More connections could likely be made which provide opportunities for further research.

The Essential Facets of Territoriality

Sack is very specific, mentioning several times that he sees three "essential facets" for territoriality: 1) the classification of a particular space as a territory, 2) the communication of that classification, and 3) the defense of that territory.[27] Any account of territoriality must include, or imply, these three. This requirement becomes important when considering other scholars' usage of his theory. Sack argues that these three facets "disclose the logic and

24. Sack, *Human Territoriality*, 2–3; 18.

25. Sack refers to both *causes* and *effects* in his text. He argues that they often look and function the same way. If one uses the strategy of territoriality knowing and desiring the likely *effect*, this turns the *effect* into a *cause*. Consequently, when I use the term *effect* here this could imply the possibility that this may also be the *cause* for why territoriality was used.

26. Sack, *Human Territoriality*, 216.

27. Sack, *Human Territoriality*, 22.

significant effects of territoriality."[28] These facets, beginning with classification, will be explored briefly before considering the other effects.

Classification

Territoriality first involves a form of classification by area. Sack states "we are classifying or assigning things to a category such as 'ours' or 'not yours' according to its location in space."[29] Classification becomes an efficient way of referring to an area without having to identify or divulge all that may be in the territory. Consequently, "territoriality . . . may be the only means of asserting control if we cannot enumerate all of the significant factors and relationships to which we have access."[30] For example, when a missionary is assigned to a particular country, or when a church planter selects a city, these assignments to a classified area supersede detailed enumeration of all that exists in the area. The details of their ministry are either unknown or too numerous to define. Classification by location becomes an efficient means of articulating that which is difficult to quantify.

The boundary lines of a classification can be negotiated, expanding the limits outward or inward. Within a classified territory, subdivisions can also be created and adjusted. The classifications of a secondary territoriality may be specific to the group's or organization's needs or they may be adopted from the primary territoriality. For example, a denomination may make use of governmental subdivisions (e.g., Michigan) or create their own divisions for the purpose of their denominational needs (e.g., The Great Lakes Region).

Classifications, at times, can be understood as neutral undertakings, but in the act of classifying there are dynamics of power and ethics at play. Classifications presuppose perspectives about what places are good or bad, valuable or worthless, central or peripheral, and even Christian or non-Christian. Power is demonstrated when one's perspectives are used to classify places while other perspectives are disregarded. The ethical dimensions of these classifications can be revealed when one asks whether these classifications are true, just, dignifying or demeaning. In the next chapter, the perspectives that underlie classifications will be considered more directly.

28. Sack, *Human Territoriality*, 21.
29. Sack, *Human Territoriality*, 32.
30. Sack, *Human Territoriality*, 32.

As one of the three essential facets of territoriality, evidence of classification is in and of itself not sufficient for determining that territoriality is present. Sack believes that, "delimitation becomes a territory only when its boundaries are used to affect behavior by controlling access."[31] By contrast, other classifications may just be ways of describing the geographic extent of certain activities.[32] Or in terms of mission practice, a person may feel burdened to minister in Panama to Muslims. This is an example of classification by area and by type. Based on the information provided, this does not sufficiently describe an example of territoriality, but it is a classification or a description of the geographic extent of one person's ministry activities. Even so, the likelihood that Panama is a sufficiently precise description of the extent of their geographic activities is not very plausible. And the use of Panama in this description likely serves to communicate geographical ideas to those outside of Panama rather than those within.

Classifications can also be formed prior to the other necessary facets of territoriality being in place. Sack provides the example of a government designating a region to receive financial assistance. The classification may predate the aid distribution, but it only acts as an example of territoriality when "the boundaries of the region are affecting access to resources and power."[33]

Communication

Once a classification has been determined, it requires a form of communication. This is the next essential facet of territoriality. The boundary of the territory is the main substance of the communication. According to Sack, "territoriality can be easy to *communicate* because it requires only one kind of marker or sign–the boundary." Sack observes that the territorial boundary "may be the only symbolic form that combines direction in space and a statement about possession or exclusion."[34]

There are other ways of communicating the boundaries of a territory. Communication could take verbal form, be articulated in writing, or drawn on a map. The type of communication can be based on the characteristics

31. Sack, *Human Territoriality*, 19.
32. Sack, *Human Territoriality*, 19.
33. Sack, *Human Territoriality*, 19.
34. Sack, *Human Territoriality*, 32.

and context of the territory. Signs, walls, and fences are appropriate for one scale but not another.

Sack distinguishes the communication facet of territoriality from merely communicating "the geographic extent of activities in space."[35] To say that a person is traveling from one side of the country to the other may be a communicated classification, but it makes no statements of possession or exclusion nor does it seek to influence an area in any particular way. In contrast, if siblings are sharing a bedroom and one subdivides the space with a line of blue tape on the carpet, this is likely not a benign communication of the geographic extent of the activities of each sibling. It is more likely a strong statement of possession and exclusion, implying a significant threat of enforcement.

Enforcement

Enforcing control over an area is the third essential facet of territoriality. To effectively exclude people or things from an area, or contain people or things within an area, requires enforcement. But it is more than defending area alone. Sack states, "territoriality need not be defended area, if by that is meant that the area itself is the object of the defense, and that the defender(s) must be within the territory defended."[36] Sack continues, "territory can be used to contain or restrain as well as to exclude, and the individuals who are exercising control need not be inside the territory" or "anywhere near it."[37] What is essential for enforcement is the belief that transgressing the boundaries of the territory has consequences.

The characteristic of intensity of force is particularly associated with enforcement. The more obvious enforcement actions would be conquest and physical domination or the threat of these. Influence and withholding resources are also forms of enforcement, though they are more subtle forms of control. While a primary territoriality can often make use of any form of enforcement, a secondary territoriality is usually limited to the more subtle forms.

As an example of a more subtle form, consider the classification of people between 10 degrees latitude and 40 degrees latitude. Imagine that this classification is received by a church mission board. Territoriality

35. Sack, *Human Territoriality*, 32.

36. Sack, *Human Territoriality*, 19–20.

37. Sack, *Human Territoriality*, 20.

comes into play when the church mission board is unwilling to support the missionary interested in serving Muslims in Panama because the activities do not fall within the geographical area classified as the *10/40 Window* The enforcement, though mild, comes in the form of withholding access to resources. This action is presumably within the scope of the church board's responsibilities. They are custodians of the missionary funds, but their actions could be understood as a form of territoriality as they seek to mold and influence missionary activity to a particular geographic area.[38]

Classification, communication, and enforcement are the three essential facets of territoriality and the first effects. While they need not develop simultaneously, all are necessary to state that something is an example of territoriality and "each instance must involve an attempt at influencing interactions."[39] What one can see from this overview of Sack's understanding of territoriality is that his theory extends beyond a mere definition, making it a useful tool for spatial analysis. But Sack's understanding of territoriality is not limited to the three facets alone. Territoriality is also associated with other kinds of effects that may or may not always be present. As previously mentioned, Sack lists ten tendencies which can also combine for a total of fourteen different effects. Some of these effects relate to specific time periods or spatial arrangements that are outside the scope of this work. Only six will be considered here–reification and displacement, container, empty space, hierarchy, inequality, and increasing territoriality.

The Six Additional Effects of Territoriality

Reification and Displacement

Reification and displacement are possible effects of territoriality used to enhance or hide power. The accoutrement of royalty, such as their robe and crown, are physical manifestations that reify the sovereign's power and prestige. Territoriality can be used in much the same way to enhance and symbolize power. Abstract ideas like sovereignty and power "are not always as tangible as are streams and mountains, roads, and houses. Moreover, power and the like are often potentialities. Territoriality can make the potential explicit and 'visible.'"[40] Reification brings abstract notions of power

38. For more discussion on the territoriality present in the '10/40 window,' see de Korte and Onnekink, "Maps Matter."

39. Sack, *Human Territoriality*, 22.

40. Sack, *Human Territoriality*, 33.

"down to earth" in physical form. Places of worship can serve as examples of this effect. "The church building, as well as the parish and diocese, reminds us, through reification, of God and the Christian community."[41] Here a kind of conflation can occur where the building becomes the church rather than the people. In time the building, or another *holy* place, can be understood to have a power of its own.

There are more subtle ways reification occurs and can thus exhibit territorial power. Increasingly, it has become common for churches or non-profit organizations to demonstrate their global influence with maps, sometimes stretching from floor to ceiling, that tell a singular story of one community's engagement with the world.[42] Those places not connected to the community are often left empty as if awaiting the church's attention. And while some organizations may use precise markers of their engagement, others will opt for visually changing the color of whole nations to demonstrate what could in fact be a much smaller location of ministry.[43] Such representations can have good outcomes. They may be effective at communicating the general mission activities the church is involved in. They may even serve to promote the idea that the work of God extends beyond one's own local setting. Or at a minimum help alleviate geographic illiteracy. However, it is worth asking, if such representations can also serve to subtly promote the aggrandizement of the institution or organization. Maps have often served as tools of power projections to communicate importance and significance.[44] Could such displays be a temptation for church leaders who feel a need to communicate their own worth and significance? The more destructive notion implied in these kinds of communications is that all that matters, in the work of God's mission, is what is done in this particular worshipping community. This creates a myopic view of Christian faith and mission.

41. Sack, *Human Territoriality*, 114.

42. The use of the word global here is intentional. While Sanneh often prefers the term *world* as in world Christianity, this kind of territorial power betrays a subtle, "from the west to the rest" ideology that Sanneh sees as implicit in the term global.

43. For example, World Vision makes use of a map in some of their correspondence and on its website. The map has two tones, orange and gray. Above the map it states "Orange-colored countries indicate a World Vision presence," from a 2011 Donor correspondence letter. The map and two-tone color strategy give the impression that a full 2/3rds of the world are being served by World Vision.

44. Klinghoffer, *The Power of Projections*, 28.

In territorial reification the power of the controller emanates out in concrete manifestations of space and place, all of which points back to the controller. Displacement and reification are similar in that both take the form of concrete manifestations of power, yet with displacement, the objective is not to point back to the controller but away.[45] Sack explains, "Reification through territory is a means of making authority visible. Displacement through territory means having people take the visible territorial manifestations as the sources of power. The first makes the sources of power prominent, whereas the second disguises them."[46] Displacement downplays the role of the influencing agent and instead creates the illusion that the place itself holds the power. Reification helps to enhance power while displacement helps to hide power.

At the same time, the difference between reification and displacement is often so slight, that it may not be possible to distinguish one from another.[47] Sack conveys how "territoriality can be used to *displace* attention from the relationship between controller and controlled to the territory, as when we say 'it is the law of the land' or 'you may not do this here.'"[48] The rules are thought of as intrinsic to the place, arising from the place, displacing the role of the human agents in constructing these rules.

When reification and displacement are united, "these effects make the sacred visible and the visible sacred."[49] Consequently, this can create what Sack calls "a mystical view of place or territory."[50] Just as reification can create a conflation between buildings and church, displacement can occur when the "holy" space or church building come to be seen as having a power of their own. Sack argues that "when the site is especially sacred and when the building contains relics," the power of that particular place is heightened.[51] Often these locations become pilgrimage destinations, thus the designation of a place as holy has often benefited those with territorial control of the location.

There are other ways territoriality can obscure power which are built on the way territory acts as a container.

45. Sack, *Human Territoriality*, 114.
46. Sack, *Human Territoriality*, 38.
47. Sack, *Human Territoriality*, 114.
48. Sack, *Human Territoriality*, 33.
49. Sack, *Human Territoriality*, 59.
50. Sack, *Human Territoriality*, 38.
51. Sack, *Human Territoriality*, 114.

Container

The idea of thinking of territory as a container was an innovation that developed over time.[52] Inge argues that place as a container can be traced to Aristotle's influence.[53] The mental habit of understanding space as a bounded geographical territory can emphasize constraint over and against fluidity.[54] This way of thinking can also be an efficient means of not having to enumerate all that is within the territory.

Speaking and writing of places as containers is often an efficient and intentionally imprecise way of addressing issues. For example, when Walls argues that "early Christianity has important African and Asian dimensions that invite the attention of Western Christians," he is using broad continental containers to express his idea.[55] In Dorottya Nagy's article, "Where is China in World Christianity?," she accuses Walls of using a kind of "territorial essentialism."[56] She holds that conversations of World Christianity have a "continental narrowness,"[57] and this perspective is seconded by Elenora Hof.[58] Yet, Walls's expression is perhaps better understood in light of Sack's argument for efficiency. Using a territorial container allows Walls the opportunity to not be weighed down by the particular and the need to enumerate all that is within the container. This is necessary, if not unavoidable, when crafting a broad narrative about World Christianity.

As a shorthand, speaking of place in terms of containers has value, but that value diminishes when precision and complexity are one's aim. In response to Nagy, one could argue that China is but another territorial container that also obscures the complexity of diversity therein. Furthermore, what one finds in Walls's writing is a fluctuation of scale. While at times he

52. Elden, *The Birth of Territory*, 322.

53. Inge, *A Christian Theology of Place*, 4.

54. Klinghoffer, *The Power of Projections*, 128.

55. Walls, *Crossing Cultural Frontiers*, 10.

56. Nagy, "Where is China in World Christianity?," 177.

57. Nagy, "Where is China in World Christianity?," 177.

58. Hof, "Re-imagining World Christianity." Hof picks up on this remark (which is actually in one of Nagy's footnotes) to define territorial essentialism as "the naturalization of a given territory by making it the primary lens of interpretation" (177). In her view, this comes through the process of an "unwarranted emphasis on a certain locality" and "is complete when it is hardly possible to acknowledge the necessary contingency of this locality" (177). Her ideas are interesting avenues to explore and draw attention to the possible distinction between territorial essentialism and ethnocentrism.

speaks in broad terms, he counterbalances this approach by also descending into the particulars of history.

While the classification of territory as bounded space is common for the reasons mentioned above, territoriality can be used to enhance or maintain the impression that territory is a container. In this way, "territoriality acts as a container or mold for the spatial properties of events."[59] For example, the legal limits of a city are bounded even while the influence and authority of a city can spread far beyond this boundary. Territoriality works to preserve the notion that, generally speaking, objects, relationships, and patterns remain in their container.

Consider how in the US, the South and the North are often spoken of as if they exist as bounded containers to which certain attributes and phenomena are ascribed. If racism is ascribed to the South this can direct attention away from instances of racism in the North, giving the false impression to some that, "we don't struggle with that here." The classification of territories and the view of territories as a container can obscure the complexity and redirect (or displace) attention from the relevancy of that issue in another territory. Those making use of territoriality can have these dynamics serve their advantage.

The combination of displacement and the idea of seeing places as containers is expressed in statements such as 'we don't do that here.' Used to justify a rule, such statements redirect attention from the authority that makes the rule, to the place itself. Sack believes that there is evidence of this way of thinking of territory as containers and displacement in the first several centuries of the church. Conflict could be thought of in terms of places rather than people: "the see of Constantinople vies with the see of Rome, Alexandrea with Jerusalem and Antioch."[60] The result is that each location is understood as a container of particular theological perspectives and adherence to that perspective and the location become intertwined.

If territory is viewed as a container, it is not hard to then imagine that container being thought of in terms of emptiable and fillable space. The next effect, looks at how territoriality works to create the impression of empty space.

59. Sack, *Human Territoriality*, 33.

60. Sack, *Human Territoriality*, 113.

Empty Space

If territoriality gives the impression that a classified territory is a container, that container can then be thought of as empty or filled. In this way of thinking "when the things to be contained are not present, the territory is conceptually 'empty.'"[61] Territoriality helps to foster the notion that a territory is an emptiable place, it is also used to empty, fill, and maintain the territory. Consider the idea of empty space in relation to a vacant lot within a city. Sack contends that "it is describable as an empty lot, though it is not physically empty for there may be grass and soil on it. It is emptiable because it is devoid of socially or economically valuable artifacts or things that were intended to be controlled."[62] The place is empty or filled based on whether it has value in the controller's perspective.

To understand the idea of empty space as an effect of territoriality, one can compare the *social definition of territory* to *the territorial definition of social relationships* (see Figure 2.1). For the social definition of territory, the geographic extent of the social group defines the area. Historically, some societies have relied on a social definition of territory; the Chippewa that once populated what is now Wisconsin, are the example Sack offers.

Figure 2.1 Social Definition of Territory Versus Territorial Definition of Social Relationships

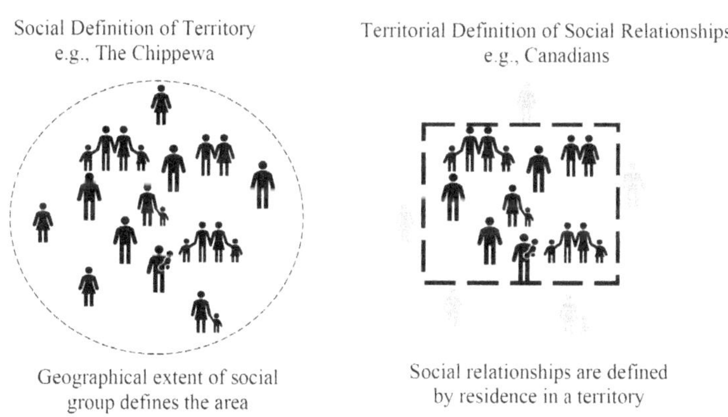

By contrast, the territorial definition of social relationships is based primarily on one's residence or domicile. The social relationships are defined by the fact that the individuals live in the same territory. An example might

61. Sack, *Human Territoriality*, 33.
62. Sack, *Human Territoriality*, 33–34.

be those that live in Canada are Canadians. Sack notes that the territorial definition of social relationships is more common for "modern societies" where "continuous and intense territorial definitions lead . . . to a conceptually emptiable space."[63] Territorial definitions of social relationships can replace ethnically defined areas and acknowledge the diversity within the location. In these places, "location within a territory defines membership in a group."[64] Thus, residency is all that is required for an individual to be entitled to the services of, for example, a city.

Alongside the inclusive aspects of a territorial definition of social relationships is a framework that creates the possibility "of continually filling, emptying, and rearranging things in a territorial mold for the purpose of efficient functional control. This constant manipulation of things within a territory would lead, on an abstract level, to a conceptual separation and recombination of things and space and thus to a conceptually emptiable space."[65] While urban environments can open the door to all kinds of residents, the increased segmentation, the continual emptying and filling, can inhibit those same residents from feeling fully integrated in a meaningful way. This can deepen the experience of isolation and inhibit a sense of belonging.

In its capacity to arrange space and give meaning to place, territoriality can appear custodial. But it is not an insignificant power to be able to declare a space empty or filled. While this effect of territoriality can often go unnoticed, it can also be a source of conflict. The European encounter with the so-called New World provides one illustration of this effect.

When Europeans came to the shores of what is now called North America, what they found was massive amounts of land that they knew little about. As Sack describes "the untamed forces of nature made it wild, and its vast unknown quality, intensified by the lack of detail in the cartographic representation of these lands, emptied it even further."[66] Klinghoffer echoes this observation, noting that in cartographical representation "blank space in an area implied that territorial claims could be made there."[67] Europeans did indeed make those claims.

63. Sack, *Human Territoriality*, 37.
64. Sack, *Human Territoriality*, 37.
65. Sack, *Human Territoriality*, 37.
66. Sack, *Homo Geographicus*, 108.
67. Klinghoffer, *The Power of Projections*, 79.

As it happened, with the use of longitude and latitude one could plot even the unknown into manageable parcels. A conceptual framework was placed on the land prior to surveys and settlements. Sack observes that "the New World charters described territorial claims abstractly and geometrically and, in conjunction with conceptually and then actually clearing the land of Indians, the geometric lines of territorial authority become sweeping space-clearing and maintaining devices for territorially instituting communities."[68] Lack of knowledge and presumed superiority over the resident population led to a belief in conceptually empty land. When it was discovered that the land was not as empty as assumed, efforts were made to make the situation match the classification. In particular, "by the beginning of the seventeenth century the characterization of Indians and their non-agricultural relationships to land as sub-human served as the rationale for white expansion."[69] The English legal doctrine of *vacuum domicilium* allowed white settlers to seize land based on their understanding of how the land should be used.[70] If the parcel of land was not being used for agriculture, did not have a proper fence, or a fixed building structure, it was theirs for the taking.

There is a tendency for decisions regarding conceptually empty land to be made far from the land itself. Classification can seem so innocuous when it is merely drawing lines on a map. The land at "its farthest reach, was over 1,000 miles from the Eastern Seaboard where the decisions were being made."[71] According to Sack, "with the stroke of a pen, Americans of European descent were to classify, divide, and control people, including Chippewas, solely on the basis of their location in space."[72] These developments had social and economic impacts at various levels. As the map of the Northwest took shape, the Chippewas found their social definition of territory deconstructed. "Eventually part of the Chippewa were to be in Canada, another part in Minnesota, another in Michigan, and yet another in Wisconsin."[73]

In the New World, the use of abstract emptying in this form of territoriality was distinct from other uses of territoriality. Sack sees this difference

68. Sack, *Human Territoriality*, 134.

69. Sack, *Human Territoriality*, 134.

70. *Vacuum domicilium* is Latin for *empty dwelling*.

71. Sack, *Human Territoriality*, 134.

72. Sack, *Human Territoriality*, 11.

73. Sack, *Human Territoriality*, 11.

in how the English brought settlers to Ireland, a land that they could not conceivably imagine as empty.

> Maps, surveys, and deeds continued to incorporate detailed landscape features and pre-existing Irish land use, practices, and divisions. Moreover, the settlement plans had Irish populations interspersed among the English. Compare this with the abstract claims of territorial control made by the charters and grants of North America. Here a physical feature may be mentioned, there an Indian place name, but the overwhelming sense is of claiming and subdividing an empty space.[74]

The comparison between Ireland and the New World underscores how the territorial effect of empty space can belie dehumanizing perspectives of people, and profound ignorance of physical space.

Viewing territory as empty space should also be considered theologically, particularly where the practice exists within the history of Christianity and mission. One of the first descriptions of creation (Gen 1:2) was filling what was formless and empty. The form and structure of creation were supplied, and the empty space was filled. There is, therefore, no corner of the earth that is truly God-forsaken. All space has been filled by God's creative design and purpose.

The next effect of territoriality also tends toward emptying, filling, and arranging, but the focus is on positions and personnel within an organization. This effect is hierarchy.

Hierarchy

At some scales, when territory is classified and subdivided, the creation of a corresponding hierarchy often follows. Sack explains that "most of human behavior occurs with hierarchies of territorial organizations."[75] What arises from the territorial hierarchy are two specific outcomes–impersonal relationships and bureaucracy. Through the geographical molding activities of territoriality, area is subdivided and basic organizational hierarchy forms with these various potential effects. These hierarchies can be extrapolated to multiple layers as mentioned in the characteristics above–such as cities, states, nations, or parish, diocese, archdiocese. Sack holds that everything that has been said of territories also applies "to hierarchical territorial

74. Sack, *Human Territoriality*, 140.

75. Sack, *Human Territoriality*, 34.

organizations."[76] Both territories and hierarchies can expand outward or subdivide within. What follows looks at impersonal relationships and bureaucracy specifically.

Classifying by area can foster impersonal relationships. This can be either the aim or the unintended result of territoriality. As Sack explains, "upper echelons of a hierarchy tend to use territories to define, enforce, and mold groups, with the result that members may be collected and dealt with impersonally."[77] As a group, empire, or religion grows, pursuing impersonal relationships may be the most equitable way to meet the needs of an increasingly large and complex organization. Contemporary cities are a prime example of large groups defined by impersonal relationships which are likely the result of the territoriality necessary to organize all the activity and people in an urban setting. In most cities, belonging is largely determined by residence within the territory which tends to foster impersonal relationships.

Bureaucracy is the next outcome associated with hierarchy. The development of territorial hierarchies can heighten "the effect of impersonality" and also "increased the bureaucratization and centralization of power."[78] When considering the effects of hierarchies, Sack combines his understanding of territoriality with that of organizational theorists. He lists the following general characteristics important to understanding organizations:

- *Specialization*—which refers to the division of labor;
- *Standardization*—which refers to the extent of procedural regularity in the organization;
- *Formalization*—which refers to the use of documentation for job definition and communication;
- *Centralization*—which refers to the locus of authority in the organization.[79]

As Sack investigates territoriality, these are elements that he identifies as associated with bureaucracy. While Sack leans on Weber in particular, he

76. Sack, *Human Territoriality*, 34.

77. Sack, *Human Territoriality*, 36.

78. Sack, *Human Territoriality*, 167.

79. Sack, *Human Territoriality*, 44. Sack also includes *Configuration*, which refers to the shape of authority and hierarchy and can often be summarized by span of control.

believes that these characteristics of organizational bureaucracy are generally consistent with other theorists.

Sack describes how Weber valued the rational and efficient aspects of bureaucracy.[80] Yet he also admitted that it had a "tendency to make relationships too uniform and impersonal, which would cause the organization to dissolve or split apart and could create opportunities for charismatic leaders to form new ones."[81] Despite these concerns, bureaucracy was still seen as something that could be used for good. Successors to Weber more fully investigated the down side of bureaucracy.

> Michels examined German socialist organizations and found that, despite their idealistic and egalitarian beginnings, these organizations became increasingly institutionalized, authoritarian, and hierarchically rigid; and the officials became more interested in perpetuating themselves and their offices than in their commitment to the original goals of the organization. This trend he attributed to bureaucracies in general and called it the 'iron law of oligarchy.' Merton disclosed another malevolent side to bureaucracy. An emphasis on strict formal procedures, disciplines, and rules, he argued, leaves officials with the view that adherence to formal procedures is an end in itself.[82]

Bureaucracy has the promise of efficiency, equality, and organization that helps institutions reach their goals. Yet this high ideal can be subverted by organizational leaders that serve their own interests.

One of the contexts where Sack explores bureaucracy is in the church. His expectation is that the theory of territoriality would "guide our understanding of the Church's use of territory."[83] More precisely, "We can expect that territoriality has gone hand in hand with the development of Church organization and hierarchy. As the latter increased so did the former, and conversely. Specifically, we can expect to see a positive association between development of Church territory and the sociological dimensions of specialization, standardization, formalization, and the organizational span of control."[84] The development of hierarchy was a response to the legitimate

80. Sack, *Human Territoriality*, 45. See also Weber, *The Theory of Social and Economic Organization*.

81. Sack, *Human Territoriality*, 45.

82. Sack, *Human Territoriality*, 45; See Michels 1968 and Merton 1949

83. Sack, *Human Territoriality*, 98.

84. Sack, *Human Territoriality*, 92.

need for greater organization. Sack believes that the Roman Catholic Church stands "as one of the most extensive, long lasting, hierarchical bureaucratic organizations in the world, and its structure in turn has affected its goals."[85] The role of territoriality in the church will come into greater focus in the following chapters, but considering how a hierarchical structure influences an organization—particularly in ways that lead to greater specialization, formalization, and control—is an important aspect of this theory.

Bureaucratic centralization can have an impact on who has access to knowledge and responsibility. For example, Sack points to the way that subdivision can separate workers from the big picture understanding of what they produce. From hospitals to prisons to schools, these institutions "were modeled on rational and efficient forms of managements . . . [which] required the minute and intense subdivision and integration of territory."[86] One type of process or group is to be contained in every partition. The sum of all these distinct parts needs to then be integrated into the whole.[87] Yet this integration is often only the prerogative of the select few at the top of the hierarchy. Territoriality can keep responsibility and knowledge clustered at the highest levels while restricting access at the lowest levels.[88] Ultimately the subdivision leads to the kind of reductionism spoken of in the previous chapter. At risk is the possibility of segmenting one's sense of self. Sack states, "increasing territorial partitioning can mean increased specialization and division of activities. But it can also present problems of unification and integration."[89] Those not afforded the whole picture can, "contain things without knowing what they are and . . . can fragment without recombining."[90] The impact of hierarchical territorial organization on access to resources and knowledge leads to the next cluster of effects resulting from territoriality.

Territorial Inequity

In terms of human evaluation, all land is not created equal and the subdivision of land or space can further complicate the distribution of resources.

85. Sack, *Human Territoriality*, 92.
86. Sack, *Human Territoriality*, 181.
87. Sack, *Human Territoriality*, 181.
88. Sack, *Human Territoriality*, 34.
89. Sack, *Human Territoriality*, 173
90. Sack, *Human Territoriality*, 173.

The hierarchical structures that are built upon territorial partitioning can also create unequal access. The exacerbation of inequality is one of the most significant results of territoriality, yet it does not necessarily begin with malevolent intentions. Territoriality "can have a *momentum* of its own *to create inequalities.*"[91] It does so by "helping to enforce differential access to things [and] can become institutionalized in rank, privilege, and class."[92] Territoriality can then be used to maintain layers of inequality, making it institutionalized. Sack argues that "once such inequalities exist in even the best-intentioned society, they can corrupt those in power."[93] Whether intentional or not, territorial inequality can be disruptive to the goals and structure of an institution.

When access to knowledge and responsibility is clustered at the top of a hierarchical structure, their scope can be "graded according to territorial levels" or scales.[94] When activities are assigned to the wrong scale, Sack refers to this as mismatch or spillover. In such instances "territorial hierarchy allows for the mismatch of power and responsibility which can further obscure the use of power."[95] The assignment of knowledge and responsibility to the wrong level, can create situations where those in control no longer know what it is that they control. Decisions can be made far from the locations where they will be implemented and where the effects will be primarily felt. Similarly, decisions can be made without consideration of the impact beyond the assigned territory. This can occur in coordination with the idea of territory as a container. For example, if Brazil decides to allow deforestation, or fails to extinguish fires in the Amazon rainforest, they may do so with the understanding that what happens in their nation-state is their responsibility and their choice. But land is not really a container. The effects of deforestation, volcano ash, flooding, and climate change, do not remain neatly isolated in nation-state containers. National decisions regarding supposed internal matters can spillover with worldwide impact.

Territorial mismatches can be unintentional or can be done intentionally to serve a purpose. In particular, scale can be used as part of a geographical strategy or subtle means of obfuscation. Sack explains how this can be. "Scale can be used to disguise power and intentions. As we

91. Sack, *Human Territoriality*, 39.

92. Sack, *Human Territoriality*, 39.

93. Sack, *Human Territoriality*, 152.

94. Sack, *Human Territoriality*, 36.

95. Sack, *Human Territoriality*, 164.

noted, geographic hierarchy of scales is frequently part of social organizations. Nations have states and counties, and the Church has archdioceses and parishes. These hierarchies may be instituted for some general purpose of organizational logic and efficiency, but they can be used for other means as well. Process and scale can be mismatched intentionally to avoid responsibility or to doom a process to failure."[96] For example, states or politicians can assign responsibility to the wrong scale (perhaps the local level) as an effective means of discharging unpopular decisions. Yet the smaller scale may not be able to solve the problem. After the civil war, President Johnson assigned the responsibility of integrating those who were formerly enslaved to the people who had enslaved them. The devastating long-term effects of this decision demonstrated how the solutions to reconstruction needed to come from the federal level of government. But by pushing the responsibility to the local level, Johnson avoided the possible negative consequences for his office.

Within a religious framework, places deemed holy became intertwined with seats of power in the church hierarchy. Sack argues that "holier places often have higher ranking Church officials in charge of them."[97] For example, "St. Peter's Tomb at Rome gives added weight to the bishops of Rome for it makes them also the vicars of St. Peter."[98] Church leaders were aware that some posts had greater power and prestige and sought to attain these positions.

On a smaller scale, territoriality is present in the partitioning of places of worship. "Temples and palaces for instance are most often internally subdivided to mark off degrees of the sacred. The more sacred the place, the less accessible it is to the average person. Only the highest priest was allowed to enter the holy of holies and only the royal family and their retainers were allowed within the heart of the palace."[99] There may be important reasons for territorial partitioning of a worship space that serve the whole community well, but it is a distinction that can reinforce a hierarchical framework that divides "important" people from the "unimportant" people territorially.

96. Sack, *Homo Geographicus*, 124.
97. Sack, *Human Territoriality*, 93.
98. Sack, *Human Territoriality*, 93.
99. Sack, *Human Territoriality*, 75.

The tendencies of inequality, along with the bureaucratic and hierarchical development of territoriality only tend to increase. The last effect reviewed here is the tendency for territoriality to beget more territoriality.

Increasing Territoriality

Whether it is intended or not, territoriality has a momentum of its own whereby it is inclined to produce even more territoriality. This increase can be seen in outward territorial expansion or inward hierarchical subdivision. As organizations grow, they tend to increase in complexity. They may acquire new property or open a new campus which adds more area to control. They may also add layers of hierarchy by subdividing their territory or organization from within. This increase in territorial hierarchy can lead to escalating bureaucracy, particularly centralization. Whether outwardly or inwardly, territoriality tends to create more territoriality.

This "multiplication and intensification of territoriality" is often related to competition for goods in space.[100] Increasing territoriality can be a response to the issues created by differential access to resources, knowledge, and responsibility. Sack argues that "when there are more events than territories or when the events extend over greater areas than do the territories, new territories are generated for these events."[101] As more territories are added, there are more opportunities for events to be created and more relationships to be molded. Sack points to political theorists that have identified the tendency for governments to "increase in complexity and scale of society."[102] Often increasing the territorial range of activity is taken to be synonymous with improvement, growth, and success.

Within an organization, territoriality can come to have a life of its own. It has the potential "to affect and control beyond what might have been originally intended."[103] Often doing so at the risk of the institution.

> Overall there is the suggestion that territoriality can help increase the efficiency of an organization (whether it be a state, a business, or a church) up to a point, and that it can help shift an organization's goals from benign to malevolent . . . These inefficiencies can lead to the need for more hierarchy and larger territories to

100. Sack, *Human Territoriality*, 89.
101. Sack, *Human Territoriality*, 34.
102. Sack, *Human Territoriality*, 161.
103. Sack, *Human Territoriality*, 219.

> coordinate the spillover and mismatches. But eventually central control will be impaired. This could result in local levels having greater autonomy *de facto* if not *de jure*. Defining responsibility by area can also be used intentionally to obscure or disguise processes, increase the advantages of those in control, and shift the organization from benign to malevolent.[104]

Recalling Michels' 'iron law of oligarchy,' even if organizations begin with egalitarian commitments, they tend to become "increasingly institutionalized, authoritarian, and hierarchically rigid."[105]

The early period of the Catholic Church provides examples of these dynamics. Sack states that "by the fifth century A.D., the powers of archbishops were measured in part by the numbers of dioceses and parishes under their control."[106] Consequently, one way an archbishop could increase his power, was by further subdividing his see, giving him the opportunity to oversee additional bishops and priests. Such maneuvering by archbishops necessitated formal prohibitions against the practice. In response, canon law developed rapidly as a means of regulating such conduct and establishing normative standards for ecclesial leadership.

Uniformity and standardization are some of the ways to manage the growing complexity of an organization like the church. Such measures can provide clarity and efficiency, but only up to a point. The same innovations that lead an institution to greater effectiveness and organization can also serve to make the institution more entrenched in bureaucracy.[107] In other words, the very activities that made the organization necessary and function well, can in time, become the thing that hinders it. At that tipping point, they can appear to some as counterproductive, inefficient, and unnecessarily bureaucratic.[108]

The ineffectiveness of an overly heavy bureaucracy can lead to alienation and hostility at lower levels of the hierarchy. As a result, this increases the desire for reform, which can ultimately lay the groundwork for division and secession. When the inefficiency and the inequity within an organization are too great, breakaway groups often form new organizations. In Sack's view, "secession describes the condition wherein an individual

104. Sack, *Human Territoriality*, 41.

105. Sack, *Human Territoriality*, 45.

106. Sack, *Human Territoriality*, 39

107. Sack, *Human Territoriality*, 39.

108. Paul Light, in *Thickening Government,* echoes Sack's observation.

or group uses territorial tendencies to lessen or remove the authority of others."[109] The new organization resulting from secession may experience the markers associated with less territoriality–equality, voluntary association, and a flat hierarchy. New organizations can avoid or at least minimize the perceived negative effects of hierarchical territoriality. Consequently, groups that secede will tend toward integrating rather than specializing, improvising rather than holding to a rigid standard, personal relationships over and against impersonalization, and a tendency toward decentralized power. New organizations can also more easily respond to changing social values, compared to heavily bureaucratic institutions which are less nimble. As a result, a group that emphasizes freedom may be particularly successful when seceding from a long-standing organization that emphasizes authority. Refreshing as seceding and forming a new organization may seem, as the group grows, they may find themselves in need of more structure and hierarchy and once again making use of territoriality. Doing so would open the door to the same or different permutations of territorial effects that have been mentioned above.

A total of nine effects have been described in this chapter, three of which are essential facets of any instance of territoriality. This list is added to the descriptive characteristics, ethical considerations, and definition of territoriality that in total provide an overview of Sack's theory. It is a dense and multifaceted theory that is not easy to concisely summarize, but its complexity adds substance, making the theory useful for understanding and analysis. The final section of this chapter explores some of the concerns related to making use of Sack's theory.

THE USE OF SACK'S THEORY OF TERRITORIALITY

The theory presented by Sack is a tool for understanding instances of territoriality and the effects that flow from it. His goal in laying out the theory is to provide "a suitably broad yet clear definition which points to the general implications of territoriality for humans."[110] Sack accomplishes this in part by creating a more usable paradigm for analyzing a wider range of contexts and for recognizing how expressions of territoriality change over time. Territorial power takes different forms in different societies, and the effects of territoriality depend a great deal on the context in which it is being used. The theory seeks to identify and categorize these differences, aiming not

109. Sack, *Human Territoriality*, 40.

110. Sack, *Human Territoriality*, 23.

only to show variation but also to explain it. Doing so allows territoriality to be seen more clearly within a social context or a historical frame. "Both the selection of territoriality and the effect it has depends on social context: on how space in general is used and conceived as well as on who is controlling whom and for what purposes. This means that the history of territoriality is closely bound to the history of space, time, and social organization."[111] Governments and institutions throughout history, and continuing into the present, have used territoriality to organize and partition their domain. Yet each organization, within its particular context, employs territoriality differently, emphasizing distinct characteristics and effects. Sack notes that some effects "have been used only at particular times in history."[112] As territoriality takes on new forms of expression and manifestation, specific effects may become more salient. Sack maintains that "territoriality is always socially constructed. It takes an act of will and involves multiple levels of reasons and meanings."[113]

The theory of territoriality can serve as a framework for anticipating the kinds of effects that tend to emerge within complex social organizations. No matter their agenda or size, organizations have to manage their goals in a spatial world, assign roles and responsibilities within a hierarchy, and influence the people and things that are under their purview. Because "territoriality of one sort or another will likely be employed, we must be aware that it possesses its own potentialities to affect and control, and that some of these may be contrary to the goals of the society."[114] The theory of territoriality is substantive enough to engage in useful analysis of past occurrences, but it is general enough to respond to changing contexts and new forms of territorial manifestations. According to Sack, this kind of thick but flexible approach to territoriality "has been missing in previous works on territoriality."[115]

How others have written about territoriality offers a valuable comparison. Sack contends that some use the term territoriality without connecting it to any particular scholarly work or definition. While others write about territoriality without using the word. Walls provides an example of writing that seems to address the issues without making use of the term. In

111. Sack, *Human Territoriality*, 52.
112. Sack, *Human Territoriality*, 23.
113. Sack, *Human Territoriality*, 26.
114. Sack, *Human Territoriality*, 219.
115. Sack, *Human Territoriality*, 23.

contrast, Sanneh's writing employs the term territoriality without elaboration on a definition and without reference to any geographical scholar in particular. Sack also observes a third usage of territoriality. There are those who use the word, and even make use of Sack's theory, but they do so in ways that merely describe spatial behavior when such behavior does not rise to the standard of the definition. Because the theory of territoriality is complex, there is a temptation to reference the theory to advance one's argument without descending into the particulars or analyzing whether the perceived instance of territoriality qualifies under Sack's definition. What follows is an examination of two scholars whose use of Sack's theory raises questions about how closely their interpretations align with his definition.

The Use of Sack's Theory by Magda and Scott

Ksenija Magda's 2009 work, *Paul's Territoriality and Mission Strategy*, endeavored to apply geographical theories to concerns within New Testament scholarship. Her focus was on one missionary in particular, Paul. Magda's aim was "to contribute to the discussion about Paul's understanding of his mission by investigating how geography can be used to illuminate Paul's missionary strategy."[116] She undertook this goal by consideration of the idea of territoriality through the work of Robert Sack.

In a search for a more comprehensive approach, Magda argues that Sack's theory is the only one she could find that adequately handles the complexity of forces inherent in territoriality.[117] This theoretical base is used to understand the perspectives of the apostle Paul. It asks questions of how the self is influenced by place, how in turn the place is influenced by the self, and how geographical perspectives are formed. Specifically, she considers how one's geographical place influences how they understand the world, how they categorize other locations as central or peripheral based on their place, and how they make goals and strategy as a result. For Magda, "territoriality is intrinsically and primarily tied to a person's geographical place . . . [where] all other realms of the human experience assemble."[118] In this view, territoriality is essentially about understanding one's place.

Magda may not be using territoriality in quite the same way as Sack. Her work is written in response to the work of James Scott, *Paul and the Nations*. Magda argues that while New Testament scholars often build

116. Magda, *Paul's Territoriality and Mission Strategy*, 4.

117. Magda, *Paul's Territoriality and Mission Strategy*, 24.

118. Magda, *Paul's Territoriality and Mission Strategy*, 33.

complex arguments based on geographical principles, they rarely delve into the specific literature of geographers. Magda commends Scott as the exception to this rule.[119] Scott claims to employ Sack's definition of territoriality from *Human Territoriality* and applies this definition to the apostle Paul. Scott then argues that "when Paul's mission is viewed in light of a territorial strategy based on the Table of Nations, many aspects of his relationship to the Jerusalem apostles and his opponents begin to fall into place."[120] In the long and ongoing debate about why Paul did what he did when he did it, Scott offers territoriality as a rationale.

Understanding Paul's territorial strategy seemingly has explanatory power and Sack's definition is Scott's theoretical foundation. Magda, while arriving at a different set of conclusions from Scott, follows his pattern of using Sack and linking territoriality to Paul. Scott rightly states Sack's definition, but limits his interaction with Sack's ideas to that statement.[121] There is no comment on the associations of power and control. Considering the fullness of the meaning of territoriality, it seems reasonable that one may become apprehensive about applying this notion to the apostle Paul. At a minimum, using Sack's theory should require that a case is made for Paul's mission strategy aligning with the essential facets Sack outlines.

The Question of Paul's Territoriality

If Scott uses Sack's theory of territoriality, then the three "essential facets" of *classification, communication*, and *defense* should be helpful for identifying territorial behavior, and consequently one should see evidence of these three conditions in Paul's actions. Scott does not state how he believes Paul's behavior satisfies Sack's requirements, but it seems worth considering. One could grant that Paul had a *classification of a particular space as territory*. It appears evident that Paul did have a kind of geographic strategy, however loosely constructed, or primarily Spirit led, it may have been. The passage significant in this regard for Magda is Romans 15:19–20, "so from Jerusalem all the way around to Illyricum, I have fully proclaimed the gospel of Christ."

With the second condition, it is possible but less clear how much Paul engaged in efforts one could consider as *communication of classification*.

119. Magda, *Paul's Territoriality and Mission Strategy*, 180.

120. Scott, *Paul and the Nations*, 150.

121. Scott, *Paul and the Nations*, 150.

Demonstrating a strategy of movement is not quite the same as communicating a classified territory for the purpose of power and control.

The third condition seems to be even harder to find evidence to sustain. If Paul were behaving in accordance with Sack's conditions, Paul might have argued that he alone was the apostle to the Gentiles and that outside of Jerusalem, the Roman empire was his exclusive evangelistic territory. To the contrary, when disputes arose such as described in 1 Corinthians 3:4, "one says, 'I follow Paul,' and another, 'I follow Apollos,'" or Philippians 1:15–18, "But what does it matter? The important thing is that in every way . . . Christ is preached," Paul's language suggests the opposite of territorial behavior. He was not seeking to control or limit access and does not seem to be motivated by power. Though Paul did mark his progress geographically, there is no evidence that he intended his evangelistic goals to be understood as gaining possession of land or area, or even a kind of spiritual conquering of a territory.

If Scott's use of territoriality does not align with Sack's, how does Scott use it? Scott presents territoriality as a cognitive activity, essentially answering the question, "what is Paul's geographical reasoning?". One can see how this approach overlaps with the first of Sack's conditions of territoriality; classification is primarily a conceptual project. However, Scott's usage of territoriality falls short of at least one, if not two, of the other conditions.

Magda follows Scott in this approach, and doubles down in the more cognitive account rather than one that includes both cognition and behavior. She does so, using Sack's work, but not *Human Territoriality*. Instead, she holds that his *Homo Geographicus* is a continuation of his line of thinking on territoriality.[122] This latter work has a paradigm for understanding one's place that Sack refers to as a *geographic awareness paradigm*. Magda prefers to call it a "Territoriality Paradigm."[123] She then uses this paradigm to analyze Paul and specifically his letter to the Romans. Given the lack of familiarity already present with this geographical term territoriality, Magda's choice potentially fosters some confusion.

Magda's approach is unexpected, mainly because Sack rarely refers to territoriality in *Homo Geographicus*. To be fair, that omission is indeed striking. The word *territoriality* appears only five times in *Homo Geographicus*, and two of those are in the footnotes. Although Sack notes that the book continues aspects of his earlier work on human territoriality, the

122. Ksenija Magda, personal correspondence (video call), September 15, 2018.

123. Magda, *Paul's Territoriality and Mission Strategy*, 22.

connection is indirect.[124] In a publication which looks back at the contribution of *Human Territoriality* to the field of human geography years later, Sack addresses the reason for why territoriality is largely absent from *Homo Geographicus*.

> I have always thought that territoriality is a special case of the part of *Homo Geographicus* . . . that develops a theory of the structure and dynamics of place. I did not devote time to argue the point (although I did address territoriality in a footnote) because I thought this connection was clear enough, and to make it more explicit would have overburdened an already complex argument, and drawn attention away from other points I wanted to make. But since then I have seen that it might be worthwhile to show how exactly *Homo Geographicus* can subsume territoriality.[125]

I have not found further statements from Sack on this topic.

If the continuation of the territoriality theme was as strong as Magda suggests, one would expect it would be more clearly stated in Sack's text. Furthermore, when Sack traces human territoriality in his monograph by that name, he does so within three realms; one of them is the church. Therein he states that the church in the early days was strikingly non-territorial in their approach. Consequently, it seems odd for Magda, or Scott, to find examples of territoriality in Paul if Sack recommends looking elsewhere, particularly as they claim to follow his geographical expertise and use his theory of territoriality. While Magda effectively traces Paul's geographical perspective, she does not extend her analysis to consider whether his spatial reasoning might constitute territoriality as Sack defines it.

Magda's Contribution

The significance of Magda's work lies in her examination of the relationship of the self and place as the bedrock for the conceptual analysis of geographical perspectives. These kinds of perspectives could lead to territorial behavior or territoriality, but not necessarily. They could instead lead to what Sack sees as merely spatial behavior. Most importantly, Magda points in the direction of how missionary strategies imply geographical perspectives in their action plans.[126] These observations, or ones like them, have

124. Sack, *Homo Geographicus*, Acknowledgments.

125. Agnew, Paasi, and Sack, "Classics in Human Geography Revisited," 96.

126. Magda, *Paul's Territoriality and Mission Strategy*, 155.

probably not received enough attention in missiological circles. Setting aside her use of the term territoriality, Magda does faithfully apply Sack's *Homo Geographicus* to understanding Paul and his place in helpful ways. Had she done so retaining Sack's language, the objection to her approach would dissolve. Yet not using the term territoriality might have jeopardized her clear link with Scott's work.

To reiterate, the first of Sack's conditions of territoriality is mainly conceptual. Or to put it another way, all territoriality begins through conceptual geographical perspectives that can lead to the *classification of territory*.[127] But this does not mean that all geographical perspectives necessarily lead to territoriality or give rise to territorial behavior. While Sack's definition of territoriality is lauded by many, later definitions seem to adjust to more fully explore this conceptual angle. Raffestin, for instance, defines territoriality as "the translation of a system of relations that neither affects only territory nor derives from it completely" and happens "within the limits of the conception that [groups or individuals] have of it."[128] Raffestin's definition takes a step closer to Magda's usage and aligns with Sack's work on place and perspectives in his *geographic awareness paradigm*.

If all territoriality begins with conceptual geographical perspectives derived from one's sense of place, Magda's research and Sack's *Homo Geographicus* rightfully belong as a part of any investigation of territoriality. For if one is to fully understand territoriality, they must give attention to the experiences and perspectives that invigorate territorial behavior at the conceptual level. It is also, at this conceptual level, where the integration of theology and ethics can extend Sack's understanding of territoriality in meaningful ways.

Taking all this into account, Magda's work on territoriality has value but may require greater nuancing. It may be that in this nuancing, one could

127. Sack makes this point by distinguishing between place and territory. "This delimitation becomes a territory only when its boundaries are used to affect behavior by controlling access. For instance, a formerly ordinary geographical place or region such as a corn belt or a manufacturing area may become designated by the government as a region to receive special financial assistance or as an area to be administered by a special branch of government. In this case the boundaries of the region are affecting access to resources and power. They are molding behavior and thus the place becomes a territory. By the same token, what geographers call nodal regions, market areas, or central place hinterlands are not necessarily territories. They can be simply descriptions of the geographic extent of activities in space. They become territories though if the boundaries are used by some authority to mold, influence, or control activities." Sack, *Human Territoriality*, 19.

128. Raffestin, "Space, Territory, and Territoriality," 126 and 124.

retain the distinction between territoriality and geographical perspectives generated by place without disconnecting them from each other. Doing so may serve to deepen and enrich the overall understanding of these ideas.

The Use of Territoriality by Walls and Sanneh

By way of contrast, Walls and Sanneh do not make use of Sack's work but do discuss territorial dimensions of Christianity and in the case of Sanneh, territoriality specifically. When Walls and Sanneh say that Christianity is no longer territorial, what do they mean and how does this compare to Sack? Repeatedly, Walls and Sanneh refer to a time period when the Christian faith was linked with specific land; where all who were within the territory were Christian (or irrelevant), and all those outside, were deemed non-Christian. This territorial expression of the faith is usually included under the idea of Christendom, and as Walls articulates, essentially coterminous with Europe.[129]

When Sanneh speaks of territory, he has in mind real land, the boundaries of which are best understood as state or country boundaries. In Sanneh's articulation "the religious case of nonterritoriality" is essentially "the separation of church and state."[130] After what he calls "Christendom's territorial meltdown," Sanneh observes that there remains an uncomfortable ambiguity in the way some Christians relate to the state.[131] Specifically, there is a tendency among some Christians toward a nostalgia that pulls them back toward the shadows of Christendom. Sanneh admits that there are advantages to religious territoriality. Yet, the kind of enforcement necessary to secure this level of widespread religious territoriality is ethically problematic for Christians.[132] Sanneh's use of the term territoriality is not inconsistent with Sack, but Sack's definition is broader.

If one were to consider Walls's and Sanneh's perspectives on territoriality in relation to Sack's conditions, they may see the following: 1) At one time, or another, Christians have *classified* particular places as Christian, and other places as non-Christian. In Sack's terms, created or classified a territory. 2) In various ways Christians have *communicated* these classifications, to those within and to those outside the territory (e.g., referring to places, not just people, as Christian or not Christian). 3) Finally, at

129. Walls, *Crossing Cultural Frontiers*, 15.

130. Sanneh, *Encountering the West*, 185.

131. Sanneh, *Encountering the West*, 185.

132. Sanneh, *Encountering the West*, 222.

particular moments, Christians have felt the need to *defend* that territory, either by actively maintaining it, guarding it, or enlarging it. These actions have been taken as if one were defending Christianity itself. Leaving aside the question of whether or how this continues today, this description seems to be consistent with the similarities in Walls's and Sanneh's approaches to territoriality and aligns with Sack's three conditions.

The following determinations can be made: 1) Sack has written separately about both territoriality and perspectives formed by place in two different monographs. 2) While Magda writes about territoriality, she is likely more properly discussing the idea of place and geographical conceptions of territory stimulated by place. 3) When Walls and Sanneh are speaking in terms of territory or territoriality they are not, broadly speaking, inconsistent with how Sack defines it. 4) It seems possible and beneficial to retain the distinction between territoriality and perspectives formed by place without disconnecting them from each other. They are best linked through the more conceptual first step of territoriality, classification. According to Sack, perspectives arise out of one's place which unites the realms of the mental, the social, and the natural. These perspectives lead to a variety of spatial behavior which could include territoriality. In this way, place is relevant to a thorough understanding of territoriality; indeed, this is why it is difficult to understand territoriality without understanding the role of place. Consequently, in the next chapter, classification will be looked at as a geographical perspective that arises from one's place. The link to territoriality will be examined but the separation of the ideas will be retained.

CONCLUSION

In this chapter, Sack's theory of territoriality was put forth as a useful and substantive tool for understanding and evaluating instances of territoriality. In addition to defining territoriality and briefly considering the ethical concerns, a list of various characteristics and effects were described.

The chapter then looked at how one should and should not make use of Sack's theory with particular emphasis on the work of Ksenija Magda. While Magda's understanding of territoriality diverges from Sack's, her understanding of his *geographic awareness paradigm* is useful for seeing how perspectives, such as territorial classifications, arise from one's sense of place. Exploring this further is the aim of the next chapter.

3

The Influence of Place on Perspectives and Classifications of Territoriality

THE ARGUMENT

This chapter continues to build the theoretical framework for understanding territoriality by looking deeper at classifications and how they are formed. While the previous chapter considered the effects that flow out of territoriality, this chapter looks at the perspectives that feed into territoriality and how these perspectives are formed by one's place.

THE SIGNIFICANCE OF PLACE

While territoriality is manifest in behavior and action, the initiation of such activity is connected to one's perspectives. As touched upon at the end of the last chapter, the first facet of territoriality, classification, is conceptually based. But where do these conceptual ideas, or perspectives originate? In this chapter it is argued that one's perspectives are formed in large measure by one's place. One's experience of place influences how they view the world and how they act in that world, including their use of territoriality. Considering the link between how one's place and their perspectives influence classifications helps to deepen one's understanding of territoriality.

In the preliminary section of the introduction, the importance of place—and its capacity to constrain and enable human activity—was emphasized. In the previous chapter, the human activity of territoriality was shown to have an effect on a wide range of people, places, and things. As

Sack states, territoriality can be used to "give meaning to place."[1] But while territoriality can influence place, place also influences territoriality.

Sack develops this idea in his text *Homo Geographicus* where he connects place and perspectives in his *geographic awareness paradigm*. This paradigm invites one to consider how their actions (including territoriality) influence the world. This chapter helps connect behavior with perspectives so that one can consider how their view of the world influences their engagement with the world.

Place in Sack's Geographic Awareness Paradigm

Sack's paradigm is a broad framework for understanding how different elements intersect to create a place and how this place then influences people. His aim is to stimulate research that is developed from a broader geographic awareness as opposed to disciplines that treat processes and activities in ways that ignore spatial elements. This framework enables one to consider "how a particular event or process (such as education, work, and poverty, or categories such as meaning, nature, social relations, and the self) occurs as a series of places."[2] When one studies education, poverty, or theology, they can do so using the framework to understand the complexity of place and how it influences abstract ideas and even the researchers themselves. Rather than viewing place as the illustration or application site for abstract ideas, Sack argues that one cannot really understand these issues without seeing them in place.

As previously stated, place is distinguished from space in that space is a physical property and not socially constructed, while "place is both physical and cultural."[3] Humans are an essential component to the process of space becoming a place. The pliable aspects of the physical environment are adjusted, yes, but humans also provide the meaning, the conceptual understanding that makes the place what it is. This meaning is often derived from the activities that occur in a place. "Places and events in ordinary, everyday life become linked and infused with meaning; and just as the group sees their society and habitat closely connected, so too does the individual see as intimately interconnected his involvement with events and their spatial configuration. Hence physical space and its properties are not abstracted

1. Sack, *Human Territoriality*, 2.
2. Sack, *Homo Geographicus*, 255.
3. Sack, *Homo Geographicus*, 33.

far from the experiences it contains."[4] One's experience shapes the meaning they attribute to a place.

Sack holds that there is very little space in the world that has not become a place through the constraining, organizing, and defining influence of humans.[5] Yet a place can seem to be empty space if it has been neglected or if it no longer functions as intended. According to Wilfred McClay, "a setting that had once been charged with human meaning" can be transformed "into one from which the meaning has departed, something empty and inert, a mere space."[6] What McClay describes is similar to one of the effects listed in the theory of territoriality, where territoriality can be used in a place clearing function to create the perception of empty space. Motivated agents can declare space empty because it does not align with the meaning they ascribe to the place.

The Forces That Make Up a Place

The idea was introduced in the first chapter that place is where the forces of the different realms assemble. The elements of Sack's framework for place come from the realms of the natural, the social, and the mental. Place is understood as the point of intersection for these forces that both enable and constrain a person.[7] The comprehension of this idea may be facilitated by the example of one's home. In a home there are natural elements–the weather outside influences activities and behavior in the home; the DNA and talents of the people present; the smells of what is being cooked for dinner; the architectural design that divides up a house into even smaller rooms. There are also social elements. Who lives in the house, who comes to visit, who is not permitted, who is heard and seen on TV or the internet, and how all of these relate to each other? There are also elements from the mental realm. There may be books shared, and family history told, jokes, legends, and stories of importance, or conversations about religion or philosophy. Place is where all these forces combine and interrelate. While place and territory are material, which is to say they are the object of "theoretical scientific, historical, and philosophical systems," they are also just as much "an invitation to contemplation, to emotion, to dreaming, and to creative

4. Sack, *Human Territoriality*, 64.
5. Sack, *Homo Geographicus*, 92.
6. McClay, *"Introduction,"* 4.
7. Sack, *Homo Geographicus*, 13.

imagination."[8] As the realms of the natural, the social, and the mental interact with and influence each other in a dynamic relationship, place itself becomes a force.

Part of what makes one place unique from another place is how much of each realm influences that place (see Figure 3.1). Generally, in the contemporary world, specific activities belong in specific places. As Sack explains, "some places stress nature, others social relations, and still others meaning, [this] illustrates that the character of places depends on how much of each of these realms they contain."[9] Differences between places occur as different elements adjust and are subjected to each other.

Figure 3.1 Comparison Between a Place which Emphasizes the Mental Realm and a Place that Emphasizes the Physical Realm.

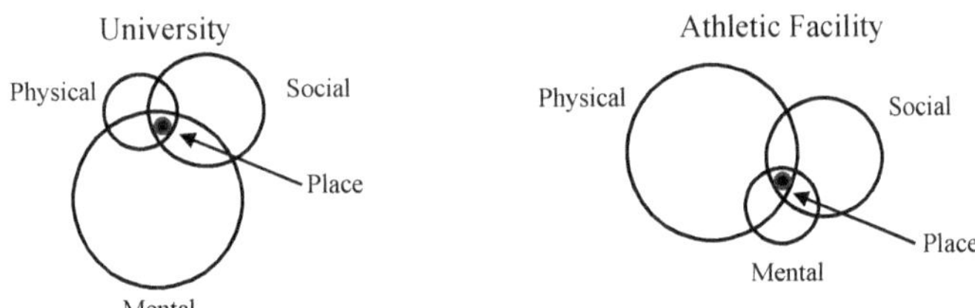

Imagine a university setting. It contains social and natural elements, but the primary goal of a university environment is to focus attention on the mental realm. If there is too much emphasis from the social realm, such as students talking too much about unrelated topics, it will get in the way of the primary goal which is focusing on the mental realm. The professor might redirect the conversation back toward the mental realm and the goals of that particular place. By contrast, imagine if after class, the professor heads to the nearby athletic facility. The professor sees their neighbor and views this as an opportunity to continue to develop the finer points of their next lecture, thus avoiding the exercise that the place is intended to facilitate. The neighbor chides the professor. This is an athletic Facility; the goal is to focus on the natural, the development or maintenance of the physical body. The professor yields because part of living in what is understood to be modern organizations of space is the recognition that specific activities belong in specific places.

Consider how this tendency of spatial separation of specific activities into specific places can influence the experience of missionaries when they

8. Raffestin, "Space, Territory, and Territoriality," 132.

9. Sack, *Homo Geographicus*, 84.

move to a different location. A missionary may have previously sent their children to school, while they and their spouse went to different locations to work, all reuniting at the end of the day. The circumstances of their relocation may now bring all of these activities together into the home. The sending mission organization may also discourage the purchasing or possessing of physical property, aside from one's own residence. The home is no longer the safe haven where the family recharges at the end of the day. Homeschooling, team meetings, and ministry obligations now transform the home into a multifunctional work-school-home space that presents a disorienting change from prior understandings of home.

Places, Change, and Routine

Places are changeable and this is what allows for activities to be separated into places. Once this structuring has occurred the activities and events that happen in the place become associated with the place. This creates a routinization which maintains the place and makes it resistant to change, creating the illusion of permanence. Until, through territoriality, places are emptied and changed again. This cyclical dynamic shows how place is changeable while also being resistant to change.

Often the resistance to change takes the form of rules about what is in or out of place. A class is taught in a classroom, the sick people are to be in the hospital, the worker to the workplace, the farmer to the field. The fireplace does not generally belong in the bathroom and the automobile tools are not appropriate in the bedroom. One's awareness of place is often stirred when something is wrong. Something smells off, there is not enough light, the floor is sticky, and this does not belong there. All of these require attention to place rather than to the activities that normally happen in the place. It is the place that, "defines what it means to have too much or too little of one thing or another."[10] Territoriality becomes one of the tools to change or maintain a place. When things are then functioning properly, place is ignored and repetition acted out spatially "unconsciously reproduce the particular forces that have helped shape these routines."[11] This routinization helps diminish awareness of place, freeing one to focus attention on the activities that the place is making possible.

Routinization and territoriality can be used together to maintain the way things are done. While such strategies can help support the structure of

10. Sack, *Homo Geographicus*, 157.

11. Sack, *Homo Geographicus*, 157.

a place, they can also serve to perpetuate injustice. When these become cultural rules solidified through regular practice, this "routinization of place can help obscure" these injustices.[12] The displacement effect of territoriality is then used with statements like, 'this is just how things are done *here*.' In so doing, the particularity of the place becomes the justification for the unjust rules.

Thick and Thin Places

Place has boundaries. Sack refers to these as either *thick* and impermeable or *thin* and permeable. A *thick* boundary serves to minimize change to a place and controls the level of interaction with those outside. Some thick places can foster fear of outsiders and exercise tight control over who belongs. They are also often effective in preserving what makes them distinctive. A *thin* boundary is porous, allowing for a greater flow of interactions, ideas, and difference. However, thin boundaries tend to erode the distinctiveness of a particular place. Over time, thin places begin to resemble one another, their remaining distinctions fading into near insignificance. Understanding the boundaries of place in terms of thickness or thinness can help one to appreciate the differences between places and how the people of the place relate to others.

Urban centers are an example of what Sack calls thinned out places. The mix of people, ideas, and dissimilarity can help foster a greater awareness of the *other*. Rural places might contrast with urban centers in thickness, but with amenities such as internet connections or satellite TV, those with means can thin the boundary. Isolation can be easily diminished. Yet in places where isolation remains, "people and the place they occupy become extremely close . . . not only because of familiarity and dependence but also because the people come to think of themselves and place as organically and even spiritually linked."[13] In these places, it is easy to understand the idea of culture tethered to land, and yet harder to make sense of the culture without reference to geography. Places with this kind of thickness are becoming less common as travel and technology continue to thin the boundaries of many places.

Places that are neither overly thick nor closed, but instead combine diverse elements and maintain permeable boundaries, "can bring us together

12. Sack, *Homo Geographicus*, 159.

13. Sack, *Human Territoriality*, 58.

so that our differences enrich one another."[14] Territoriality can be used to change the thickness and thinness of a place's boundary, but it is not merely a matter of collective or individual determination. The thickness of a location may be explained by geographical elements from the physical realm that significantly shape that location.

For example, David Radford writes of the geographical elements that have reinforced the thickness of the place occupied by the mountainous peoples of northern Kyrgyzstan. He tells how "the great Tien Shan mountain range forms a natural barrier to conquerors, imperialistic or religious."[15] A place's quality of being thick or thin is influenced by the forces (mental, natural, and social) that assemble in that location. Walls, his extensive understanding of mission history, provides another example of how the natural realm can affect the activities of a place. He observes how Norway, though small has been noteworthy for its missionary consciousness and engagement. In contrast, Hungary has "produced only a couple of missionaries—and those from the German minority—in the whole of the nineteenth century, and no mission agency before the twentieth."[16] Walls attributes this difference to Hungary's landlocked geography and to the fact that roughly 90 percent of Norway's border lies along the coast.

According to Sack's *geographic awareness paradigm*, place is the assemblage of mental, social, and natural forces. Place is changeable, but it also resists change depending on factors like the thickness and thinness of its boundaries. Territoriality is one strategy people use for changing or maintaining a place. But just as a person can influence a place, place can influence a person and their perspectives. These perspectives can then inform new forms of territoriality.

The Influence of Place on a Person

There is an inherent complexity to the relationship of humans and place. Places are distinct by the mixture of forces present, but people also introduce different kinds of variability to the relationship. Sack explores this dynamic with reference to "the self," as in "how does place influence the self and how does the self then influence place?"

Two people may experience the same place, but they do not experience it in the same way. The size or scale of a place is one factor for understanding

14. Sack, *Homo Geographicus*, 254.

15. Radford, *Religious Identity and Social Change*, 12.

16. Walls, *The Cross-cultural Process in Christian History*, 200.

how it can be experienced differently by two people. The larger the place, the more likely it is that experiences of the place will not be equivalent. Two people can live in California and have vastly different experiences and influences. The place is large, and a commonality is more difficult to establish. Two people can live in the same home and have different experiences and influences. But the place is smaller, and they are more likely to share significant commonality compared to those outside the home.

Part of the difference between how two people may engage a place differently is due to a different set of life experiences and the person's own social or biological make-up. One's historical geography or the prior events of one's life can also influence how they experience place and therefore how place influences them. People can move, they can travel, they can stretch beyond their origin, and they encounter place in light of other places they have been. They compare and contrast new places and old places. In many ways, humans cannot make sense of new places without thinking of it in light of the places they have already experienced.

For some the significance of two or more places has such an effect that their experience is thought of in terms of duality or hybridity. For others, the complexity of their experience is difficult to describe. Sanneh observed that, if you "ask many Americans which state is their home . . . they will wobble for an answer just to think of all the in-betweens that defy the singular idea of a fixed abode."[17] But living in a variety of places can make one feel that they do not belong anywhere. Even those from places with thick boundaries, for religious, economic, or familial reasons, may come to feel detached from the place that was once home. Yet even for those who feel a sense of detachment or dislocation, Sack maintains that people still have an uncanny ability "to try to make a place feel like home."[18] They may never feel as though they truly belong, but that does not stop them from filling their place with those things that say they are truly there.

While some may seek to ignore the influence that comes from the places of their past, others who leave can feel a continued connection. They are in a sense bound to the places that have shaped them, particularly the foundational places of their childhood. McClay speaks to the kind of loss that comes when one is detached from such a place.

> There is no evading the fact that we human beings have a profound need for 'thereness,' for visible and tangible things that persist and

17. Sanneh, *Summoned from the Margin*, 126.
18. Sack, *Human Territoriality*, 74.

> endure, and thereby serve to anchor our memories in something more substantial than our thoughts and emotions. Nor can we ever predict in advance the points at which our foundational sense of place will be most vulnerable, though surely a childhood home is a very likely candidate. In any event, when one of those anchors disappears or changes . . . we are left alone, bereft and deserted, our minds and hearts burdened by the weight of uprooted and disconnected memories which can no longer be linked to any visible or tangible place of reference in the world outside our heads. So the memories wither in time like cut flowers, and the more general sense of place, or 'thereness,' is lost with them.[19]

The persistence of memory, both intellectually and emotionally, is rooted in the enduring presence of place, revealing the deep bond between memory and the spaces we inhabit.

A person can see their life experience as a series of discreet places that form their historical geographies. For example, I have lived in Western Pennsylvania, Minnesota, Indiana, Ohio, Illinois, and Michigan. A person can also tie these historical geographies together in a way that sees the particular places as a part of a larger whole. I could alternatively speak of being from the Midwest. In this way, place is an expandable idea that can be quite large and depends where one anchors oneself, where one has been before, and how one conceives of the outer limits of their place.

Two examples of the individual experience of place may be helpful. Benson contrasts the experience of place by missionaries and their children. The missionaries had prior life experience of other places which influenced how they interacted with the place of their ministry. Their children often have much less experience to draw on. "We children of missionaries lived in 'thick' places during our childhoods that influenced us our whole lives and continue to influence the way that we connect with new places."[20] As a result, in many cases, missionary children form such a close attachment to the place their parents serve that they come to see the place as home in ways their parents never fully could. Both the children and the parents encountered the same place and yet the place influenced them differently because of their prior life experience.

Sanneh provides another example of how being in the same place as others does not always equate to having the same experiences. In a generalized statement, Sanneh describes how European missionaries occupied the

19. McClay, "*Introduction*," 2.

20. Benson, *Missionary Families Find a Sense of Place and Identity*, 85.

same place as Africans in Africa, yet they often lived apart having vastly different experiences. "Europeans could be in Africa, but, thanks, to their technology and messianic ideology, they could afford not to be of it. Familiarity here was the opiate of empathy. Geographical range affected little of the imaginative capacity for intercultural exchange or the willingness for equality."[21] These missionaries lived in Africa but all the while shielded themselves from many of the forces that made that place what it is. Instead, they worked to recreate their prior experiences of 'home' in another place. They became isolated European islands diminishing the influence Africa could have on them, and in return diminishing the influence they could have on Africa.

The biological elements and the life experience a person has had adds layers of complexity to one's relationship with place. As a result of this complexity, if one goes from this place to that, the change of place may be understood in terms of freedom, or power, or vulnerability.[22] One may feel a sense of belonging or exclusion. Places can empower individuals and enable them to achieve goals as members of a community. In the same way, places can also disempower, potentially making one "homeless, stateless, refugees."[23] One's particular experience of place is therefore critically important to one's sense of self and how one views and responds to the world.

The variability of place and people create different dynamics of influence, but how do these differences help to stimulate perspectives?

Awareness of Other Places

In Sack's paradigm, knowledge of other places is important for building awareness. "The landscape must be differentiated for the child to see things disappear and reappear . . . There also must be other places or 'elsewhere' for him to imaginatively enter. And his interest in them depends on how different they are from [his] own."[24] Place can help a person transcend their location and consider the world that exists beyond them. Awareness comes when the mind is able "to lift a person beyond her place."[25] This kind of awareness instigates questions. The process of reevaluation and reflexiveness that comes from seeking answers to these questions can help to further

21. Sanneh, *Disciples of All Nations*, 139.

22. Sack, *Homo Geographicus*, 253.

23. Sack, *Homo Geographicus*, 254.

24. Sack, *Homo Geographicus*, 161.

25. Magda, *Paul's Territoriality and Mission Strategy*, 40–41.

develop one's perspectives. New perspectives are then formed in the light of one's experience. As a result, awareness of other places helps one to move beyond partiality.

The varieties of places in one's life "lead us to different types and degrees of awareness."[26] For many people, their experience is complexified by the influence of more than one place. Their lives are best understood as a series of places lived in or visited. For each person, "perspectives are shaped by their historical geographies," not just their current location.[27] Even after leaving a place, it continues to have its effect as it lives on in the perspectives and memories of the self. For example, in his book *Encountering the West*, Sanneh details his relationship with the locations that have shaped him.[28] He articulates the connection between his experience of being physically located "on four continents" with a rich diversity of perspectives that are not separate but distinct and interwoven.[29] Sanneh's experiences have made him more aware of the influence place has had on him and his view of the world.[30]

Place can constrain or enable one's awareness. Sack describes how "the interthreading of place and self can oscillate from having places make us more aware of ourselves and our distinctiveness, to making us less aware, to the point where place and self are fused and conflated."[31] When the boundaries of a place are so thick that they inhibit knowledge of other places, then the place becomes a constraining force making one less aware. Sack explains that "place can so thicken culture and decrease porosity that it

26. Sack, *Homo Geographicus*, 160.

27. Sack, *Homo Geographicus*, 175.

28. Sanneh states in *Encountering the West*, "This book is . . .a personal intellectual testament, [of] one individual who was educated on four continents and who carries within him some of the formative strands of several distinct cultural traditions: the African, the Islamic, the Christian, and the modern West. Often these four strands are unalterably intertwined, and when one strand is drawn out to provide a perspective, the others resonate in sympathy, and their combined synthesis becomes the unspoken rationale for whatever merit there is in a multicultural vocation such as mine," pg. 24–25.

29. Sanneh, *Encountering the West*, 24–25.

30. There is further evidence of Sanneh's belief that place influences the self. In *Summoned from the Margins*, Sanneh, when recounting an experience in a new location, says in passing, "the phenomenon was unknown to me, since there are no mountains in my part of West Africa, and it made me appreciate all the more how terrain could shape one's attitude to the world and to people" 114.

31. Sack, *Homo Geographicus*, 136.

imprisons us. We cannot then see through our own culture and distance ourselves from it to see others . . . We are unable to transcend its partiality."[32]

Places that are thinner may enable one to connect with the world beyond their place more easily. But just as thick places can be constraining, more porous places can also develop a kind of constraining particularity. Sack states,

> This tendency toward globalization of place and culture can then push us willy-nilly in the direction of a shared perspective, but one that has not been critically examined. We all become more aware of the world as the world becomes smaller and its places more alike. Clearly, the tendency toward homogenization can threaten a geographical awareness if it seriously limits the variety of perspectives. And if a single perspective emerges, a geographical awareness must be able to recognize if this is due to the measured and reasoned acceptance of a position, or to the domination of one culture's partial view over all others.[33]

In this way, places with thinner boundaries may be tempted to look down on thick places as narrow-minded or parochial, without realizing that their own outlook reflects not true variety but a globalized, homogenized, and ultimately partial perspective.

Sack offers several ways one's awareness can move beyond the constraining force of the particular.

> The local home can provide a place to launch us on the quest for such a view, though our imaginations are not always sufficient to carry us. The physical act of leaving home and visiting other places can help. But we can also open our homes to the ideas of others and thereby link our place to the world. And once we see things from these other perspectives, we may never return home because it now looks too provincial and constraining. Or if we do return, we may strive to transform it into something more open.[34]

One's imagination, their physical movement, or their social network can all increase one's awareness of places other than one's own. Connectivity may differ from one place to another, but it is not determined solely by physical distance. Particularly at this time, when mass media can bring even young children into contact with distant places, Sack notes that these

32. Sack, *Homo Geographicus*, 254.

33. Sack, *Homo Geographicus*, 19.

34. Sack, *Homo Geographicus*, 18.

connections are not random but rely on "complex networks" of social, mental, and natural elements.[35] When one inhabits a sufficiently thin place, its web of connections can awaken a deeper sense of awareness. A child in Uganda may learn through the medium of television about the snow in Alaska. They need not be in the physical place of Alaska to be influenced by it. In this case, the place of Alaska stimulates questions about the experience of snow or the scientific factors necessary to produce it.

Through technology one can be more aware of other places without being physically present in them. But without a change of place the right questions may be difficult, if not impossible to ask. There is a connection between abiding in a place and the cultivation of certain questions that cannot easily occur otherwise. It speaks to why proximity for decision making matters. This idea is echoed in Walls's belief that "the conditions of Africa . . . are taking Christian theology into new areas of life, where Western theology has no answers, because it has no questions."[36] The questions that a place prompts leads to the development of perspectives.

THE DEVELOPMENT OF PERSPECTIVES

Through the interaction of the different realms assembled in a place, the self formulates perspectives. Magda conveys the idea in this way, "the place is the point of reference in a person's existence which helps determine what elements/forces from all realms are drawn in and how the forces of these elements can then be understood to define the person."[37] Out of the self, come perspectives, or reflections upon one's self and one's world. These perspectives help one to conceptually order their world, to attempt to understand and explain that which is so immense and complex.

One can hear echoes of this idea in Sanneh's own recognition of place influencing perspective. He states, "we are speaking from a North American vantage point, and consequently we cannot escape the pressure of the forces that have produced our kind of religion in our kind of society. We are both beneficiaries and victims of that heritage."[38] Sanneh uses the word "society" but references the specific place of North America. His location in North America influences how he understands religion in both admittedly positive and negative ways.

35. Sack, *Homo Geographicus*, 85.
36. Walls, *Missionary Movement in Christian History*, 146.
37. Magda, *Paul's Territoriality and Mission Strategy*, 43.
38. Sanneh, *Encountering the West*, 222.

Magda uses this framework to understand the Apostle Paul. She holds that it is unnecessary to adjudicate whether the supreme influence on Paul's missionary strategy was his Roman citizenship, his Jewish theology, or his Greek education. All of these influences come together in an understanding of Paul's place. In this way, a variety of influences on the self can come together and be understood in their collective complexity "without reducing the individual significance of any of them."[39] And from Paul's place come his perspectives which are specified in his epistles.

While linked to and formed by a place, perspectives are not restricted or contained in that place. Furthermore, just because perspectives develop in a place, this does not "necessarily limit that perspective, or explain it away" as if all perspectives are merely parochial.[40] Sack believes in the human ability to not just evaluate one's own place but to also intellectually engage those perspectives that originated from different places. He holds that humans are not mired in relativism, but can transcend their place enough to understand the perspectives of someone else from another place, even if imperfectly.[41]

Before moving on to examine the relationship between perspectives and classification, it is worth noting that Sack's understanding of perspectives is not too different from that of Walls and Sanneh.

Comparing Mental Maps with Perspectives

In his *geographic awareness paradigm* Sack uses the language of perspectives to describe how one thinks about themselves and the world. What is of particular interest to me is the perspectives that flow into a classification which then are part of territoriality. Walls and Sanneh have a concept similar to these types of perspectives but they use the language of 'mental maps.' Consider this statement by Walls.

> Worldviews are the mental maps of the universe that contain what we know, or think we know, about the universe and, how it operates, and about our own place in it. We use these maps to navigate our way through daily life. The maps are compiled from many sources: from our own observation and experience, from our family and our education, from the outlook and customs of

39. Sack, *Homo Geographicus*, 122.
40. Sanneh, *Encountering the West*, 175.
41. Sack, *Homo Geographicus*, 57.

> our community, from the accumulation of sources we believe we have reason to trust.[42]

Walls expresses a view of mental maps as significant for the operation of one's daily life and as drawn from a variety of sources.

Sanneh uses the language of 'mental maps,' but also employs equivalent concepts such as 'mental habits,' and 'mental picture of the world.'[43] One of the key arguments in Walls's and Sanneh's work is that there has been a profound shift in Christianity's center of gravity. Sanneh bases this on demographics shifts of Christianity rising in some places of the world with seeming decline in other places. He describes how despite the demographic changes, updates to the mental map are slower to be realized. The "surviving mental habits still locate Christianity's intellectual and political center of gravity in Europe and North America."[44] The disparity between the mental map and the physical or demographic map is problematic because "most people take their cue from the mental picture of the world."[45] Despite what seems to be the apparent case, the intellectual and political influence (or power) located in the places of Europe and North America stubbornly retain an outdated "mental map of Christianity as Christendom."[46]

Sanneh's observations regarding the slow changing adjustments to mental maps converges with statements made by Walls. Adjustments to one's mental map can be "intellectually threatening," requiring "new ideas and skills" and "the sudden irrelevance of too many accepted authorities."[47] His comments suggest that there is a willful ignorance regarding the adjustment of one's mental map because it comes at a cost some are unwilling to

42. Walls, *Crossing Cultural Frontiers*, 35.

43. There are also similarities in Sack and Sanneh's ideas of place. Sanneh demonstrates a crossroads of influence in a way that echoes Sack's realms assembling in a place. "These parish-style villages transformed Freetown into a black diaspora, a bustling entrepot of refuges at large, with Freetown becoming a creolized, Caribbean-style cultural experience on African soil, a teeming crossroads of African and Western ideas stirred with an admixture of religious elements, Muslim, Christian, and indigenous. African recaptives who originated from many different parts of the continent, some from as far away as the Congo and Mozambique, intermingled with those from Nigeria and elsewhere. They had in common only the experience of being uprooted and banished from village, hearth, and shrine, and of the bewildering effects of a life of forcible migration in slave ships and slave camps." Sanneh, *Disciples of All Nations*, 127.

44. Sanneh, *Disciples of All Nations*, 94.

45. Sanneh, *Summoned from the Margin*, 231.

46. Sanneh, *Disciples of All Nations*, 94.

47. Walls, *The Cross-cultural Process in Christian History*, 38.

pay. Yet Sanneh is optimistic about the potential for change and even more determined about its necessity. He states that, "the case today for an alteration in our mental maps, and in our corresponding cultural sensibilities, has never been more urgent and necessary."[48] Similarly, Walls argues that the "national distinctives" which include, among other things, the "shared mental processes . . .are within the scope of discipleship."[49] One's mental maps may be slow to change, but they can have a substantial influence on the world.

Walls and Sanneh use the language of 'mental maps' but there are similarities to Sack's notion of 'perspectives.' In reviewing Sanneh's and Walls's writings and comparing them with Sack's, there is an overlap with respect to these two ideas, but they are not exactly equivalent concepts. Walls and Sanneh use the language of mental maps to build toward larger arguments while Sack is directly explaining how perspectives are formed in relation to one's place. Consequently, Sack's understanding provides a greater complexity than what was required for the purposes of Walls and Sanneh. While mental maps could be described as 'ways of thinking about geographical space,' perspectives can relate to any subject (mission, law, butterflies), yet they begin and take shape due to the forces present in one's geographical location. I use the language of perspectives for the remainder of this work to draw attention to the way that perspectives are influenced by one's place. However, like Walls's and Sanneh's "mental map," the perspectives that are of interest in the present study are the ones that are about geographical space. Specifically, this study is interested in the perspectives that feed into territoriality.

Walls and Sanneh suggest a connection between mental habits and actions, Sack just makes this more explicit. As the ethical culmination of his framework, he believes that one can evaluate their perspectives and even the perspectives of others to understand how each of them influence the world.

The Connection Between Perspectives and Classifications

How do one's perspectives relate to territorial action? There is a link between Sack's theory of territoriality and his *geographic awareness paradigm* by way of perspectives taking shape as territorial classifications. For example, Sack notes that "a conceptual order and understanding are imposed

48. Sanneh, *Disciples of All Nations*, 96.

49. Walls, *Missionary Movement in Christian History*, 27.

upon the land even before a physical order."[50] The conceptual order that is one's perspective is there from the start of any act of territoriality. Place influences a person and their perspectives. Not all perspectives are about territory. Of those perspectives that are about territory, only some develop into a specific classification. And as addressed in the last chapter, not all classifications necessarily lead to territoriality. Yet for any act of territoriality, there must be a classification and this classification is derived from one's perspectives which have been influenced by one's place.

Why is connecting perspectives and territoriality important? Perspectives, and their connection to place, are worthy of consideration because they are presupposed in human territoriality. The connection between place and territoriality is not intended as an absolute means for determining exactly how a specific place influences territoriality. It certainly is not grounds for dismissing an idea because one came from a particular place. But as Magda argues when addressing how Paul's place influenced his mission strategy, "we need to take into consideration that even a perspective which seems independent of the place develops from the place of the self, because the self that produces it cannot exist unless it is bound to the place."[51] The classification of territory, the formation of one's understanding of 'home,' all arise from the self as perspectives. These perspectives influence how one understands Christian faith and mission. They influence how one tells the story of their faith, how they categorize, how they conceive of their place, and how they conceive of the place of others. All of these perspectives can be played out in one's use of territoriality.

The argument here is that understanding territoriality has continued relevance for Christian faith and mission. The link between one's place and perspectives should lead to questions about how this influences their classifications and territoriality. This is the goal of Sack's paradigm, to encourage awareness of how one's perspectives and actions impact the world on various scales. In particular, territoriality can be used to alter one's place or the place of another (see Figure 3.2). These changed places can then influence new perspectives, classifications, and possible territoriality.

50. Sack, *Homo Geographicus*, 14.

51. Magda, *Paul's Territoriality and Mission Strategy*, 51.

Figure 3.2 The Connection Between Place, Perspectives, and Territoriality

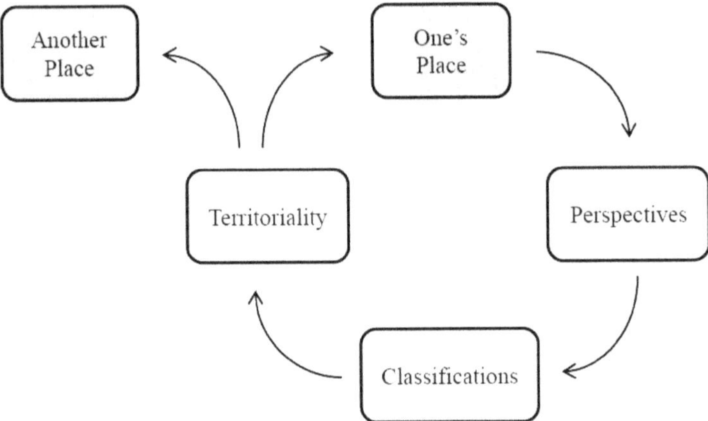

Global Influence

Human actions, such as territoriality, can have far-reaching influence. Awareness of this potential can influence one's sense of moral responsibility for others. But such evaluations are not easy. There are impediments to thinking about how one's actions affect the various spatial scales. Particularly at the global scale, one may find that tracing the full reach of one's influence in the world can become a complex task.[52] One may prefer to think in terms of universal morality but ignore the reality of their particular place and the limits of their situatedness.

> Those who possess a global or universal view of morality-cosmopolites if you will-often claim a more encompassing sense of moral concern and responsibility. They are 'liberated' from ethnic strictures and strive to treat everyone with equal care. But can one be equally responsible for everyone, everywhere? Isn't universalism doomed to superficiality? Don't we have to draw boundaries simply for the sake of efficiency? Can our global and more inclusive view overcome the fact that we are individuals localized in space with partial and personal perspectives, and with limited capacities to attend? Whether one emphasizes the local or the global it remains the case that a geographical awareness of the consequences

52. Sack, *Homo Geographicus*, 254.

> of our actions—the understanding of the links of actions through space—is essential for acting responsibly.[53]

In other words, one's perspectives will always be, at some level, partial. This is one of the cornerstones of appropriate epistemic humility. Humans are limited by the fact that they exist in only one place at a time. Yet increasing one's awareness of the world will impact how one acts with respect to that world. Without this awareness "we then have the worst of worlds: one in which our actions affect all of the cultural and natural systems, but one where our lack of awareness prevents us from anticipating and assessing these effects."[54] This is the risk in large scale acts of territoriality today. One's actions can have global consequences but without a commitment to being more geographically aware, one cannot begin to anticipate or assess the extent of that impact.

One could apply Sack's paradigm to an evaluation of their own personal mission strategy and find that the strategy has connections with their place. One's mission strategy could be related to the realm of meaning. For example, one's eschatological perspective may impact how they prioritize one place over another in their goal of communicating the gospel. Or it could be related to one's social network, what other missionaries have invited them to serve or raised their awareness about needs in another place. Or it could be related to their physical environment, their health or the health of their family. It could be related to one's perceived proximity to spiritual need, "why should I travel far when there is need near?" Or it could be the converse belief, that missionary work requires that one must go far. Using Sack's understanding of place and perspectives can help one to uncover the mental, social, and physical factors that influence their missionary strategy.

One could also apply Sack's paradigm to understand how large-scale evangelistic strategies are formed by a particular person existing in a particular place. For example, what is the connection between mission strategies like the *Back to Jerusalem Movement* or the *10/40 Window* and the people who first articulated them? How did their presence in or outside the targeted mission territory influence their perspectives? These strategies cannot be understood to be the definitive universal evangelistic strategy. But given the complexity of the world today, the increased diversity within Christianity, crafting a universal world strategy for mission implies a kind of omniscience that no particular group of Christians can achieve.

53. Sack, *Homo Geographicus*, 23.

54. Sack, *Homo Geographicus*, 11–12.

Understanding the relationship between place, perspective, classification and territoriality can help one better understand and evaluate their actions. In the remainder of this chapter, specific kinds of classifications relevant to this study of territoriality are examined.

CLASSIFICATIONS

Classifications are a kind of perspective. In terms of territoriality, they are a demarcation that defines one area from another, made by a person or group who hold some amount of power whereby their demarcation is understood as meaningful. There are many different examples of classifications that are relevant to discussions of territoriality. A place can be classified as a *paradise* or a *wasteland*, *Christian*, or *non-Christian*, *holy* or *enemy territory*. A place can also be classified as central and significant, or peripheral and of marginal importance.

Given the subjective nature of perspectives, one's bias can be expressed in the classifications one may make. The determinations may not be factually supported or the reasons for the decision could be capricious. Yet often classifications can be received as objective.[55] When one's distorted perspective of the other takes shape as a classification of area, coupled with the power of enforcement, this increases the likelihood that the territoriality will become a tool of oppression.

Some general ideas regarding classification were covered in the previous chapter. This chapter looks closer at three specific kinds of categories of classification: Religious Classification, Classifying Center and Periphery, and Classifying Empty Space. This is not an exhaustive list of the kinds of classifications that can become part of territoriality, but these classifications are relevant to understanding territoriality within Christian faith and mission.

Classifying Religious Places

Throughout history places have come to be identified with particular faiths. Many religions have places that are classified as holy which hold important symbolic and ritualistic value. Classification can also be made of larger

55. The assignment of particular people to particular places is another classification that cannot be explored in this work but is worthy of much greater examination. Sack explains how myths of origin are used to anchor people to a place. He points to Plato's plan of willful deception of the people, contemporary nationalism, and ideas of "homeland, motherland fatherland, and blood and soil." Sack, *Homo Geographicus*, 185.

swaths of geographic area. Places can be classified as 'Christian land,' 'Islamic land,' 'reached,' or 'unreached.' Such classifications have occurred regularly in Christian history.

Holy Places

The dialectical relationship between the ideas of the abstract immaterial world and a physical location are clearly present in the idea of holy places. With holy places, the spirit world is "linked back to [the] landscape because their actions explain and empower it. They make this or that place sacred and magical–a gift of the gods–and provide *home* and *world* with weight and meaning."[56] Classifying a place as holy is therefore significant. It can be perceived to provide peace, strength, or power. A person can recognize a place as holy even if they are physically far from and have had little personal experience with the location. Within Christianity and for some people, Jerusalem may be an example of this type of place. A person can also strive to bring the holy nearer to them and by doing so endow their location with "weight and meaning."[57] For those Christians in Mexico, the origins of Our Lady of Guadalupe might be an example of this approach to holy places.[58] And of course, one place can have different significance for different groups. This becomes increasingly complex when territories considered holy overlap and are contested.

Scholars of Islamicjerusalem make clear statements about the importance of proximity when they speak of the *Barakah* blessing emanating in concentric circles from the al-Aqsa Mosque in Jerusalem. Within Islam, the mosque and the surrounding area are classified as holy. This is the center of the blessing, and consequently, to receive the fullness of this blessing, proximity is a necessity. While *Barakah* may reach all over the world, it is "not on the same scale" as for those living near the center.[59] El Awaisi therefore has a global vision of blessing in Islam, but it has a fixed center and "is gradually diminished" the farther one is from that center.[60] According to El Awaisi, "this global common space of openness and *Barakah* made Islamicjerusalem an ideal destination region for everyone to live there and

56. Sack, *Homo Geographicus*, 8.
57. Sack, *Homo Geographicus*, 8.
58. Sanneh, *Disciples of All Nations*, 93.
59. El-Awaisi, *Introducing Islamic Jerusalem*, 33.
60. El-Awaisi, *Introducing Islamic Jerusalem*, 33.

enjoy this *Barakah.*"[61] When a place of such religious significance is combined with the perceived power of a blessing, it becomes easy to understand why one would desire access to it. Once access is granted, the site would naturally need to be controlled and defended. Territoriality thus emerges as a strategy for achieving this aim.

Jerusalem is just one of the holy places that have a symbolic role in Islam. Sanneh speaks of Mecca and Medina as "Islam's territorial core."[62] From the beginning of Islam, Mecca and Medina have been the fixed geographical points central to the faith. The classification of these places as holy has been so central to the Islamic faith that it is without question. Sack argues that "directions, shape, and location can be combined to enhance magical powers even more. A settlement can be located at a sacred site, have the sacred shape, and be oriented in the sacred direction."[63] Within Islam, praying toward the Kaaba in Mecca (qibla) and making the pilgrimage to Mecca (hajj) reinforces the idea of a locational supremacy.[64] Sanneh argues that the focus on Mecca can undermine the significance of one's own place. In this way, place becomes ranked in a hierarchy of significance. But this is not unique to Islam.

Some who practice Christianity have similar understandings of holy places. Islam requires pilgrimage when possible. Christianity does not make this requirement, but trips to Jerusalem for Christians have become a similar practice. Based on what Sanneh argues, it is worth asking, do trips to Jerusalem obscure the significance of one's own place? Do these pilgrimages reinforce a kind of territorial idea of Christianity that mirrors rather than contrasts with Islam? It is possible, as Christians, to say that Jerusalem is distinctive because of what happened in that place. One could argue that such classifications of holiness are benign.

The challenge that can occur once a place is classified as holy for religious purposes, is that it can encourage a posture of defense. It is not difficult to imagine that loss of access to a particular holy place, such as the Holy Sepulcher in Jerusalem, could cause some (even those from outside the location) to lobby for control of the space. Sack warns that such situations can be explosive. While many disputes regarding territory can be approached based on logic, fairness, and economic factors, disputes over

61. El-Awaisi, *Introducing Islamic Jerusalem*, 29.

62. Sanneh, *Disciples of All Nations*, 79.

63. Sack, *Homo Geographicus*, 183.

64. Sanneh, *Summoned from the Margin*, 234.

places considered sacred cannot be so easily settled. Sack holds that "many participants in the Middle East conflicts" are in agreement about the notion that places can be sacred and holy. "The argument is about whether God gave a particular place to the care of a particular group. Social science 'solutions' that would allocate responsibility on the basis of proximity or efficiency of access would be entirely secondary to the issue of the sacred."[65] If classifications of holy places tend to imply controlling or defensive territorial behavior, it is worth asking if such behavior is consistent with the values of one's faith. The distinctly non-territorial behavior of the Christians of Palestine, referenced in the first chapter, may testify to something more consistent with Christian values.

Large Territorial Religious Classifications

Holy places are one kind of classification, but larger portions of land can also be classified as Christian, Buddhist, or Islamic territory. The classification of a land as Muslim by Muslims can have negative effects on the Christians or other non-Muslims who inhabit that place. Sanneh states that,

> There are many communities that share a territorial boundary with Muslims but not necessarily a religious one. Such people as Arab Christians, Iranian Zoroastrians . . .are a reminder of the restricted value of territorial designations for religion. And qualitatively and quantitatively, the world is becoming more and more so. Can we as believers witness to faith without the coercive recourse implicit in religious territoriality or numerical preponderance?[66]

Awareness of the pressures experienced by Christians living in majority Muslim countries, should motivate Christians, who find themselves in different circumstances, to treat religious minorities with compassion. When Christians champion religious freedom, do they eagerly or begrudgingly seek to extend this to others? When Christians classify a place as Christian, how does this contribute to the religious marginalization of others? As Sanneh suggests, religious classifications have restricted value.

There are examples of Christians making these kinds of classifications in the chapters that follow. One of the main features of later Christendom was dividing up the world into groups of Christian countries and non-Christian

65. Sack, *Homo Geographicus*, 184.

66. Sanneh, *Encountering the West*, 222–23.

countries. Sanneh describes counter narratives that emerged challenging what countries better fit the definition of Christian, but not whether such classifications should occur.[67] However, Sanneh's writings often question or subvert the understood religious classifications. For example, Sanneh speaks of how "missions under colonialism have sought by the back door to retrieve a failed Christendom by looking to the 'Dark Continents' of the non-Western world."[68] The notion rests on the idea that Africa was in spiritual darkness. Yet in agreement with Lesslie Newbigin, Sanneh argues that, "the West may be a 'darker continent' for having reneged on its religious heritage."[69] The idea of large geographic space easily labeled as 'converted' or 'heathen,' 'light' or 'dark,' does not speak to the complexity of places or the people who inhabit them.

Many holy places begin as the central location of a religion but do not necessarily stay that way. The classification of places as central and peripheral happens in many traditions.

Classifying Center and Periphery

The idea of center implies significance, meaning, weight and a value of proximity to the place. For example, some who classify Rome as central to the Christian faith, may view Indonesia, by comparison, as marginal. The classification of a place as central may endow the place with greater power and decision-making capabilities. Territoriality is expressed in the creation of designating a place as center or periphery. This is done "by the exaltation of certain places and the casting aside of others."[70] Just as in the hierarchical manifestations of territoriality, proximity to the center may increase one's opportunities and access to resources.

There is often a complicated relationship between the center and the periphery. In light of the power and importance of the center, the periphery may be ignored and viewed as less significant. Those at the center, or the top of the hierarchy, may be unaware or less involved in the movements away from center, at the periphery. Innovations from the margins may be understood as mere sideline projects that serve to extend the reach of the center. The margins may be used to further underscore the strength and significance of the center by increasing the span of control. Such situations

67. Sanneh, *Disciples of All Nations*, 252.

68. Sanneh, *Encountering the West*, 206.

69. Sanneh, *Encountering the West*, 163. See all Newbigin, *Foolishness to the Greeks*.

70. Raffestin, "Space, Territory, and Territoriality," 137.

can once again create an unequal distribution of resources, knowledge, and access to long-term planning. In the end, they become the foundation for disunity or secession.

Walls and Sanneh use references to center and margin repeatedly in their writings. When Sanneh states that "Freetown was the center of that New World African impulse," or that "increasingly, Europe is a new Christian margin," he is using this kind of spatial logic.[71] He is categorizing and making claims about significance, meaning, and weight. From the outset of *Summoned from the Margins*, Sanneh presents a contrast between centers of importance and marginal places. His text is a retelling of his "intellectual journey from the margin of remote Africa to the center of the world."[72] In this example, Sanneh plays with the ideas of center, margin, and gravity, calling attention to the typical understandings of these ideas, and then subverting them. It is Sanneh's conviction that "no culture is so advanced and so superior that it can claim exclusive access or advantage to the truth of God, and none so marginal and remote that it can be excluded."[73] This theme reverberates throughout Sanneh's work.

Walls speaks of the "massive southward shift of the center of gravity of the Christian world, so that the representative Christian lands now appear to be in Latin America, Sub-Saharan Africa, and other parts of the southern continents."[74] Here one can see Walls's understanding of center as connected to that which is representative. Throughout his writings, the theme of center (or alternatively heartland) emerges as significant for tracing the movement of Christian history. For Walls these terms refer to locations of various scales, where the Christian message has flourished and where a significant number have claimed Christianity as their faith. The concept of a *heartland* may also carry a temporal dimension, suggesting that the flourishing of the Christian message in that place has endured over a significant span of time. Often the center is presented as a place with a certain amount of power and privilege, and yet this power is more fragile than it seems. Walls describes how "the expansion of Christianity does not plant churches that endure forever."[75] In his perspective the story of Christianity is not one of "steady, triumphant progression" instead it is one that can be

71. Sanneh, *Disciples of All Nations*, 177, 275.

72. Sanneh, *Summoned from the Margin*, 16.

73. Sanneh, *Disciples of All Nations*, 25.

74. Walls, *Missionary Movement in Christian History*, 9.

75. Walls, *The Cross-cultural Process in Christian History*, 29.

thought of in terms of both "advance and recession."[76] Classifying a place as Christian, or as central to the Christian faith, obscures the fragility that Walls references. The classification becomes a false sense of security. Classifying a place as non-Christian can also serve to diminish the significance of Christians who are present in that place. This kind of classification is very similar to the classification of empty space.

Classifying Empty Space

In the previous chapter it was shown that territoriality can be used in a place clearing capacity. Such usage of territoriality is built on and furthers perspectives and classifications of space as empty. For example, when fifteenth century Europeans encountered land outside of Europe, they often thought of it in terms of being empty. The land was unknown and unstructured in ways that were familiar to them. It was viewed as mostly devoid of that which they valued. Classifications of empty space obscured the complexity of the pre-existing place. By contrast, land and people within Europe were more difficult to conceptually erase. It had already been charted and other Europeans were understood as undeniably Christian and human. Outside of Europe, land was more easily conceived of as empty and the use of territoriality to subdue and clear the place was therefore more easily justifiable.

The classification of space as spiritually empty works in similar ways. The land is devoid of what is spiritually valued by the one making the classification. For example, if one believes that being Baptist is the only legitimate expression of the Christian faith, locations without Baptists would be classified as spiritually empty and if present, spiritually filled. Such perspectives can ignore previous religious or even Christian history in a location.

Applying grids of longitude and latitude over land is also associated with the classification of empty space. By applying an external abstract grid, those outside a place can make the vast seemingly unknowable space more manageable. But the use of these space clearing tools of territoriality can create challenging dynamics for those on the ground, where the logic of longitude and latitude makes less sense.

As a way of summarizing the relationship between place, perspectives, classification, and territoriality, the final section of this chapter considers the formation of a well-known classification. This classification was made

76. Walls, *The Cross-cultural Process in Christian History*, 29.

using several of the methods mentioned above, including latitude as a space clearing device.

THE 38TH PARALLEL NORTH LATITUDE ON THE KOREAN PENINSULA

The use of longitude and latitude to subdivide an area is a telltale sign that the territoriality that is being employed originated from a source external to the place. The dividing line between North and South Korea on the 38th parallel north after the Second World War is an example of this principle. Of this demarcation, it has been said, "no division of a nation in the present world is so astonishing in its origin as the division of Korea; none is so unrelated to conditions or sentiment within the nation itself at the time the division was effected."[77]

Japan had been exerting a primary territorial control over Korea since the early part of the twentieth century. Consequently, the terms of the Japanese surrender with respect to Korea became an important issue for both the US and Soviet leadership. At the Yalta conference, both sides had expressed interest in an independent Korea free from external control. But the Japanese in Korea would need to surrender to someone, and ostensibly an infrastructure would need to be set in place before Korea could stand on its own. A guardianship of some kind would need to be established. While the US was not in the position to occupy the entire peninsula, Korea was supposedly of too much strategic importance to relinquish the opportunity to the Soviets alone. Even though the Secretary of State at that time had to ask a subordinate to explain where exactly Korea was located.[78]

It was determined that a deal could be struck to temporarily divide Korea into areas of custodial control between the US and Russia. The important question remaining was where to divide the country. If the US delayed in making the proposal, Soviet troops were in place to easily take the entire peninsula. A line of demarcation needed to be proposed quickly, it needed to be in line with US interests, and it needed to be acceptable to Stalin.

On the night of August 10, 1945, the demarcation task was assigned to Colonel Charles H. Bonesteel III and Lieutenant Colonel Dean Rusk who were stationed in an office building next to the Whitehouse in Washington

77. Oberdorfer and Carlin, *The Two Koreas*, 6.

78. Oberdorfer and Carlin, *The Two Koreas*, 4.

DC.[79] They had thirty minutes to divide a country they knew little about. Neither of the colonels had ever been stationed in Korea at the time they made the proposal,[80] and by their own admission, neither were Korean experts.[81] They had both been stationed in a variety of places that may have had an influence on their perspectives, but Korea was not one of them.

Ideally and initially, the territoriality they sought to impose would have taken into consideration mountain ranges, waterways, and the provinces that the Korean people themselves used to separate one place from another.[82] Unfortunately, the map used by Bonesteel and Rusk was a regional map of "Asian and Adjacent Areas" produced by the National Geographic Society for a US audience.[83] It did not provide the necessary topographical details or provincial subdivisions. In other words, Bonesteel and Rusk were hoping to rely on information from outside their place to supplement their limited knowledge of Korea and broaden their perspective. But the only information available had been produced in and for their place, reinforcing rather than broadening their perspective.

What the map did clearly show was that the 38th parallel north latitude could divide the country into roughly equivalent land masses. This abstract and geometrical demarcation was logical, particularly for those who did not know much about Korea. Latitude has a way of making the vast and unknown intelligible and manageable. With the capital of Seoul and several significant ports located in the Southern portion, the subdivision would work for US interests and military capability. The classification was made, the boundary lines of their territoriality were chosen.

For leaders in Moscow and Washington, the demarcation had a beautiful simplicity about it. A line of latitude on paper has an appealing clarity and precision for purposes of communication to audiences, at least for audiences not in Korea. A detailed and complicated subdivision of the land could have further extended the negotiations. The US was pleasantly surprised that Stalin agreed. He even called back some of his troops who had already crossed the line.[84] There was clear communication and the

79. Oberdorfer and Carlin, *The Two Koreas*, 5.

80. New York Times, "Charles H. Bonesteel 3d, Army General Who Lead U.N. Command in Korea."

81. Rusk, *As I Saw it*.

82. Schnabel, *United States Army in the Korean War*, 9.

83. Fry, "National Geographic, Korea, and the 38th Parallel."

84. Black, "The Korean Crisis."

beginning of an enforcement, it seemed both sides were pleased with the temporary arrangement of this territoriality.

Korea was not empty space. It was not uncharted nature nor was it devoid of established communities of people. Yet the use of latitude worked as a kind of space clearing mechanism, as if the land was empty. Empty, that is, of anything meaningfully important to those who placed the line. In the US Army Center of Military History's record of the demarcation, in a chapter entitled, *Korea, Case History of a Pawn,* James Schnabel offers the following description regarding the impact of the hastily expedited decision.

> The new dividing line, about 190 miles across the peninsula, sliced across Korea without regard for political boundaries, geographical features, waterways, or paths of commerce. The 38th Parallel cut more than 75 streams and 12 rivers, intersected many high ridges at variant angles, severed 181 small cart roads, 104 country roads, 15 provincial all-weather roads, 8 better-class highways, and 6 north-south rail lines. It was, in fact, an arbitrary separation.[85]

What is not listed, but can be presumed, is the impact on the smaller units of farms and families. The *paths of commerce* that were divided by the demarcation also separated the differentially resourced parts of the peninsula. The agriculturally rich South would no longer serve as the complement to the metal and mineral rich North.

There was no intention to create the kind of mess Schnabel describes. Placing lines on maps thousands of miles from the actual place can seem benign and there were other objectives, deemed more important, that needed to be obtained. The line that was created did not need to be acceptable to the Koreans nor was it proposed by Koreans or created in consultation with Koreans. It was a classification made in Washington, by military officials who had not been to Korea, with a map created for a US audience, produced for the purpose of US interests, and for the easy comprehension and acceptance of the Soviet Premier. The territoriality of the 38th parallel was created by and for an external audience. The messiness was the collateral damage produced by time limits, a bad map, and a preference for clear communicable boundaries.

This is not a full account of what could be described as Bonesteel's and Rusk's place. It does not include all the mental, social, and physical elements that have shaped them individually. What is clear is that Korea was not part of their sense of place. And yet their place influenced their

85. Schnabel, *United States Army in the Korean War*, 11.

perspective of Korea. Even when they attempted to broaden their perspective, the tools at their disposal reinforced an external perspective of Korea. From this perspective, classifications and territoriality were created. Because they were in a position of power within a powerful country, the territoriality they determined had significant influence on a place far from where the decision was made.

There were a variety of effects due to this territoriality. It created the impression that one could easily divide and contain people and things to the provided classifications. That the places where the line fell were sufficiently empty of meaningful things (such as ports and major cities). And from this assumption of emptiness, territoriality acted as a place clearing mechanism with provinces split, families divided, and roads to nowhere.

The precision of the line did not last long as war broke out on the peninsula. Even as it is still referred to as the 38th parallel, the actual demarcation between North and South Korea is now more winding and complex. It is a new territoriality created by soldiers on the ground and frozen in place by an armistice. The hope of reunification continues to perpetuate the belief that this too is just a temporary line.

The example of the 38th parallel on the Korean peninsula provides a glimpse of what is sometimes difficult to see in its fullness–the connection between place, perspective, classification, and territoriality. Place, and in this case the geographical tools assembled in one's place, can influence the perspectives which form classifications, and therefore territoriality. While the classification was formed far from the place in question, and for the purposes of an external audience, the results had unintended and far-reaching consequences.

In the next three chapters, the use of territoriality will be explored in the history of the Christian church and mission. The characteristics, facets, causes, and effects of territoriality will be highlighted and how these change over time. These are comparatively easier to recognize and categorize. It is a much harder task to identify the person or group of people responsible for each decision, harder still to understand how their place influenced their perspectives. That level of granular detail may be lost or at best waiting to be uncovered in the historical record. While the focus for the remainder of this work will be on instances of territoriality, it should be understood that behind every instance of territoriality are perspectives that arise from a person or group of people influenced by their place.

CONCLUSION

In this chapter, the influence of place on perspectives, classification, and ultimately territoriality was investigated. This was done by linking Sack's *theory of territoriality* with his *geographic awareness paradigm* to clarify how one's classifications, derived from their perspectives are influenced by their experience of place.

This chapter is part of a larger section considering territoriality in geographical perspective. The section has presented geography as a highly integrative discipline and that spatial analysis offers opportunity to understand a variety of human behavior. Territoriality has been explored by considering the effects that flow out of it, and in this chapter, from the perspectives that feed into it. With these tools in hand, this study turns to understanding instances of territoriality in Christian and mission history.

4

The Foundation of Territoriality Prior to Christendom

THE ARGUMENT

The preceding chapters provided a theoretical understanding of territoriality. In this chapter, the theory is applied to show that territoriality was present before the advent of Christendom in Christian history. While Christianity began as a largely deterritorialized religious group, territoriality developed and increased over time. This chapter will provide evidence that a foundation for territoriality, along with some examples of territoriality, existed prior to Constantine and therefore prior to the earliest date of Christendom. Constantine's influence empowered a broader range of enforcement to support the increasingly territorial church.

THE MANGER AND THE BASILICA

Luke's announcement of the birth of Christ concludes with a statement about a manger in a makeshift location because there was no space available for the young couple and child (Luke 2:7). The statement underscores the humility of Christ's incarnation and foreshadows his future itinerant ministry. This theme continues in Luke 9:58 when it is stated, "foxes have dens and birds have nests, but the Son of Man has no place to lay his head." Through the threat of persecution, many of the early followers of Jesus experienced dislocation and placelessness. The memory of the humble beginning of their Savior's life provided a measure of solidarity.

In contrast to the manger, St. Peter's Basilica in Rome is a 227,060 square foot concrete and marble edifice. Intricate mosaics and priceless sculptures all speak to the magnificence of this place. The baldachin, the canopy covering the alter, is adorned with over 100,000 pounds of bronze. Above the baldachin, inside the dome are the words of Matthew 16:18, "you are Peter, and on this rock I will build my church." It is claimed that the calcified bones of Peter lay beneath the Basilica, inviting the reader to appreciate this promise in startling literality.

The dissonance between the improvised manger and the immovable Basilica exists because they are both symbols of the Christian faith. How did this come to be? The church's development from its early stages into an institution that is increasingly visible and made manifest in physical structures is one example of how territoriality was used as a strategy. While the early church exhibited elements of a deterritorialized religion, expressions of territoriality increased as the church developed. These increases occurred prior to the beginning of Christendom.

PRELIMINARY MATTERS

Clarifying the Beginning of Christendom

Before demonstrating how territoriality became increasingly important to the function of the church, it is necessary to deal with some preliminary matters. As the intention of this chapter is to establish that territoriality was taking shape prior to Christendom, then it is necessary to clarify when Christendom began. Endeavoring to do so should not be taken as a tacit acceptance of the notion that Christendom is exclusively a temporal phenomenon. Christendom, as will be shown in the next chapter, should not be understood merely as a period of time. The purpose for determining the beginning of Christendom has to do with the relationship between Christendom and territoriality. Wilbert Shenk states that these notions are often assumed to be "twinned."[1] Evidence to show that territoriality begins prior to Christendom, and furthermore extends beyond it, indicates that these notions are not equivalent.

Exploring the question of when scholars believe Christendom began reveals the variety of viewpoints on the nature of Christendom itself. This will be explored in greater detail in the next chapter. For now, there are at least two groups of thought on when to date the beginning of Christendom.

1. Wilbert R. Shenk, personal correspondence (email), April 13, 2017.

For the first group, Constantine initiated Christendom around the beginning of the fourth century.[2] Muggeridge summarizes this position well when he states "Constantine, as an act of policy, decided to tolerate, indeed positively favour, the Church, uniting it to the secular state by the closest possible ties."[3] The second group, which includes Walls and Sanneh, prefer a later date.

Sanneh, following Pirenne, dates the beginning of Christendom later, around the time of Charlemagne (roughly 800 AD).[4] He recognizes Constantine as a symbol associated with Christendom and concedes that the idea is present in some of the initiatives taken by Constantine. But "the unitary institution" of Christendom was founded under the Carolingians, "who made territoriality a rule of religious life and made the principle of political organization the 'unrestricted adhesion of the Western Church to the Empire.'"[5] From this explanation one can see the close association between Christendom and territoriality in Sanneh's understanding.

Walls agrees with much of this assessment arguing that the Roman world was too pluralistic for the specific characteristics he would attribute to Christendom. He is even less inclined to draw the connection between Constantine and Christendom and prefers to date the beginning of Christendom even later, as an entity created by the inclusion of people further north.

If it can be established that territoriality began prior to the Carolingians, and in a limited sense even prior to Constantine, then this establishes that territoriality existed prior to Christendom. I agree with Walls and Sanneh that the changes Constantine initiated do not constitute Christendom, but instead they reveal, not the beginning, but a further increase in territoriality. Constantine built on a foundation of classifications and hierarchical subdivisions already in place which made his even more powerful enforcement effective. While the church prior to Constantine provides limited but specific examples of territoriality, a substantial foundation was created independently of Constantine. If the churches had not been linked

2. Elliott-Binns, *The Beginnings of Western Christendom*; Mudderidge, *The End of Christendom*; Carroll, *The Founding of Christendom*; Kreider, *The Change of Conversion and the Origin of Christendom*; Brown, *The Rise of Western Christendom*.

3. Mudderidge, *The End of Christendom*, 14.

4. Pirenne, *Mohammed and Charlemagne*.

5. Sanneh, *Encountering the West*, 185–86.

in this way, Constantine would not have been able to influence in the ways that he did.

The Use of Sack

The second preliminary matter has to do with the use of Sack's analysis of the Roman Catholic Church. In Sack's *Human Territoriality*, he lays out the details of his theory and then turns to understanding territoriality in particular contexts. Presumably he could have chosen from any number of human organizations, but the Roman Catholic Church and its ascendant hierarchy were, in his perspective, the ideal place to begin. "The interconnections among hierarchy, bureaucracy, and territoriality" make the church, "one of the most enduring and best-documented examples of an institution using territoriality as an integral part of its organization."[6] The humble beginnings of a faith uninterested in establishing permanent physical structures or meticulously organized territorial leadership, stands in contrast to the later opulence, fixity, and hierarchy expressed in the Roman Catholic Church. According to Sack, from the archdiocese, the diocese, the parish, and even to the partitions in the layout of the church building, there is a clear and growing "reliance on territoriality" by the church.[7]

Sack's case study of the Roman Catholic Church teases out some dynamics that are outside the scope of this work. Likewise, I am also interested in territoriality beyond the scope of the Roman Catholic Church. Yet Sack's analysis of the church, and in particular his review of the various letters and cannons are helpful. Consequently, along with Sack's understanding of territoriality as the theoretical basis for the following chapters, his analysis of territoriality in the church is also helpful.

Discerning Territoriality

The remaining preliminary matters are a few general comments for discerning evidence of territoriality. The focus will be on the visible church, the outward and upward expansion of territoriality, and its continuity and discontinuity from previous manifestations. Sack clarifies from the outset what he sees as the two natures of the church, the visible and the invisible, with the latter including such things as the abstract belief patterns and heavenly participants. In contrast, he understands the visible or physical church

6. Sack, *Human Territoriality*, 51.

7. Sack, *Human Territoriality*, 51.

as "church buildings, properties, holy places, parishes, and dioceses," but it also includes "the social institutions of the Church and encompasses its members, its officials, its rules and regulations."[8] Sack's clarification distinguishes between how one may imagine the church ideally, or perhaps theologically, and how the church is made manifest in earthly reality.

As Sack describes the visible church, the definition extends across multiple scales and is certainly more than physical buildings. The laws and canons, the members, and the hierarchical offices are included in Sack's understanding of the visible church. For many of these visible aspects of the church, Sack would refer to them as territories. They are "places set apart by boundaries and within which authority is exerted and access is controlled."[9] Church buildings are more obviously territory, but according to Sack's description so are hierarchical offices. This was in no small part due to how church hierarchy was built on and corresponded with physical territory, such as anointing the Bishop of Alexandria.

This broader sense of territory aligns with how territoriality was described in chapter 2 as expanding a territory outward as well as subdividing a territory from within. Subdivision can be seen in the delimitation of physical space or in the subdivision (or stratification) of hierarchy, particularly when that hierarchy is built on land jurisdictions. Within the church, development of territoriality is presented in both its outward territorial expansion and its upward hierarchical subdivision. These two types of territorial increase have often gone together. Sack states that one can observe "a positive association between development of Church territory and the sociological dimensions of specialization, standardization, formalization, and the organizational span of control."[10] As Christians came to be present in more places, the church expanded outward and the hierarchy of the church leadership expanded upward. Both increases are part of the visible church and evidence of territoriality.

The third general comment about discerning territoriality has to do with its development. The essential ingredients of territoriality can take shape independently. Classifications of place are often formed before instances of enforcement can be identified and motivations for enforcements may never be made clear.[11] These classifications become part of territorial-

8. Sack, *Human Territoriality*, 93.

9. Sack, *Human Territoriality*, 93.

10. Sack, *Human Territoriality*, 98.

11. Sack, *Human Territoriality*, 33.

ity when a person or group seek to express their power over an area. When the church was not officially recognized by governmental authorities, the enforcement available to the church was limited to smaller scales of area, such as the congregation. However, much of the foundation upon which territoriality comes to be built is laid down by the upward and outward expansion of the church. Consequently, even if specific examples of territoriality are minimal, the essential ingredients of later territoriality are taking shape.

As territoriality may develop in parts, one should also expect "persistence and change in territorial use through succeeding social contexts."[12] There is continuity and discontinuity between expressions of territoriality and past manifestations. Some effects look strikingly similar to prior patterns, while other effects demonstrate fundamental difference. This is exemplified in various Christian churches, denominations, societies, and organizations. When reflecting on the history of territoriality in relationship to the Christian faith, innovations of territoriality should be anticipated.

The next several chapters will trace evidence of territoriality in both its outward and upward manifestations in the visible church. This evidence will reveal how territoriality has persisted and changed over time. The early development of the Christian faith was itself born out of change as it defined itself off from the Jewish faith and formed its early territorial characteristics. The context of this change is where the account of territoriality in Christian faith and mission should begin.

THE FORMATION OF A DETERRITORIALIZED FAITH

Deconstructing Jewish Territoriality

Christianity developed at a time when a complex relationship existed between the Jewish people and the land they inhabited. Religious symbolism was tied to the landscape which was defined by places of remembrance for the acts of God in the life of the community. The land was understood to be uniquely blessed, divinely given to the people. Jerusalem was the center and the temple within Jerusalem was holy. There were layers of holiness and access was strictly controlled. Sack describes the temple as "a territory of worship" which "contained a hierarchy of sub-territories with the holiest place reserved only for the High Priests."[13] Jerusalem contained the only

12. Sack, *Human Territoriality*, 91.

13. Sack, *Human Territoriality*, 91

legitimate temple and those worshippers of Yahweh that lived outside of Jewish land would make regular pilgrimages back to this temple.

That the Jewish land was actually a Roman colony added further complexity to the relationship between the people and the land. While the Jewish state was maintained, their control over the territory was not autonomous but subsidiary. Primary control of the land belonged to the Roman Empire and it was therefore subject to the laws of Roman society. This was yet another layer to the multifaceted political history of that area. The desire to reestablish and maintain territorial possession and primary control of the land was part of the narrative that shaped the community and their view of the Messiah. Into this context, Christianity emerges.

Sack understands Christianity to be "one of several dissident Jewish experiments" that would rebel "against the rigid hierarchical structure of Judaism."[14] He argues that groups like the Essenes "anticipated the early Christian conceptions of the temple or the church as not a building but a community of worshippers."[15] While the followers of Jesus were not the only ones to imagine replacing the temple with a group of people, this non-territorial, non-physical approach to the worshiping community was a distinct marker of early Christianity. It was a clear divergence from the Jewish attachment to land and the necessity of the temple.

Walls, in contrast to Sack, stresses the continuity between the early Christ followers and their Jewish faith and culture. In his perspective they were more reformers than rebels. The first Christ followers were keepers of the law and continued to see the temple as a holy meeting place. "They worshiped in the temple, and they loved it, and saw it as their home . . . These people loved God's law, and lived the law the Jesus way. This led them to radical new expressions of that law: they willingly shared their property, for instance, and they shared their meals in the enjoyment of the company of other followers of Jesus."[16] Walls presents the Jewish Christians as committed to continuing their worship in the temple and reluctant to deterritorialized their religious practice.[17]

There are elements of truth in both Walls's and Sack's representation. The earliest followers of Jesus were less like the intentional rebels that Sack imagines. They were slow to appreciate the implications of their leader's

14. Sack, *Human Territoriality*, 102 and 99.

15. Sack, *Human Territoriality*, 102.

16. Walls, *The Cross-cultural Process in Christian History*, 75.

17. Walls, *Missionary Movement in Christian History*, 3.

teaching. But the teaching of Jesus, and the New Testament as a whole, laid the foundation for a radical departure from the territoriality present in the Jewish faith.

Relevant New Testament Texts

In Sack's perspective, the New Testament contains numerous instances of "pronouncements against religious organization."[18] Here he cites the warning against those praying in the street (Matt 6:5), and sees social definitions of territory in Matthew 18:20, "where two or three gather in my name, there am I also." Paul's portrayal of Christians as the "temple of the living God" in 2 Corinthians 6:16 is another example. Sack also held that the eschatological focus of the early church made levels of ecclesiastical hierarchy, in clearly defined territories, initially unnecessary.[19] These are the passages that Sack provides to show the deterritorialized tendency of Christianity, but more could be added that show how many passages of the New Testament created the foundation for a more deterritorialized faith.

The Gospels

In Luke 7:1–10, Jesus heals the centurion's servant, but his physical presence was not required for the healing to occur. In response to the Samaritan woman's question about the right place to worship in John 4:19–24, Jesus refocuses the discussion away from place and toward the priority of worshiping in Spirit and truth. In a statement that subverted the conventions of the Jewish physical establishment, Jesus tells Peter in Matthew 16:18, "on this rock I will build my church." The church would not be built on a place but on a person, defining the community socially instead of territorially. It is therefore striking how the church would revert to the preference for physical establishment, the inscription at the Basilica demonstrating this turnabout.

Jesus's teaching on the temple was also a shift from the expected norm. As mentioned in chapter 2, one of the effects of territoriality is reification, where the abstract notion of the holy becomes tangible in physical forms, such is the case with the temple. In light of the significance of the temple to Jewish faith, consider Jesus's response to his disciples stated in Mark 13:1–2,

18. Sack, *Human Territoriality*, 101.

19. Sack, *Human Territoriality*, 101.

> As Jesus was leaving the temple, one of his disciples said to him, "Look, Teacher! What massive stones! What magnificent buildings!" "Do you see all these great buildings?" replied Jesus. "Not one stone here will be left on another; every one will be thrown down."

Such statements by Jesus decentralized the temple, countering the idea that it was the source of God's power on earth. The splitting of the veil in Matt 27:51 further deconstructed the reification of God's holy place and foreshadowed a faith where the barriers between religious leaders and congregants were diminished. As stated by Clark and Johnson, "sacred place has thus given way to sacred person . . . the aim of Israel's temple is fulfilled and transformed by the incarnation of God."[20] Jesus, in his teachings and in the events that his incarnation initiated, challenged the physical forms of religiosity presented by Judaism. The implications of these truths have impacted the formation of the church, even if the earliest disciples were hesitant to make the connections.

Acts of the Apostles

The book of Acts records three movements in the life of the early church that signaled a new direction, "a fresh view concerning God's impartial activity."[21] Before the ascension of Jesus, the disciples were told that they would be witnesses "in Jerusalem, and in all Judea and Samaria, and to the ends of the earth" (Acts 1:8). The author of Acts presents the development of the Christian faith in this way, expanding across multiple boundaries associated with human particularity–language, culture, and territory.

The first movement was Pentecost, "which set a seal on mother tongues as sufficient and necessary channels of access to God."[22] Acts 2 describes the proclamation of God's good news in multiple languages among the Jewish Christians of Jerusalem and the diasporic Jews who had come to Jerusalem for worship. Sanneh sees this moment as "a piece of cultural innovation that enabled the religion to adopt the multiplicity of geographical centres as legitimate destinations for the gospel."[23] It was the start. The seed of change

20. Clark and Johnson, *The Incarnation of God*, 100.
21. Sanneh, *Encountering the West*, 134.
22. Sanneh, *Encountering the West*, 134.
23. Sanneh, *Encountering the West*, 134.

was developing but there was not yet a clear challenge to the idea that Jews and Jerusalem were central to the life of the Christian community.

Beginning in Acts chapter 8, the second movement sees the good news reach people in Samaria. Persecution had begun to scatter the followers of Jesus and Philip preached in one of the towns of the region. Walls notes that Luke broadly follows a westward trajectory in Acts, with the exception of a eunuch from Ethiopia who is introduced at the end of chapter 8. According to Walls, "It is as though the author is telling us 'My own story is about how the gospel traveled the highway to the West; but there are other stories of the gospel's progress besides the one I am telling. One day we will see that the stories join up and the gospel is preached to the whole world.'"[24] The encounter between Philip and the Ethiopian is managed end to end by an angel of the Lord and the Holy Spirit. The reader of Acts is left unaware of the implications of the moment, with only the suggestion that the movement is larger than what is captured in the current frame. Here, as throughout Acts, the disciples are presented as slow to understand what was being divinely initiated.

Acts 10 continues this theme as Peter, in a port town of Samaria, receives a vision during prayer. His commitment to the Jewish food laws was challenged by the command, "Kill and eat." Peter's interpretation of the vision signaled that this was not about the food though, it was about Cornelius. The movement of the Holy Spirit had once again caught the Jewish Christians off guard. According to Sanneh, "Peter's insistence that true religion cannot be restricted to mere institutional adherence signals a radical shift to the idea of God as boundary-free truth, of God as one who is without partiality."[25] This second movement breached ethnic and national boundaries.

The culminating third movement extended the geography further, intermixing all of the boundary breaking of before. Crossing the third threshold would be the inaugural step toward bringing the message of Jesus across the borders of language, culture, and territory. Sanneh states that "when the faith was taken from Jerusalem to Antioch, Christianity acquired a worldwide cultural and geographical orientation."[26] Walls elaborates further:

> Luke quietly describes one of the most critical events in Christian history. So far as we can see, it was no part of any grand missionary

24. Walls, *Crossing Cultural Frontiers*, 79.
25. Sanneh, *Disciples of All Nations*, 4.
26. Sanneh, *Disciples of All Nations*, 3.

> strategy on the part of the Church; it grew out of circumstances wholly unforeseen. Nor were the people who initiated it, so far as we know, any of the apostles and elders of Jerusalem who were the Church's pillars. It was a few Jerusalem Christians–we do not even know their names–who, driven away from home to Antioch, began to talk to their Greek pagan friends about Jesus, whom they and all other Christians of that time thought of as the Jewish national savior.[27]

Antioch represented the beginning of a different kind of vision. Till this point much of salvific history had echoed the vision laid out by Isaiah 66:20, "and they will bring all your people, from all the nations, to my holy mountain in Jerusalem." The momentum pulling toward Jerusalem as the physical fixed center of God's worship was being reversed.[28]

The broad theme of the book of Acts shows how God was creating a new people, linguistically and culturally diverse, and geographically dispersed. The good news was moving out from the center and changing, among other things, the territorial makeup of the church.

Epistles

In the New Testament epistles, one sees evidence of reframing physical places in spiritual, abstract terms. In Galatians 4:26, Paul created distinctions between the Jerusalem above and Jerusalem below. Magda understands such statements as beginning a process of distinguishing the *place* as a more universal spiritual symbol from the *place* as a particular physical location.[29] Jerusalem could become an abstract ideal. Where once places such as *the holy mountain* or Jerusalem mediated access to God, these places could now be redefined in a spiritualized perspective, making God accessible anywhere. Sanneh notes that in time, Bethlehem was treated similarly. "Bethlehem was emptied of cultural content and elided to a universal incarnation."[30] Likewise, gathering in the temple was no longer required, since the believer was now understood to be the living temple, as articulated in 2 Corinthians 6:16.

27. Walls, *Missionary Movement in Christian History*, 52.
28. See also Peters, *A Biblical Theology of Missions*.
29. Magda, *Paul's Territoriality and Mission Strategy*, 52.
30. Sanneh, *Disciples of All Nations*, 13.

The epistles teach that when believers did meet, the place was generally not a physical structure specifically built for religious purpose. They were most commonly in the home of one of the church members (1 Cor 16:19; Rom 16:3–5; Phlm 1:2; Col 4:15). The church was the body of believers and the focus was on the people who gathered there.

Communities were voluntary associations with low hierarchical arrangements. Robert Banks argues Paul understood the responsibility for the community as belonging to all the members of that community.[31] He asserts that Paul "rejects any formal distinction between clergy and laity."[32] Where there was a notion of leadership it was tied to service and if a member of leadership was worthy of respect it was on the basis of their service. Banks holds that Paul did not stress authority and writes of himself as "belonging to the church, not the church belonging to him."[33] While Paul sought to engender a fellowship between churches, Banks states that "there is no suggestion of a visible, earthly, universal church to which local gatherings are related as a part to the whole. Nor does Paul speak of any organizational framework by which the local communities are bound together."[34] Paul's letters contained expressions of unity in the form of personal connections rather than a formally structured federation of churches.[35]

The community that Paul helped to produce deemphasized the need for physical and hierarchical establishments. Eschatological teachings presented the world as broken, longing to be remade (Rom 8:19). Christ's return was eminent, and a Christian's time on earth was therefore transient. They were pilgrims, exiles, and sojourners, temporary residents focused on an eternal home (1 Pet 2:11). Such ideas could produce a form of detachment from a place.

Evidence from the Gospels, Acts, and the epistles demonstrates that Scripture was an important part of creating a deterritorialized faith. These early writings helped to establish and maintain a different kind of religious community.

31. Banks, *Paul's Idea of Community*, 117.

32. Banks, *Paul's Idea of Community*, 114.

33. Banks, *Paul's Idea of Community*, 153.

34. Banks, *Paul's Idea of Community*, 38.

35. Banks, *Paul's Idea of Community*, 39.

The Church as a Deterritorialized Community

The Christians grew in number as the good news spread beyond Judea. The seemingly deterritorialized beliefs opened doors for a faith not bound to one location. Sanneh tells how early accounts of the church seem to reflect a "new conception of religion [which] accounted for the birth of new communities of faith and new forms of social life, independent of official endorsement and without the necessity of a promised land or the advantage of cultural privilege"[36] Following Jesus did not entail worship in a specific location. Sanneh expresses this conviction as follows: "Christianity was not a belief in an axis mundi, and so could flourish anywhere as experienced-based personal faith. The idea of holy place was not an immutable, timeless place or dwelling; it was wherever believers found God."[37] Sack identifies a similar perspective at work in the origins of the faith. Early Christians did not think of their worship as "in any sense place specific, and there is little to suggest that they thought of Israel, or even Jerusalem, as especially sacred."[38] Without the requirement of "religious territory [this] enhanced the Christian claim to universality. It made conversion easier. It made Christian communities more flexible."[39] The universalizing potential of a religion cut free from anchors that tied it to one exclusive place alone allowed the gospel to move across physical and cultural barriers.

The church was also free from the confines of state religion and systems of stifling hierarchical leadership. Unconnected to established governmental entities and without a complicated infrastructure, the Christian faith could be integrated in whatever soil it was planted.[40] Sack acknowledges that "the early Christian communities were geographically dispersed and often multi-cultural."[41] Without a controlling hierarchy to manage the growing network of churches, uniformity was impossible to achieve. Yet Walls is struck by the "sense of mutual belonging" that characterized the early church.[42]

The earliest followers of Jesus were shaped by convictions that deemphasized the importance of territory and therefore the use of

36. Sanneh, *Disciples of All Nations*, 14.
37. Sanneh, *Disciples of All Nations*, 13.
38. Sack, *Human Territoriality*, 106.
39. Sack, *Human Territoriality*, 102.
40. Sanneh, *Encountering the West*, 118; and Sanneh, *Disciples of All Nations*, 53.
41. Sack, *Human Territoriality*, 102.
42. Walls, *Crossing Cultural Frontiers*, 4.

territoriality. Their perspectives contrasted with Judaism and were solidified by their sacred texts. The good news of Jesus could cross barriers which would have otherwise been insurmountable for a religion more rooted in cultural particularity and fixed in a location.

The outward expansion of the church indicated the potential for Christianity to become a worldwide religion. But with this outward expansion, came growing organizational needs. These needs were met by building a foundation of territoriality in the early church.

THE FOUNDATION OF TERRITORIALITY IN THE CHURCH

Jerusalem as Central and Antioch as Peripheral

In spite of the potential for Christianity to have a more universal appeal, incorporating groups further away from Jerusalem presented challenges. For the first followers of Jesus, Jerusalem was central. It was the location for many key events in the life, death, and resurrection of their Lord. The Ascension happened in Jerusalem and that would be the place of the Lord's return. They had been told to wait in Jerusalem to receive the Holy Spirit and at Pentecost thousands more joined their movement. But the good news moved beyond Jerusalem.

The Gentiles in Antioch had "believed and turned to the Lord" according to Acts 11:21. The followers of Jesus in Jerusalem were not always sure how to respond to such surprising activities of the Holy Spirit. Walls suggests that they chose to take on an authenticating role. "It was Jerusalem that sent out commissions to decide whether the conversion movements among Samarians and Antiochene Gentiles were really acceptable; [and] it was Jerusalem that had to settle the question of how far non-Jewish believers in Jesus must conform to Jewish cultural norms."[43] Walls's summary of the dynamics above is described in terms of place, as he repeats the phrase "it was Jerusalem," but people are implied. In time conflict described in terms of locations became more common as places came to have symbolic meaning. But at this time, there was no question that Jerusalem was the center and Antioch was the periphery. When, in Acts 21:19, Paul reported in detail on the movement of God among the Gentiles, the response from those in Jerusalem was tepid. While it was cause to praise God, they wanted Paul to reassert his own commitment to Jewish particularity by acts of

43. Walls, *The Cross-cultural Process in Christian History*, 32. He cites Acts 8:14.; 11:22; and 15:1–2.

worship in the temple. Walls states that "while being decently glad of the 'mission field' conversions . . . they continued to think of Jerusalem as the regulative center of God's saving word."[44] Paul acquiesced, even though according to Banks, "the founding apostles in Jerusalem are not accorded any privileged position" in Paul's perspective.[45]

The movement of the Spirit in Antioch aligned with what was promised in Acts 1:8; a step toward the someday when the Christian message would be heard in even the furthest places on earth. But nothing of that promise challenged the centrality of Jerusalem. For those in Jerusalem, the response to the gospel from the Antiochenes served to underscore the significance of their Jewish Messiah. The developments in Antioch were understood to be complementary to the far more consequential work God was doing among the Jews. Walls imagines the reasoning from Jewish perspective. If the Gentile Christians were truly dedicated, within time they "would come to look as much like Jerusalem Christians as was possible for such benighted heathen."[46]

The relationship between Antioch and Jerusalem provides the opportunity to consider some limited early effects of territoriality in the context of the church. As noted in chapter 3, the mental, social, and physical forces of one's place help form the geographic perspectives one comes to hold. For the Jewish believers, they knew the Scriptures, they were part of God's chosen people, and they had walked with Jesus personally. It was not unreasonable for them to view Jerusalem as central and any other place as peripheral. In terms of territoriality, these classifications of center and periphery were assumed. When the Jewish believers took up the role of authenticating those in the periphery, they reinforced their own classifications.

As believers in Jerusalem took on a regulatory role, doing so placed themselves hierarchically above others.[47] Sack refers to this organizational development as an example of standardization.[48] As the church grew, Jerusalem set the standards and made the decisions. Considering the underlying conflict in the letter to the Galatians, it is likely that even the Greek believers assumed the appropriateness of this "cultural apprenticeship under the

44. Walls, *Missionary Movement in Christian History*, 8.

45. Banks, *Paul's Idea of Community*, 149.

46. Walls, *Missionary Movement in Christian History*, 8.

47. Walls, *Crossing Cultural Frontiers*, 20.

48. Sack, *Human Territoriality*, 97.

Torah."[49] Some Gentiles Christians accepted the Jerusalem centric classifications but Paul challenged these ideas directly. Based on Galatians 2:6–9, Banks states that "though others regard them as pillars of the Christian movement, Paul appears quite unconcerned about their status."[50] Evidence of this can be found in Galatians 4:25 where notions of the earthly Jerusalem as the center and standard were dismissed. The fact that the New Testament was written in Greek and often far from Jerusalem also contributed to a decentralizing of Jewish particularity within the Christian faith.

The inclusion of the Antiochene Christians presented a contrast between here and there. The growing multiplicity of locations brought about circumstances that would eventually develop into territorial subdivisions. The church's hierarchy of leadership was built on this foundation.

Evidence of Organizational Development in the New Testament

While the teachings of the New Testament emphasized a deterritorialized faith, Scripture could also be used to justify the need for territoriality. The ministry and writing of the early Apostles expanded over an increasing geographical network of churches. Paul's epistles were addressed to the churches in that network making use of the place's name, as in 'to the churches in Galatia.' A similar pattern appears in the letters of Revelation chapters 2 and 3. The place's name was usually a city, not a larger region or smaller subdivision. In Sack's view, "the letters recognize that the congregation or community is in the city and that normally there is one per city."[51] Sack states that this practice continued in the correspondence of the next two centuries.

The epistles provided opportunity to connect, encourage, and exhort at a distance. Paul sent and received other believers and his letters were punctuated by introductions and greetings from those who were with Paul (Eph 6:21–22; Col 4:7–9). The epistles also gave an opportunity for the Apostles to express their esteem and solidify links between Christians where physical distance made the expression of solidarity more difficult. The link between churches should not be understood as a formalized arrangement. As Banks comments "the idea of a unified provincial or national church is as foreign to Paul's thinking as the notion of a universal church."[52] But these

49. Sanneh, *Disciples of All Nations*, 7.
50. Banks, *Paul's Idea of Community*, 149.
51. Sack, *Human Territoriality*, 105.
52. Banks, *Paul's Idea of Community*, 28.

connections helped address the needs of a growing network attempting to relate to each other.

Some of the issues facing the early churches are mentioned in the New Testament. There were relational disputes, both interpersonal (Phil 4:2) and religious/cultural (such as the divisions between the Jews and Gentiles in Romans and Galatians). There were moral concerns (1 Cor 5:1–13) and the need for more orderly worship (1 Cor 11). In response to the perceived need for standards, discipline, and control, greater leadership structure was provided and submission to leadership was encouraged. Paul instructed the Corinthians to submit to the household of Stephanas who "were the first converts in Achaia" and "have devoted themselves to the service of the Lord's people" (1 Cor 16:15–16). Paul clarified spiritual gifts, guided the appointment of leaders and provided a framework for qualifications (Rom 12:6–8, 1 Pet 4:10–11, 1 Cor 12:1–31, 1 Tim 3:1–7, Titus 1:6–9). Gatherings of believers established elders who were assigned to teach, and deacons to serve. Sack holds that the fact that the Christian communities received visitations by respected Christian leaders who also authored letters distributed broadly "suggests the willingness of a community and its bishop to recognize and submit to a higher authority."[53] While Banks would argue that this was not Paul's intention, the evidence is that "by the end of the second century the hierarchy both within a community and among communities was becoming solidified and explicit."[54]

A principal concern for the early church was keeping the Christian message from being distorted and that those within the community behaved in ways consistent with that message (Rom 16:17; 1 Cor 15:2; 15:33; 1 Tim 1:3, 20 and 4:1–5). A process of church discipline was developed to meet these needs (Titus 3:9–11, 2 Thess 3:6, 1 Tim 5:19–20). Facts needed to be confirmed by two or three witnesses (2 Cor 13:1), the immoral unrepentant were to be expelled (1 Cor 5:1–13), and, once repentant, ways of reentering the community needed to be established (2 Cor 2:6–11).

As the early church developed, the growing need for organization led its leaders to form new patterns of religious life. Sack states that "early Christians became more accepting of organization and hierarchy [because], like all groups, they needed internal discipline to continue to exist."[55] As the

53. Sack, *Human Territoriality*, 103.

54. Sack, *Human Territoriality*, 103.

55. Sack, *Human Territoriality*, 102.

social definition of the Christian territory expanded, so did the need for upward organizational hierarchy.

The New Testament provides the substance for a deterritorialized faith, but it also shows why some may have found territoriality to be an effective strategy for meeting organizational goals. The teachings of Jesus, Luke, Paul, and Peter effectively deconstructed much of the territoriality of Judaism. These values persisted and Christianity was still far less territorial than the religious forms present within Judaism, but one can see certain elements begin to align for more territoriality to occur. Limited instances of territoriality are present, but more importantly an organizational foundation was beginning to take shape.

The Effects of Persecution

Rapid growth and geographic dispersal of the church went hand in hand with internal and external pressures. The Roman Empire's persecution of the church is one example. The Romans made attempts to unify their own geographically widespread empire through Romanization. This was particularly important in places like North Africa, in part because of their distance from Rome. Such territorial outposts needed to be Roman first whatever their religious views. Walls states that while the Roman Empire was not uniquely religious, it did have an "underlying civil religion concerning the state itself."[56] As the primary territoriality, the Romans required allegiance, but it was difficult for Rome to understand a Christian's loyalties.[57] In its urban settings, Romanization and the establishment of Christianity seemed to occur simultaneously, which further complexified the issue.[58] Sanneh states that "Pliny resorted to panic in describing the Christian movement as the contagion of a superstition that had infected cities and had festered in villages and hamlets."[59] Persecution resulted from Christians failing a Roman "patriot test."[60] This external pressure instigated a variety of reactions.

There were three broad responses to the persecution among the Christian community. One could deny their faith to avoid the most severe repercussions. Both leaders and laity who had capitulated under the pressure

56. Walls, *Crossing Cultural Frontiers*, 80.

57. Sack, *Human Territoriality*, 102.

58. Decret, *Early Christianity in North Africa*, 4.

59. Sanneh, *Disciples of All Nations*, 31.

60. Walls, *Crossing Cultural Frontiers*, 80.

of torture were labeled *lapsi* and would need to be disciplined before they could re-enter the community.[61] Alternatively, one could flee. Persecution tended to be more cyclical than constant and leaving the region for a time was an effective solution for those who could afford to do so. But situations arose where more wealthy church leaders abandoned their congregants while poor laity bore witness to Christ through their suffering.[62] At times this created hierarchical challenges when church leaders left their flock and needed to be replaced.

The third response to persecution was for one to stand firm in their commitment to Christ and withstand the testing of persecution. Those who did were held up as heroes and their courage stood in contrast to the formal leadership of the church. If they survived, they had the potential to create an alternative leadership structure that was a challenge to the authority of the official church. Consequently, when persecution inevitably died down, the church was left with a greater need for internal discipline. Penalties and means for re-entry into congregational life would need to be managed for both laity and church leadership. Some leaders would need to be replaced. These dynamics increased the need for clear structural authority.[63] In these three responses to persecution territoriality would be used to replace leaders, to limit congregational access until reentry requirements were met, and to reassert the official structures of authority.

Change in Attachment

In spite of the persecution, Christians were becoming more rooted in their locations. In the first century, and the beginning of the second century, the church had strongly preferred to think of themselves as exiles and sojourns passing through. It was a relationship with one's place that was more characterized by detachment and the community's low territorial values. According to Sack, this was made manifest in the visible church. "Perhaps due to eschatology and to the peripatetic characters of the Apostles, the Church fathers go out of their way to make it seem that the Church visible is not anchored to territory. Early church letters (Paul's letters to the Corinthians, Clement's first epistles to the Corinthians, the epistles of Ignatius to the Ephesians, Magnesians, Trallians, and Romans) refer to a church being at

61. Hefele, *A History of the Christian Councils*, First Synod of Carthage, 93–95.

62. Decret, *Early Christianity in North Africa*, 46–59. See also Oden, *Early Libyan Christianity*.

63. Sack, *Human Territoriality*, 104.

(not of) a place and sometimes sojourning at a place."[64] This self-descriptive tendency changed over time. Sack explains that the first evidence of this can be found in one of Ignatius' letters, where "at one point he refers to himself as the bishop *of* Syria."[65] By the end of the second century, and certainly by the third, this becomes common practice. In this way, "the connection between a bishop and a place, if not a territory, becomes explicit."[66] The use of *in* or *at* a place could imply a kind of punctiliar impermanence, a momentary passing through. By contrast, *of* a place implies a more rooted fixity and attachment.

The subtle difference that Sack notes is suggestive of Walls's indigenizing and pilgrim principles. The principles are an articulation of how attachment to a place can often shift between the two tendencies. While the indigenizing principle makes one's faith "feel at home" within a location and culture, the pilgrim principle whispers to the Christian, "that he has no abiding city and warns him that to be faithful to Christ will put him out of step with his society."[67] Despite external pressures, the church was beginning to feel much more at home in the Roman world.

FURTHER EVIDENCE OF ORGANIZATIONAL DEVELOPMENT IN THE EARLY CHURCH

Christians began to make use of the existing ideas of place and territory by adopting the civic boundaries as church boundaries. This was true of the metropolitan areas first. Conceivably, the church could have chosen another means of subdivision, but instead it chose "to conform itself to the territorial divisions of the states or of the provinces in establishing its own territorial divisions."[68] This choice may have been a conscious attempt to use the framework already present, or they had not thought to do otherwise. The classifications that were already part of their world were brought into the church. In North Africa there is evidence that these jurisdictions also served to contain Christian expansion. Decret states that no "episcopal seat [was] located beyond the provincial boundaries and the regions controlled

64. Sack, *Human Territoriality*, 105.
65. Sack, *Human Territoriality*, 105.
66. Sack, *Human Territoriality*, 105–6.
67. Walls, *Missionary Movement in Christian History*, 8.
68. Hefele, *A History of the Christian Councils*, 381.

by military detachments."[69] Territory was beginning to be viewed as a container and the link between leadership and locations was strengthening.

The foundation of the hierarchical system was built on the idea of one bishop for one city. Banks contends that it was in "the third century that the words of clergy and layperson came into Christian usage."[70] In comparison to the traveling apostles, "the position of a bishop or cleric had become geographically fixed."[71] This shift away from itinerancy inclined the church leadership toward stationary ministry. S. L. Greenslade suggests that early church leaders understood that they had a territorial responsibility, but it is hard to tell what the limits of that responsibility were and if it was understood to be bounded by the limits of the city.[72] There is also no evidence "of using the city limits or some other specifiable boundary as a means of defining and enforcing jurisdiction over the congregation."[73] But that was the direction of the new shape of leadership and power in the church and it was built on stationary bishops assigned to locations.

The move toward more stationary ministry also helped to develop the notion of churches as physical structures. Informal temporary meeting places were moving toward more structured and permanent spaces. By 305 it was uncommon to meet in a private home for church purposes.[74] The idea of *church* as a social group was changing toward the idea of *church* as a building, and "the convenience of meeting at a specific place gradually led to the use of that place as constituting a basic part of congregating."[75] Within these more permanent dedicated worship spaces, territory was divided creating tiers of access differentiated by one's status of leadership within the church. Sack describes how "by the third century A.D., the church building was already becoming a sanctified place containing a hierarchy of sites within it that were accessible to different levels of the Church hierarchy."[76]

On the larger scale, the number of councils in the church to adjudicate disputes gradually increased in the second and third centuries. Councils were convened with representatives from the different locations. The

69. Decret, *Early Christianity in North Africa*, 5–6.
70. Banks, *Paul's Idea of Community*, 116.
71. Sack, *Human Territoriality*, 105.
72. Greenslade, "The Unit of Pastoral Care in the Early Church," 106.
73. Sack, *Human Territoriality*, 105.
74. Hefele, *A History of the Christian Councils*, 129–30.
75. Sack, *Human Territoriality*, 106.
76. Sack, *Human Territoriality*, 114.

establishment of regional assemblies provides evidence of a developing hierarchy within the church. Within this hierarchy, authority was gradually shifting away from Jerusalem toward Rome. The councils held in Carthage starting in 251 AD addressed concerns of a bishop leaving his territory due to persecution. The question of authority in this territory was initially decided in Rome and after the councils in Carthage met, they turned to Rome to affirm their decision. Sack argues that the fact that, "decisions of this and other synods were often sent to Rome for approval indicates that even at this early period the occupant of that see was considered first among equals."[77] Certain ministerial locations having greater prestige than others, created opportunity for inequality and a view of place as an end rather than a means. While the see of Jerusalem was still significant, Rome was beginning to take the lead.

Ministry was becoming more stationary, and the church was increasingly synonymous with the physical structure used for worship. Territorial boundaries were adopted, and bishops were assigned to locations. Councils were increasing in number, and power was being redistributed to other city centers. All of this is evidence of further organizational development and the foundation of territoriality.

Summary of Pre-Constantinian Territoriality

The clear and specific examples of territoriality in the early church are evident in instances where congregations excluded heretics or expelled the immoral brother or sister. They had the capability of restricting people from their assembly and people from leadership positions. Outside of these limited examples of territoriality, one can see evidence of the visible church expanding outward across spaces of land and upward in terms of hierarchical organization. While enforcement was minimal, classifications of territory were steadily developing on multiple scales.

There was a perceived need for clear structures of organization and authority. Power dynamics between places that were central and peripheral developed. Persecution encouraged the standardization of processes for discipline and reentry to the congregation. Simultaneously, there was an increased attachment to place, ministry was becoming more fixed in location, and ministerial domains were becoming more conformed to state subdivisions and territory. According to Sack, "by A.D. 300, Christians were on the

77. Sack, *Human Territoriality*, 104.

verge of using territoriality to help define their community, their places of worship, and their relationships to each other."[78]

The elements of classification by territory were becoming clearer and the foundation of territoriality was laid. Sack depicts the pre-Constantinian church in the following way:

> On the eve of its acceptance by Rome, Christianity however reluctantly, had begun creating a visible and territorial Church. Church hierarchy had become explicit and Church officials had become to some degree separate from the rest of the community of believers. Worship was being confined more and more to the church buildings, the sacred part of life having been separated to some extent from the secular. The church building and its parts increasingly reified Church government as well as the sacred. The community itself and the authority of its bishops were coming to be more and more territorial. Bishops were of a city, and city size affected the prestige of the office.[79]

A substantial organizational structure was in place when Constantine came to power.

THE INFLUENCE OF CONSTANTINE

It was some time shortly after the Battle of Milvian Bridge in 312, that Constantine's soldiers began carrying the sign of the cross in battle and the emperor wore *Christos* insignia on his helmet.[80] The army of the emperor, tasked with defending and expanding the territory of the Empire, was now adorned with symbols of Christianity. Many Christians who had lived under the threat of persecution were now on the precipice of a new era. Constantine influenced the church, but what was the extent of that influence?

Limits of Influence

Constantine has often been the pivotal character in a narrative that explains larger complex ideas such as Christendom. But the argument could be made that the impact of Constantine has at times been overstated. For example, Sack claims that "from the mid-fourth to the end of the sixth centuries the geographic limits of the Church were the practical limits of the

78. Sack, *Human Territoriality*, 99.

79. Sack, *Human Territoriality*, 107.

80. Leithart, *Defending Constantine*, 69.

Empire."[81] It is perhaps fair to state that Sack's assertion represents the conventional understanding of church history in the Western world, particularly at the time Sack wrote his monograph. It is a position that Walls has rightly critiqued because of its inaccuracy, and yet he has recognized the persistence of this perspective even among teachers of church history As Walls explains, "what Western scholars studied as the history of the church was in reality the history of the church in 'our village.'"[82] To put it another way, Walls's argument is that some iterations of church history fail in their geographic breadth based on unexamined ethnocentrism which privileges one's own place. Constantine has been understood to be important to the narrative of the church in part because he is so important to the history of the church in Europe.

The history of the church in places of Asia and Africa are often missing from the standard narrative. For example, Walls explains that while "Egypt and North Africa were among the notably Christian areas in the world . . . by no means did the whole of African Christianity lie within the Roman Empire, nor was it subordinate to the empire."[83] Sanneh states that "Christianity pursued its mission beyond the empire eastward into Central and East Asia."[84] Missionary effort by the Syriac-speaking Christians also substantially increased the spread of the faith in Asia. "It sent the faith to India, across the heart of Central Asia, penetrated the peoples bordering the Chinese Empire, and in 635, reached the capital of that empire and gained the ear of the emperor . . . At this period, Christianity is a global faith, present, active, and growing from the Atlantic almost to the Pacific and with outposts from Siberia to Sri Lanka."[85] Properly framing the relationship between Christianity and the Roman world must take seriously the fuller geographic range of the faith outside the Empire. Constantine himself wrote to commend King Sapur for the growth of Christianity in his kingdom, writing, "I am delighted to learn that the finest districts in Persia also are adorned with the presence of Christians."[86] At the time of Constantine, the Christian faith was diverse and diffuse, more than just the practical limits of the Roman Empire.

81. Sack, *Human Territoriality*, 95.

82. Walls, *Crossing Cultural Frontiers*, 72.

83. Walls, *The Cross-cultural Process in Christian History*, 88.

84. Sanneh, *Disciples of All Nations*, 32.

85. Walls, *Crossing Cultural Frontiers*, 9.

86. Sanneh, *Disciples of All Nations*, 32.

Sack's characterization of the geographic limits of the church is inaccurate, but one could reasonably argue that Christianity under Roman influence was possibly the dominant Christian expression of the period.[87] The changes Constantine inaugurated are one piece of a larger cultural influence that began prior to Constantine and continued after him. For instance, Sanneh credits the Roman empire for uniquely influencing Christianity in the areas of organization and "institutional character."[88] As has been argued, influence in this area was under way before Constantine came on the scene.

Examples of Influence

Constantine did influence a portion of the world's Christians in measurable ways. Of greatest significance, he put an end to the Roman imperial policy of discrimination against Christians. The role of Christianity in the Empire went from persecuted to privileged in a relatively short amount of time. It was not the result of a slow acceptance by the majority of the ruling class, but the decision of an emperor. Which may have been why, with persecution still in their vivid memory, it was easier for Christians to adapt to the "advantages of social organization provided by Roman imperial life."[89] Furthermore, as Leithart argues, persecution may have also had the unfortunate effect of eliminating the more determined and idealistic church leaders, leaving behind a group all too willing to accept a more comfortable arrangement.[90] Constantine provided something never before promised to Christians in this life—safety.

The implications of this new situation impacted the church on a variety of territorial scales. With security from governmental reprisal, the development of territoriality moved to a new level of possibility. No longer did the church have to conduct their affairs in the shadows. They could turn their attention to meeting the spiritual needs of the people with greater clarity and efficiency. Sack argues that territoriality was an effective tool for

87. It is worth noting that one may find that there is a development here in Walls understanding. His earlier remarks lean toward the Roman period as representing the dominant expression of the time, but his more recent publication, *Crossing Cultural Frontiers* is interested in the more geographically broad dimensions of the faith. It is possible that he may be less definitive regarding the dominance of the Roman Christianity, but he has not, as far as this author knows, contradicted his earlier position.

88. Sanneh, *Disciples of All Nations*, 57.

89. Sanneh, *Disciples of All Nations*, 57.

90. Leithart, *Defending Constantine*, 29.

achieving the church's goals. "The Empire had a vast population, geographically dispersed and with varying degrees of mobility, and such conditions would make territoriality the simplest and clearest means of defining and dividing populations into groups and of assigning them to the supervision of Church officials."[91] The foundation of classified territory could now be solidified and maintained through territoriality.

While the organizational and territorial structures of the church were not created by Constantine, he did heighten and extend them. Sanneh states that generally "when kings and rulers converted, they facilitated the process of religious institutionalization."[92] For example, the church continued to adopt the boundaries of political jurisdiction. But through the Constantinian transformation "the power of Church officials, backed up by the state, became defined according to such territorial administrative boundaries of the Empire as dioceses."[93] The word diocese sounds specifically religious to our ears today, but it "was not an exclusive term to connote a territorial division of the church until the 13th century."[94] The territorial containers of the Roman world were used as a mold for the church's own structure and authority.

The association of the territorial lines of the empire with Christianity's subdivisions created the impression that the two were linked. Furthermore, "once the Roman empire adopted Christianity . . . the entire apparatus of Roman government was at the disposal of the Church, and Church officials became part of the government."[95] This was to Constantine's benefit as well as his Roman successors, by giving the impression of a unified church in a unified empire. As Walls states, "the unity of the church was a priority for imperial domestic policy."[96] This did not mean that everyone in the empire was Christian. Furthermore, Christianity was not a monolithic entity speaking with one voice. But if Constantine was going to champion the Christian faith, there should not be a question of which Christian faith.

When Constantine convened the Council of Nicea, he only included a small number of Christians who were not part of the Roman empire. Constantine sought to influence within a classified territory, the Roman

91. Sack, *Human Territoriality*, 110.

92. Sanneh, *Disciples of All Nations*, 57.

93. Sack, *Human Territoriality*, 108.

94. Millet, *Dioceses in Ireland Up to the 15th Century*, 1.

95. Sack, *Human Territoriality*, 107.

96. Walls, *Crossing Cultural Frontiers*, 13.

Empire, effectively shaping how the church understood itself. This was a classification that Constantine made based on his sense of place and his understanding of the world. The result, either created or exacerbated, the idea that those outside the empire were less significant. Constantine did not divide the church, but these acts of territoriality were another example of how places became conceptualized as either central, and significant, or peripheral, and therefore insignificant, within the church. Walls observes that the impact of leaving out those beyond the empire was felt in the fifth-century Christological controversies when "no one thought of consulting the Christians beyond the Roman empire."[97] He concludes that this divided the church in "three ways, and broadly along cultural and linguistic lines: Greco-Latin, Syriac, [and] Coptic."[98] One could add geographical lines as well. The church was free from state policies of persecution, but they were for the first time experiencing the influence of a different kind of state intervention.

Prior to Constantine, the church had some clear but limited examples of territoriality. The three essential facets of territoriality–classification, communication, and enforcement–could be seen in the internal discipline of the church at the smallest scale–the congregation. At the broader level of church leadership, they had no strong enforcement available until Constantine. However, the power of enforcement is strengthened when one can appeal to the primary territoriality. As Canon 5 of Antioch 341 concludes, if the bishop persists "in troubling and disturbing the Church, let him be corrected, as a seditious person, by the civil power."[99] If the church could appeal to the civil power to carry out aspects of church discipline this indicated a significant change in their capacity for enforcement and empowered new expressions of territoriality.

The privileging of Christianity under Constantine was a hinge event that changed a portion of the church in profound ways. The ties between the state and the church are best described as fluid and negotiated all throughout their history. However, within the Roman Empire, the state and a portion of the church were united as they had never been before under Constantine. The intention of the Roman state and a particular group of Christians was to exhibit close personal ties and thus portray a hegemonic authority. There was maneuvering by church leadership to court the favor

97. Walls, *Crossing Cultural Frontiers*, 13.

98. Walls, *Crossing Cultural Frontiers*, 14.

99. Percival, *The Seven Ecumenical Councils of the Undivided Church*, 110.

of the emperor, and the emperor, for his purposes, courted the favor of the church. The imperial shift in policy toward privileging Christians is what Anabaptists such as Yoder understood to be a departure from what they deem to be authentic Christianity displayed in the early church.[100]

Christianity's limited power was merging with that of the primary territoriality of the state. With even clearer classification and communication, now the church had the enforcement of the empire behind them. A rowdy bishop at one time may have been excommunicated, but under the new power arrangement they could now be exiled from the empire.[101] That kind of exclusion was now available to them and specifically used to control the mounting tiers of leadership.

> The Church, however, could and did attempt to control the geographic location of its officials and used territoriality to keep them in place, to define and delimit their authority, define channels of communication, and to circumscribe hierarchically Church responsibilities. But in so doing the Church left itself open for other territorial effects such as the possibility of mismatches and spillovers of authority and territory, the possibility of having territory become an end rather than a means, the possibility of having territory create inequalities in access to resources and authority.[102]

With increased territorial control came the effects of territoriality that change an organization.

EVIDENCE OF TERRITORIALITY

One of the ways the church demonstrated their control was by codifying rules in canons created by synods and councils. These canons provide evidence of territoriality, with all three facets of classification, communication, and enforcement present. The canons demonstrate a church attempting to organize, limit, and influence their own activities but now with a greater power to do so.

Stationary Church Leadership

The various canons speak to keeping bishops in their geographical place. The Synod of Antioch in 341 had several canons on this topic. Canon 3

100. Yoder, "Is There Such a Thing as Being Ready for Another Millennium?"

101. Sack, *Human Territoriality*, 108.

102. Sack, *Human Territoriality*, 110–11.

speaks of the deacon or presbyter who may "forsake his own parish" and come to reside in another. They were prohibited from officiating in their new location.[103] Canon 5 prohibits establishing another church because one is not getting along with their bishop.[104] Canon 13 states that "no bishop shall presume to pass from one province to another" unless he has written permission from the metropolitan bishop of the place.[105] Canon 21 prohibits a bishop from leaving his post to go to a different post, whether by his own suggestion or compelled by others without the appropriate permission.[106] Canons 41 and 42 of the Synod of Laodicea state that "none of the priesthood nor of the clergy may go on a journey, without the bidding of the Bishop" or "without letters canonical."[107] In all of these canons one can see the church attempting to control the movement of its leadership.

The tendency for church leaders to move from one place to another was motivated by a variety of factors. As previously mentioned, persecution was a significant impetus for fleeing a territory. The disputes created by such actions may have been in mind when such canons were written even if persecution was no longer a factor. Conflict between leaders could also drive a bishop from their post. Geographical distance between Paul and Barnabas in Acts 15:36–41 seemed to be an example of this approach to conflict resolution. As Sack notes, "a prime means for Church officials to resist authority was to leave their territory."[108]

In Canon 1 of the Council of Sardica 344, another motivation for a bishop to leave their post is explained. There was a tendency for bishops to leave lesser assignments for more prestigious ones.

> A prevalent evil, or rather most mischievous corruption must be done away with from its very foundations. Let no bishop be allowed to remove from a small city to a different one: as there is an obvious reason for this fault, accounting for such attempts; since no bishop could ever yet be found who endeavored to be translated from a larger city to a smaller one. It is therefore evident that such persons are inflamed with excessive covetousness and are only serving ambition in order to have the repute of possessing greater authority. Is it then the pleasure of all that so grave an

103. Percival, *The Seven Ecumenical Councils of the Undivided Church*, 109.
104. Percival, *The Seven Ecumenical Councils of the Undivided Church*, 110.
105. Percival, *The Seven Ecumenical Councils of the Undivided Church*, 115.
106. Percival, *The Seven Ecumenical Councils of the Undivided Church*, 118–19.
107. Percival, *The Seven Ecumenical Councils of the Undivided Church*, 152.
108. Sack, *Human Territoriality*, 111.

> abuse be punished with great severity? For I think that men of this sort should not be admitted even to lay communion.[109]

The strong condemnation of this practice perhaps reflects the extent at which it had become an issue.

That bishops were strategizing for higher posts was not unreasonable. Sack states that, "although treated in many respects as equivalent levels within a hierarchy, each see was not in fact equal in wealth and prestige."[110] From the time of Constantine onward, large churches were being built in metropolitan centers of influence. Archbishops exercised considerable authority over resources, policies, doctrine, and decision making. Holding such a position conferred significant privileges "and being the archbishops of Constantinople or of Rome gave one even more."[111] As a result, positions could become ends in themselves rather than means to an end, since the more prestigious posts carried greater power, wealth, or both.

Bishops who attempted to move created problems for the territorial structure of the church. Whether for reasons of conflict or for enhancement, a priest's unsanctioned mobility could threaten the internal discipline of the church. Heretics could leave one congregation and go to another. A dynamic or wealthy priest could manipulate or bribe congregations to unseat less popular bishops. Movements could further exacerbate issues of mismatch and spillover. Control must belong to those who know better. The solution was found in having "larger territorial authorities enforce prohibitions against such movements and coordinate the activities of smaller territories."[112] The church used territoriality to keep bishops in their assigned areas with prohibitions and consequences to limit mobility. The increase in canons was intended to keep individual bishops in their place, but it also increased the overall stationary nature of the church. One wonders how this strict stationary ministry approach impacted the missionary impetus of some. These canons give the impression that good leaders stayed where they were, faithfully serving where God had assigned them.

109. Percival, *The Seven Ecumenical Councils of the Undivided Church*, 415.

110. Sack, *Human Territoriality*, 112.

111. Sack, *Human Territoriality*, 112.

112. Sack, *Human Territoriality*, 112.

CLARIFIED AND STRATIFIED CHURCH HIERARCHY

The church organized itself into a nested system of territorial hierarchies in which each level of ecclesiastical rank corresponded to a defined territory. Although the territories themselves were not sacred, they formed part of the Church's visible expression, not unlike its buildings and other holy spaces.[113]

A bishop's span of control over territory and other bishops became an indicator of prestige. Some bishops would name a bishop to an area that was territorially more appropriate for a priest until it was forbidden by Canon 6 of the Council of Sardica 344.[114] As some bishops strategized to attain higher positions in the church other bishops found they could raise their stature by subdividing the territory under their responsibility. This effectively increased their span of control until it too was prohibited by Canon 12 of Chalcedon 451.[115]

The increasing hierarchy of the church and the new power arrangements with the state made it necessary to clarify the chain of command. Canon 6 of Antioch 341 explains that if someone was excommunicated, they needed to return to the bishop that had excommunicated them, they could not reenter the church in another bishop's territory.[116] Likewise, in Canon 9 it was required that "bishops of every province" must "acknowledge the bishop who presides in the metropolis."[117] The metropolitan bishop had priority in rank and other bishops were instructed to "do nothing extraordinary without him."[118] Communication between sees was then reserved for the higher levels of leadership. Canon 11 forbids a priest or a bishop from going to the emperor, without the permission of their metropolitan bishop.[119]

Defining the channels of communication was another facet of increasing upward expansion of the church. This also decreased the personalization of the church organization particularly in metropolitan areas where

113. Sack, *Human Territoriality*, 95.

114. Percival, *The Seven Ecumenical Councils of the Undivided Church*, 420.

115. Sack, *Human Territoriality*, 113; L'Huillier, *The Church of the Ancient Councils*, 239.

116. Sack, *Human Territoriality*, 95; Percival, *The Seven Ecumenical Councils of the Undivided Church*, 111.

117. Percival, *The Seven Ecumenical Councils of the Undivided Church*, 112.

118. Percival, *The Seven Ecumenical Councils of the Undivided Church*, 112.

119. Percival, *The Seven Ecumenical Councils of the Undivided Church*, 114.

congregants numbered in the thousands.[120] According to Sack, in the latter part of the fourth century, "personal knowledge of congregants and informal peer pressure would not suffice to define a community or enforce discipline." Instead, "effective authority could be had by enforcing territorial assertions of control."[121] Church members were defined and related to the church by where they lived. If someone was denied communion, they were not able to just go to another church. They were required to return to the original location where their communion was denied. Sack states that "the cannons used an individual's place of residence within a church territory as a means of assigning that person to a particular set of clergy and to a particular church."[122] The relationship between the laity and the leadership was becoming more formal and impersonal. The church as an organization was also becoming more centralized.

The increased stratification of the church hierarchy exemplifies Sack's belief that territoriality "has a momentum of its own to increase the need for more hierarchy and bureaucracy."[123] To Sack this is an example of how for the sake of efficiency, an organization can diminish their own effectiveness by adding additional layers of bureaucracy. There were those that resisted these developments. The monastic tradition is one example of such resistance. However, "the general direction was toward greater hierarchical centralization, differentiation, and territoriality."[124]

Conflict Between Places

As the metropolitan bishops became more powerful, their see became "an object of pride" for the people who lived there.[125] Attachment to place among Christians continued to increase. Walls describes how theological differences could often be a kind of proxy war for locational supremacy and power. While much of the theology produced in the fourth, fifth, and sixth centuries of the church appears as protracted arguments for the appropriate formulations of key doctrines, Walls points out that there is also another way to look at them. He states, "if we choose, we may look at the same period, and many of the same events, in terms of the power struggles within

120. Sack, *Human Territoriality*, 107, 113.

121. Sack, *Human Territoriality*, 110.

122. Sack, *Human Territoriality*, 110.

123. Sack, *Human Territoriality*, 110.

124. Sack, *Human Territoriality*, 108.

125. Sack, *Human Territoriality*, 113.

church and state, or between metropolitan centre and outlying provinces."[126] In this way, places came to symbolize theological difference.

As noted in chapter 2, territoriality can facilitate the understanding of places as symbols which can obscure other sources of conflict. Positioning the conversation in terms of metropolitan sees could direct attention away from causes of social conflict such as unequal access to resources. A conflict, described in terms of place, can also obscure the people who may be central to the disagreements. While the concern may have been defined in terms of orthodoxy, adherence or rejection of a position may have also been about defending the dignity and value of one's place. This growing sense of attachment and ownership of place was true on the larger scale of the metropolitan area as well as the smaller scale.

Territoriality at the Scale of Church Buildings

Once a socially defined gathering, the church had moved toward becoming a physical and permanent place in a structure built for the purpose of worship. Under Constantine the visible presence of the church went another step further. Sack states that "funds became available to build churches and Christians could use former Roman basilicas and temples."[127] Constantine Christianized public space and built churches crafted with architectural elements borrowed from Roman temples. The first St. Peter's Basilica was one of the projects initiated by Constantine. The growth of physical churches with increasingly complex architectural design assisted in the reification of the churches' increasing political power.

The canons reflected the move toward churches being understood as physical church buildings and ordering the behavior therein. Canon 6 of the council of Gangra in the fourth century, prohibits holding private religious assemblies outside of the church, particularly when performing ecclesiastical acts.[128] Such meetings could threaten the legitimacy of the church, but limiting worship to church buildings created a separation between sacred and secular. Canon 5 speaks out against anyone who despised the house of God and its assemblies.[129]

126. Walls, *The Cross-cultural Process in Christian History*, 33. See also L'Huillier, *The Church of the Ancient Councils*, 251.

127. Sack, *Human Territoriality*, 108.

128. Percival, *The Seven Ecumenical Councils of the Undivided Church*, 94.

129. Percival, *The Seven Ecumenical Councils of the Undivided Church*, 94.

Canons also codified and clarified rules that may have already been in practice, such as forbidding heretics from entering the church.[130] What was once exclusion from the social community was now described more explicitly in terms of a prohibition on entering a church building. Canons also established rules about who was allowed or forbidden from going to the altar.[131] A hierarchical separation between church leadership and the laity as well as between different ranks of ministers played out in spatial directives as well. Canon 18 of the Council of Nicaea prohibits deacons from sitting among priests.[132] Canon 20 of the Council of Laodicea, goes a step further when it declares that deacons are only permitted to sit at the discretion of the priest.[133]

The Emergence of Sacred Space

Sacred spaces were also becoming more important to Christians. Many early Christians did not think in terms of sacred space mediating one's relationship with God. This was especially true after the destruction of the temple in Jerusalem. But as worship became more tied to physical places in the form of church buildings and cathedrals, sacred space was no longer such a foreign idea. Pilgrimage had a long history of tradition in other religions and it too found its way into Christianity. Not long after Constantine's mother Helena took a religious pilgrimage to Palestine, Constantine began efforts of excavation and removal of other religious elements from the supposed sites of Jesus's death and resurrection.[134] Locations identified with the apostles or where miracles had occurred took on greater significance as they were classified as holy places.[135]

In terms of territoriality, holy places were examples of reification. The abstract universal God could be made concrete at a bounded place. The holy places were understood to have the power to bless by bringing healing or comfort. Alternatively, improperly entering a holy place, destruction or defilement of a consecrated building could bring a curse or harm.[136]

130. Percival, *The Seven Ecumenical Councils of the Undivided Church,* 127.

131. Percival, *The Seven Ecumenical Councils of the Undivided Church,* 132, 136, and 153.

132. L'Huillier, *The Church of the Ancient Councils*, 76–77.

133. Percival, *The Seven Ecumenical Councils of the Undivided Church,* 140.

134. Leithart, *Defending Constantine*, 136–37.

135. Sack, *Human Territoriality*, 107–8.

136. Sack, *Human Territoriality*, 114.

The emergence of holy places also had the effect of creating inequality within church hierarchy. Given that church buildings themselves were understood to have the power of God, that power could be further enhanced by relics or if attached to a particularly sacred place, such as the burial of St. Peter. Of course, not every bishop had access to such limited resources.

Rome as Central and Jerusalem as Peripheral

In less than three hundred years, Jerusalem went from being central to the leadership and function of Christianity, to being marginal, and then reimagined as a symbolic holy place. Walls states that "the urban centres of the Eastern Mediterranean replaced Jerusalem as the workshop of the Christian world."[137] According to Chalcedon, Rome was unique among these metropolitan areas. Canon 28 of Chalcedon states, "for the Fathers rightly granted privileges to the throne of old Rome, because it was the royal city."[138] By 637 Jerusalem was conquered by Muslims. The supposedly Christian empire ceased to define the physical city of Jerusalem as a central territory for their Christian faith. While Jerusalem may have continued to be of symbolic importance, it was not valuable enough to fight for militarily.

That Christianity could be cut off from its Jerusalem roots and continue to flourish makes it unique among world religions. This development is observed by Sanneh. "Christianity is almost alone among world religions in being peripheral in the place of its origin. Ever since Pentecost and the Antiochean breakthrough, Christianity has turned its back on Jerusalem and Bethlehem, regarding them as secondary signposts, with the consequence of the religion becoming preponderant in regions once considered outside God's promises."[139] Sanneh refers to this as the principle of serial origin which is "here today and there tomorrow."[140] For Walls, the decentering of Jerusalem is part of a broader theme in Christian history of what he calls "erosion and attrition," or alternatively "advance and recession."[141] Walls states that what kept Christianity alive is the repeated occurrence of "cross-cultural diffusion," that went hand in hand with geographic dispersion.[142]

137. Walls, *The Cross-cultural Process in Christian History*, 34.
138. L'Huillier, *The Church of the Ancient Councils*, 267.
139. Sanneh, *Encountering the West*, 118.
140. Sanneh, *Disciples of All Nations*, 36.
141. Walls, *Missionary Movement in Christian History*, 19.
142. Walls, *Missionary Movement in Christian History*, 19.

As Christianity continued its outward territorial expansion, the church under Constantine continued to expand its upward hierarchy. This process started before Constantine and continued long after him, but the changes occurred slowly. That an organization can begin with such deterritorialized commitments and become so hierarchically structured and territorially focused is not a surprise to Sack. But the church is a particularly strong example of this dynamic.[143]

The Contrast of the Manger and the Basilica

The New Testament portrays the founder of Christianity as born in a lowly place. By 360 AD when St. Peter's Basilica was consecrated, the church was comfortable being associated with physical spaces of more grandeur. What began as a deterritorialized faith developed into a religion much more accustomed to making use of territoriality. The need for internal organizational discipline helped to establish a foundation of classified territory that increasingly materialized into new forms of territoriality.

As locations were classified, the leadership of the church developed based on territorial definitions. They adopted the civic boundaries of the Roman Empire and increased their expressions of attachment to a place. The church went from being a socially defined gathering to a physical structure with increasing definition, ornamentation, and rank. They became more stationary, with ministers more geographically fixed. Bishops first understood themselves as being *at* a location but in time they saw themselves as *of* a location. As attachment grew, conflict was territorialized as places became symbols of people and positions. And places continued to be thought of in terms of central and peripheral, but which places were central changed as Jerusalem became marginalized.

Territoriality developed first to remove heretics or the unrepentant from the social gatherings. In time it was used to control the movements of bishops, to exclude heretics through exile, and to define and protect consecrated places. Constantine provided new possibilities of enforcement as the relationship with the primary territorial structure was established. This heightened and extended the organizational structure that was already present. Increasingly the church was showing marks of a more stratified organization: impersonal and formalized relationships, clarified chain of command, and centralized leadership. The number of synods and councils

143. Sack, *Human Territoriality*, 98.

increased and canons became an important means for expressing and communicating the church's territoriality.

The canons indicated several effects of territoriality. There was evidence of reification in church buildings and holy places, territory as an end rather than a means by bishops seeking promotion to better territories, and enforcement of territorial rules. Territoriality beget territoriality as places were subdivided, territory was added, and hierarchy stratified. While the church organizational structure began from a sincere need for internal discipline, the proliferation of canon law shows how this desire can lead to increasing bureaucracy and structural rigidity.

CONCLUSION

If the claims of non-territoriality by Walls and Sanneh are based on the fact that Christendom has ended, then evidence of territoriality prior to Christendom and the continuation of territoriality beyond Christendom shows its continued relevance. The argument of this chapter has been that while Christianity began as a largely deterritorialized religious group, territoriality developed and increased over time. The foundational territorial structure and some examples of territoriality occurred prior to Constantine. It was on this previously laid structure that Constantine was able to further increase the territoriality of the church and empower broader enforcement. Even if the earlier dating of Christendom is granted, territoriality predates it. The evidence prior to Constantine establishes that territoriality is not coterminous with the period of Christendom, particularly as Walls and Sanneh define it.

In light of this, what was the relationship between territoriality and Christendom? In the next chapter, Walls's and Sanneh's understanding of Christendom in connection with territoriality is explored in greater detail.

5

Territoriality During Christendom and Continuing After

THE ARGUMENT

In this chapter it is argued that Christendom represented a particularly powerful expression of territoriality. But as Christendom begins to break down, territoriality continues to find new forms of expression and manifestation. The extent of territoriality within Christendom will be explored with attention to the effects and descriptive characteristics of proportion, span of control, and intensity of force on multiple scales. As new forms emerge, one sees instances of subdivision and secession. The effects of territoriality related to the breakdown of Christendom will also be explored by considering the Spanish colonization in the Americas and the Protestant Reformation. The chapter begins with clarifying how Walls and Sanneh understand Christendom.

WHAT IS CHRISTENDOM?

Conveying the precise nature of Christendom is not an easy task. According to Alan Kreider, "there has been little attempt to define Christendom as a term or to discuss it systematically."[1] Part of the complexity is that the term is used by different authors to refer to different characteristics. To suit their purpose, authors may emphasize a particular characteristic over and

1. Kreider, *The Change of Conversion and the Origin of Christendom*, xiv. Peter Brown, *The Rise of Western Christendom*, is a notable example of scholarly development in this area that was written since Kreider made his claim.

against another. For example, Muggeridge's belief that Christendom began when Constantine united the church with the secular state is a definition of Christendom that leans heavily on the configuration of state and church relations.[2]

Alternatively, it could be that the characteristic that is emphasized is only part of a cumulative case. Such authors would understand Christendom as a phenomenon with various essential (or even nonessential) characteristics which combine and converge. These authors may highlight different characteristics at different times, but they avoid summarizing the fullness of the phenomenon in one characteristic. While there may be a variety of ways to understand Christendom, certain similarities allow one to speak meaningfully of Christendom as a category.[3] Ideally, a framework should seek to elucidate the common threads that continually recur. This cumulative characteristic approach to Christendom is Kreider's preference and can be exhibited in the tendency of Walls's and Sanneh's approach as well.

Walls and Sanneh on Christendom

What do Andrew Walls and Lamin Sanneh mean when they write about Christendom? Neither author addresses Christendom in a systematic way as Kreider does. However, certain themes emerge when reviewing their work. The descriptions of Christendom provided by Sanneh tend to emphasize the relationship between church and state, while the singularity of cultural custom is a nuance Walls tends to highlight. Both Walls and Sanneh address the similarities of Christendom with Islam and the importance of territoriality. The concept of territoriality is of particular interest to these authors because they understand Christendom as not just a period of time but as a territory.

Christendom as a Relationship Between Church and State

Sanneh emphasizes the way in which Christendom was made manifest as a unification of church and state. The form this unification took during Christendom was both similar and dissimilar to what existed in the Constantinian era. Just as under Constantine and the Roman rulers who followed him,

2. Muggeridge, *The End of Christendom*, 14.

3. Kreider, *The Change of Conversion and the Origin of Christendom*, 92.

the faith of the ruler was the center of the system. Sanneh states that "the central principle of Christendom had been not so much the converting of individuals as having a stem in a pious emperor or ruler from whom official society draws its orthodox sap."[4] The ruler must be the visible representation of the invisible God. Furthermore, Sanneh understands the church and state alignment inherent in Christendom as a continuation from the Roman idea of "religion as political prescription."[5] But while the Romans tolerated a somewhat more pluralistic religious environment, Christendom tied religion and politics together in a way where membership in the political sphere was synonymous with membership in the church.[6] Christianity became "a mandate of political submission" something much more akin to Islam than the pre-Constantinian church. It was a "*Republica Christiana* . . . a Church and a State fused wherein morality and legality shared an indivisible even invisible boundary."[7] The relationship between church and state was not static. Struggle and change shifted power dynamics across the time and space of Christendom. But the fate of both institutions was understood to be fundamentally linked, in a way that was distinct from the relationship that existed in the Roman world.

A Singular Code

Like Sanneh, Walls does not associate Christendom with Constantine, despite the existence of a strong bond between the church and the state.

> I believe it is time that we stopped blaming Constantine for Constantinianism. The Roman Empire is not the place to seek the birth of Christendom. That empire had too much built in pluralism, too many discordant interest groups to allow such an event. The cement that held Christendom in place so long had a cohesive strength beyond anything that a Constantine, a Theodosius, a Justinian could derive from state power or political engineering. To understand it we must go to the period of conversion of the northern and western peoples of Europe, whom the Romans called barbarians.[8]

4. Sanneh, *Encountering the West*, 187.
5. Sanneh, *Disciples of All Nations*, 51.
6. Sanneh, *Encountering the West*, 187.
7. Sanneh, *Encountering the West*, 188.
8. Walls, "Ecumenical Missiology in Anabaptist Perspective," 192.

The religious pluralism of the Roman world superseded whatever earthly power Christianity had at the time. Sanneh draws a similar conclusion, stating Constantine was "too preoccupied with his personal rule in a diverse, multicultural empire to think about a cohesive, unitary institution like Christendom."[9] The arrangement under Constantine may have brought the church and state together, but one must look further north to find the kind of cohesive unity that characterized Christendom.

Those to the north, that the Romans would have considered barbarians, had a more collective reception of the Christian faith. They exchanged their local kinship groups for a broader and united vision under Christianity. As Walls describes it, "this is the birthplace of territorial Christianity . . . the northern peoples, with no easy way of dividing sacred and profane custom, produced territorial Christianity by their need to have a single body of custom."[10] Momentarily setting aside his remarks on territorial Christianity, Walls stresses the way that the sacred and profane were part of a singular, inseparable code of custom. For Walls this is one of the key characteristics for what constitutes Christendom.

The singular code that pervaded Christendom presumed the notion that "there is one desirable pattern of life, a single 'civilization' in effect, one model of society, one body of law, one universe of ideas."[11] Those who believed differently were the new barbarians. In contrast to the pluralism of the Roman world, the emphasis was on conformity to the one sacred language, the one literary tradition, the one apostolic see, the one code of law and the one custom.[12] They collectively rejected idolatry, heresy, and blasphemy and understood themselves to be "subject to Christian custom and the law of Christ."[13] This was the kind of cohesive unity that the singular code of custom brought to the notion of Christendom.

Christendom and Islam

Walls and Sanneh both stress the similarity between Christianity and Islam during Christendom. Prior to the changes brought by the fifteenth century, Christendom was mainly shaped and defined by its contact and clashes with

9. Sanneh, *Encountering the West*, 186.
10. Walls, *The Cross-cultural Process in Christian History*, 35.
11. Walls, Missionary Movement in Christian History, 18.
12. Walls, *The Cross-cultural Process in Christian History*, 36.
13. Walls, "Ecumenical Missiology in Anabaptist Perspective," 193.

Islam. In the seventh and eighth-century Islam conquered large expanses of land in North Africa and the Near East, lands with extensive Christian populations. The loss of territory was accompanied, albeit not immediately or completely, by a decline in the number of those identifying with the Christian faith. Such losses helped solidify the idea that the defense of territory was equated with a defense of Christianity. Furthermore, "the presence of an Islamic world to the east and south as Europe's only near neighbor reinforced the association of Christianity with territory."[14] Dar al-Islam and Dar al-Harb paralleled Christendom's division of Christian land and non-Christian land. Accordingly, Islam and Christianity showed a mutual approach to conquest, conversion, and religious territoriality.

Christendom as Territory

For Walls and Sanneh, the connection between territory and Christendom is of primary importance. Christendom is not just an era; it is a territory. In various ways Sanneh expresses his conviction that "'Christendom' as an idea and institution" was "the territorial expressions of religion."[15] It was under the Carolingians that "territoriality [became] a rule of religious life and made the principle of political organization the 'unrestricted adhesion of the Western Church to the Empire.'"[16] If Constantine's period co-mingled the throne and altar, Christendom went a step further by making the European land synonymous with the Christian faith.

The experience of religious territoriality turned "the very ground on which we stood into a natural privilege."[17] The Greek notion of autochthony flourished in Christendom as it "consecrated the idea of a divinely designated race and Church" rooted in a place.[18] Christendom was a matter of "birth and soil" making those who lived in the land and who were not Christians, perpetual foreigners.[19]

14. Walls, *Crossing Cultural Frontiers*, 174.

15. Sanneh, *Encountering the West*, 187, 185, and 206.

16. Sanneh, *Encountering the West*, 186.

17. Sanneh, *Encountering the West*, 214.

18. Sanneh, *Encountering the West*, 188.

19. Sanneh, *Encountering the West*, 188. Kreider holds similar perspectives. He developed a systematic framework using a three-fold lens to understand Christendom–belief, behavior, and belonging. He understands conversion and belonging to be "rooted in the primal realities of genes and geography." Kreider, *The Change of Conversion and the Origin of Christendom*, 94.

Walls repeatedly stresses the importance of territory in his understanding of Christendom. The word "Christendom" appears regularly in his three major texts, at least 123 times. Of those, forty-six times Walls uses the word without qualification or definition. In other words, he does not define it explicitly within the surrounding words, or it is assumed from prior context. The other seventy-seven times, Walls uses some kind of phrase or description to specify what exactly he means by Christendom. More than half of the definitions provided for Christendom look something like this, "Christendom . . . the idea of territorial Christianity, of geographically contiguous Christian states,"[20] or "Christendom, a conception in which Christianity was essentially linked to territory and the possession of territory."[21] or from his more recent work, "Christendom, which is only another word for Christianity, [but] became a geographical expression, 'the Christian part of the world.'"[22] Including references that imply land or territory acquisition, then all total, fifty-two of the seventy-seven times when Walls defines Christendom, he uses territorial language. This is not the only definition or qualification that he gives,[23] but the role of territory is first in Walls's expression of Christendom.

References one might see as geographic advancement of the gospel are not absent from the New Testament (Acts 1:8; Acts 16:6–10; Rev 2–3). Yet even as people belonging to a particular geographic region received the gospel, this did not result in the understanding that the territory or

20. Walls, *Missionary Movement in Christian History*, 258.

21. Walls, *The Cross-cultural Process in Christian History*, 34.

22. Walls, *Crossing Cultural Frontiers*, 174. Other examples from Walls, *Missionary Movement in Christian History* include "Christendom, the territorial Empire of Christ" (39); "Christendom . . .territorially identified Christianity" (75); "Christendom . . . the territorial connotation" (237); With respect to Christendom, and from Walls, *The Cross-cultural Process in Christian History,* "to be Christian was also to belong to specific territory-Christian lands" (36); "distinction between Christianity and Christendom . . . identification of Christianity with territory" (44); "that territorial expression of Christendom" (211); "On one side lay Christendom, Christian territory . . ." (220); And from Walls, *Crossing Cultural Frontiers* "Christendom, a word that means Christianity but which in Europe acquired territorial significance" (15); "Christianity territorially expressed" (50).

23. Walls, in *The Cross-cultural Process in Christian History,* also uses "a pure and godly commonwealth" (37); "customary law" (198) "throne and altar" (44); "political, military, and economic power" (42). And in Walls, in *Crossing Cultural Frontiers*, "Christian community" (42). But even when using terms like "society" they are paired with words having spatial connotations such as "enter Christendom" or "lying outside" from Walls, *Missionary Movement in Christian History*, 237 that bring to mind a physical space.

region had become Christianized or that it was now "a Christian nation."[24] This close association of land and religion was a process that developed over time, but under Christendom the notion was increasingly taken for granted. Walls highlights this change repeatedly.

Walls's and Sanneh's way of writing about Christendom acknowledges that it is not just an era that stretches over time but a territory that stretches over expanses of land. The complementary nature of these descriptions is summarized by Walls when he says that Christendom is "an entity with temporal dimensions, something that can be plotted on a map."[25] Like other authors when writing about Christendom, Sanneh and Walls address issues of the church and state, the way that Christianity became customary, and the similarities with Islam, but their preferred way of engaging the idea of Christendom is through the territorial lens. Their perspectives may constitute a unique nuance to the understanding of Christendom.

The close association between Christendom and territory, as opposed to an exclusively time related description, lets Walls and Sanneh place discussions of Christendom in a broader world perspective. In their view, Christendom is not merely part of the history of Christianity, but a specific European cultural expression of Christianity, limited to a specific time and space. They see it in contrast to earlier more diffuse Christian expressions, but more importantly, in contrast to the current state of Christianity–a world religion not bound exclusively to one particular place.

The False Equivalency of Territoriality and Christendom

Walls and Sanneh base their idea that territoriality has ended on the fact that Christendom has ended. This is built on their close association of territoriality and Christendom. But the association of territoriality with Christendom can be affirmed without requiring that they be coterminous. The reason for their assumed equivalency is the fact that territoriality takes a particularly powerful form during Christendom. One could say that, for the church, the Christendom time period provides a superlative exemplification of territoriality. But the fact that Christendom exemplifies territoriality does not require that territoriality only exists during or in the space of Christendom.

If Christendom is the superlative exemplification of territoriality, how does the church during and within Christendom provide evidence of this

24. Walls, *Missionary Movement in Christian History*, 20.

25. Walls, *The Cross-cultural Process in Christian History*, 36.

strategy? Moreover, how does the fragmentation of Christendom indicate not the end of territoriality, but new patterns of territorial thought and behavior? These two questions will be pursued in the remainder of this chapter.

EVIDENCE OF TERRITORIALITY DURING AND WITHIN CHRISTENDOM

In this section evidence will be given for territoriality during the era of Christendom. As in the last chapter, the evidence will mainly come from the work of Walls and Sanneh and their own expression of Christian history. Sack's work and his theory of territoriality will be used to further the conversation and organize specific causes and effects. Evidence of territoriality will be found in Christendom's classification of territory, its continuation of hierarchical development, and enforcement. If Christendom stands as a kind of high-water mark for territoriality there should be evidence of increasing span of control and intensity of force on a multiplicity of scales. Evidence of these aspects speak to the extent of territoriality. To begin, it will be helpful to sketch out the basics of the historical setting.

Historical Setting

In the portrayal of the early Christian church, Walls and Sanneh stress the diversity of people, language, and geography. Such diversity was evidence of the universal appeal of the Christian faith. The message could find a home in any culture, what Sanneh refers to as "boundary-free truth."[26] Some Christians, though not all, could claim to live within the boundaries of the Roman world, but that put no particular restriction on the ability for the message to cross borders into other places.

This arrangement changed for Christianity over time. Canon law was used to keep bishops in their parish slowing the gospel movement outside their assigned territory. Constantine joined Christianity to the governmental apparatus stuffing a universal faith into a space made for an Imperial religion. There was also the rise of Islam which changed the religious dynamic and religious geography in profound ways. Places in North Africa, Syria, and even Jerusalem found themselves no longer under the protection of a government privileging Christianity. Muslim expansion turned

26. Sanneh, *Disciples of All Nations*, 4.

Arab Christians into "cultural exiles on home ground."[27] Their experience of dhimmitude also made them effectively invisible to the Christians of Europe.

As a result of these new arrangements, "local solidarities [were] much more potent than transnational ones," even if Christians understood themselves to be "part of a universal, catholic church."[28] The division between Christians in the *west* and in the *east* was further reinforced by different languages and conflicts over authority. The political void created by the breakdown of the western half of the Roman Empire meant that new leaders and dominions were rising to prominence north of Rome. In the words of Walls, "new Christian lands emerged, replacing the old and shifting the Christian centre of gravity as drastically as it had shifted after A.D. 70."[29] The Christian faith, diverse and yet united, was now being pulled in different geographic directions.

The power of the church increased as governmental entities reorganized and Western Christianity retained a form of unity under the Apostolic See of Rome.[30] The church had increasingly extended its territorial power, and the use of territoriality could be backed by any means of force necessary. If territory for the early church was mostly understood as their stewardship over a building, then developing into parishes, Christendom increases the scale to another level while including all the rest. It was understood as, "unbroken Christian territory, subject to the law of Christ, from the Atlantic across the European land mass."[31] Consequently, Christendom had the largest possible span of control and the largest proportion of the population the church had ever known in one particular place.

Classification of Territory

Christian Land

On the broadest scale Christendom is a classification of Christianity. Walls emphasizes that, "people were Christians because they were born in a Christian country . . . born into the sphere of salvation."[32] The classification

27. Sanneh, *Disciples of All Nations*, 82.
28. Kreider, *The Change of Conversion and the Origin of Christendom*, 96.
29. Walls, *Missionary Movement in Christian History*, 256.
30. Walls, *Missionary Movement in Christian History*, 69.
31. Walls, *The Cross-cultural Process in Christian History*, 198.
32. Walls, *Crossing Cultural Frontiers*, 42.

of Christian land furthered the notion of religion as "authorized official edict."[33] By the 1500s the linking of Christianity with European land reached its zenith when "the last pagan people (apart from some in the extreme north), the populations of the Baltic region, had been dragged within the orbit of Latin Christendom."[34] At that point, the borders of Europe were thought of in terms of religion. According to Walls, "Europe was Christian territory over against heathen territory, Christendom over against heathendom."[35]

The places of center and periphery continued to influence the relationships within Christendom. Walls sees evidence for this in the way Patrick had to defend himself before "the cultured, well-organized older Christian centres in Italy and Gaul."[36] Long after the end of the Roman Empire, the See of Rome continued to be the unifying center and regulatory power of the church and Christendom. The perspectives of the *other* in the periphery continued to be considered of lesser consequence.

One of the challenges related to the classification of territory for Christianity was the location of Jerusalem. As Sanneh states, "unlike Islam, Christianity was born with the cultural complex of having lost for good its birthplace in the Holy Land."[37] The land where Christ lived and died was not within Christendom. At least two options to remedy this situation were available–take back the land or reframe the situation. Recapturing the territory was thoroughly attempted with the Crusades, but the other option was probably more effective. A hermeneutical parallel developed between Christian land and Israel. Walls comments, "once nation and Church are coterminous in scope, the experiences of the nation can be interpreted in terms of the history of Israel."[38] Reclassifying the European landmass had the advantage of drawing on religious symbolism furthering the reification of God's kingdom on earth. Jerusalem could be spiritualized and Christendom could now be the land of promise filled with the chosen people. This kind of symbolism is demonstrated in the T-O map, which places Jerusalem at the center, with Africa, Asia, and Europe flowing outward from it. According to Sack, "the import of this conception was that wherever one

33. Sanneh, *Disciples of All Nations*, 51.

34. Walls, *The Cross-cultural Process in Christian History*, 198.

35. Walls, *Crossing Cultural Frontiers*, 15.

36. Walls, Missionary Movement in Christian History, 75.

37. Sanneh, *Disciples of All Nations*, 78.

38. Walls, *Missionary Movement in Christian History*, 20.

actually is located in physical space is immaterial unless one is at the center in the heavenly city, Jerusalem."[39]

On the smaller scale, church buildings were classified as fulfilling a particular religious function. Sack states that "church law remained unyielding in its view that the church was a consecrated place, that worship should occur within its walls, and that the church territory should be divided into more and less sacred parts to which members of the community would have differential access."[40] These were specialized places intended to be set apart for holy purposes. Yet the classification of the church building was challenged when certain needs arose. In towns or cities where the church was the largest structure, it could be useful as a secure defensive stronghold, a makeshift hospital, or a meeting house.

Classification of Other Places

Underneath any use of territoriality are the perspectives that inform that behavior. The perspectives that shaped the territoriality present in Christendom were built from the long-standing Greco-Roman prejudice against the so-called barbarians, a label that shifted to different people as new land was incorporated into the fold. Classifications from these perspectives developed into a dichotomy of "Christian territory, which was subject to the rule of Christ, and pagan territory, which was not."[41]

These perspectives shaped Christian awareness of other peoples and places. Walls states that, "for centuries Europe knew nothing of the Americas, and little of Africa or Asia; Europeans thought of 'Christendom' as Christian territory . . . and hardly thought of Christians beyond it."[42] Global awareness of other Christians outside of Christendom was significantly diminished. In time, "European Christians came to think of themselves as, if not exactly the only Christians, at least the only authentic Christians." It was in this isolation that Christianity in its European form, "developed features that impeded its later attempts to take the Christian faith to peoples beyond Europe."[43] This close identification between the Christian faith and

39. Sack, *Human Territoriality*, 85.

40. Sack, *Human Territoriality*, 116.

41. Walls, *The Cross-cultural Process in Christian History*, 199.

42. Walls, *The Cross-cultural Process in Christian History*, 92.

43. Walls, *The Cross-cultural Process in Christian History*, 14.

the European landmass endangered the understanding of Christianity as a world religion.[44]

Within Christendom, the church's settled character—with its large stone buildings and clearly defined parishes—led to a context in which "mission often receives little emphasis, for the churches concentrate upon the pastoral care of their people and the maintenance of their structures."[45] By binding faith tightly to national custom, Christendom fostered a "shrinking capacity for tolerance" within society.[46] The isolation and lack of awareness of other Christians in the world led to the development of mythical stories of distant Christian kingdoms and the search for Prester John. These stories further established the notion of other Christians being distant and remote from the regular functioning church.

When missionary activity was present, it was usually "outside the geographical territory of the Christendom church, to foreigners." When Christians were "faced with accessible territories where Christ was not known, the manifest duty of Christians was to bring their peoples into the sphere of Christendom, to make those lands Christian territory."[47] Shenk observes that under Roman Catholic canon law, a mission was sent "to prepare the way for the church when the territory [had] not been present. Once a viable church is 'established' the territory is declared to be 'Christian.'"[48]

Christendom as a Container

Through classification, territoriality creates places that work as a kind of container to mold and shape that which exists in the space. Though Christendom, as a large territory of land, was not actually a container, it was perceived and classified as if it were, functioning as a mold for beliefs and behavior. This was also true for the diocese and parishes subdivided within it. As a container, Christendom was highly effective. Routinization and thick boundaries helped to maintain the beliefs and behaviors of a high proportion of those claiming to be Christians within the territory.

Christendom acted as a territorial container to mold, shape, and maintain beliefs and behavior in accordance with the singular code of

44. Sanneh, *Disciples of All Nations*, 51.
45. Kreider, *The Change of Conversion and the Origin of Christendom*, 96.
46. Sanneh, *Disciples of All Nations*, 285.
47. Walls, *The Cross-cultural Process in Christian History*, 199.
48. Shenk, Personal Correspondence, email.

custom. In Walls's perspective the conversion of Northern peoples helped to strengthen the idea of Christianity with a particular territory. The people as a collective body, "whole societies complete with their functioning political and social systems integrated around their ruler," would come to follow a single code of custom.[49] Their desire to uphold the single code of custom helped to bring about the territorial framework of Christendom as cause and effect. Walls's may be right that the custom precedes the territory, but it is also true that the territory served to uphold the custom.

Territorial containers and displacement are often revealed through statements such as, "We don't do that here." Such phrases articulate an assumed set of prescribed and prohibited beliefs and behaviors that define the boundaries of belonging. This dynamic reflects what Walls describes within Christendom: "On one side lay Christendom, Christian territory, the assembly of Christian princes and their peoples, subject to the law of Christ, territory in which idolatry, blasphemy, and heresy could have no place; on the other side lay heathendom, the world outside."[50] In another text Walls states, "all born within that territory were born under the law of the King of kings; within that territory idolatry, blasphemy, or heresy should have no recognized place."[51] In both of these quotations Walls speaks to the way that the territory of Christendom served as a molding container. The worship, the moral code, the things that are rejected or accepted, all of this is reinforced by the place. Christendom knits together the social, mental, and physical aspects of their lives in one coordinated system. Outside the container, the situation was very different.

Christendom created high moral ideals that were difficult to always live up to. This created a gap "between the established norms of a society and its actual procedures" that revealed the fraudulence of Christendom's morality.[52] If the container cannot serve to actually produce the ideals, it will at a minimum create the appearance of compliance. Walls claims that this kind of submission required by Christendom created an environment where false professions of faith were common and Christianity could become mere "custom."[53]

49. Walls, *Missionary Movement in Christian History*, 81.
50. Walls, *The Cross-cultural Process in Christian History*, 202.
51. Walls, *The Cross-cultural Process in Christian History*, 198.
52. Walls, "Ecumenical Missiology in Anabaptist Perspective," 193.
53. Walls, "Ecumenical Missiology in Anabaptist Perspective," 193.

Within the broader container of Christendom, the parish was a unit used to define and mold the Christian community on a smaller scale. Walls describes how, the "geographically expressed Christianity of Europe was organized in territorial units of which the basic unit was the parish."[54] The parish had been used since the Roman period, but the church's span of control was not as extensive as in Christendom. Within Christendom "the parson (the 'person') of the parish notionally had the 'cure of souls' of every resident within the boundaries of the territory. All were baptized in infancy, all, notionally, were taught the Christian faith and shared in the Christian worship of the community."[55] The proportion of the population that adhered to the faith is what made Christendom distinct from earlier parish models that existed in a more pluralistic society.

When space is understood to be a container, new territory can be understood to be empty. In this sense, the church used the concept of empty space when they thought about places without churches. Sack states that, "the Church decreed in the twelfth-century that parishes should be erected wherever there were none."[56] New territory was empty but it could be subdued, portioned, and Christianized, incorporated as part of the Christendom container.

Thus far the evidence for Christendom being the superlative exemplification of territoriality is rooted in the way that the classified territory served as a kind of container. In this conceptual container, all the inhabitants, or a sufficient amount to give that impression, claimed the Christian faith as their own. In contrast to the pluralistic society of the Roman Empire, the proportion of Christians in a place was very high.

Hierarchy

In the last chapter, the hierarchy of the church, which was built on a territorial framework, was an important example of territoriality. In this chapter, that dynamic extends further. According to Sack increase of territorial hierarchy often looks like an increase in centralization, standardization, specialization, and impersonalization. The development of hierarchy in Christendom was not an even steady rise in all of these areas, but Christendom saw increases in each of these areas at different times.

54. Walls, *Crossing Cultural Frontiers*, 174.

55. Walls, *Crossing Cultural Frontiers*, 174.

56. Sack, *Human Territoriality*, 113.

Centralization

On the larger territorial scale, the process of Christianization created an opportunity to coalesce power. Sanneh describes how "a motley patchwork of tribes and clans" developed into "social institutions, national communities, organized states, regional power blocs, and long-range trading contacts, sweeping triumphant kingdoms and empires."[57] Christianity helped to provide this framework for unification. Similarly, Walls saw conversion as facilitating "stable relationships with other peoples–a discourse of Christian nations."[58] These developments brought groups of people along with their territory into the hierarchical structure of the church. As a result, organizationally it created a massive increase in the span of control.

The conversion of Olaf Tryggvason of Norway is a particular example that Walls identifies. The decision for Christianity may have been in his people's best interest, "but he was also building up the power of the monarch more than any King of Norway before him." Indeed, "widespread adherence to the universal faith which he promoted so enthusiastically would assist the process of centralization."[59] Tryggvason likely understood the benefit of bringing his people into religious alignment with the powerful Holy Roman Empire while retaining state autonomy. In his domain, where locations were new and peripheral to the church's center, the acceptance of Christianity did not yet signify a conflict of power with Rome.

Standardization

As more people came under the authority of the church, more dioceses, parishes, church buildings, and monasteries were put in place. A greater proportion of the population was increasingly claiming the Christian faith as their own. The building of the church's infrastructure in the more peripheral lands required funding. The council of Orleans in 541 stated that, "any person desirous of having a parish upon his property, must, in the first place, give a sufficient endowment for the clerks who shall serve it."[60] The practice of wealthy landowners building churches and maintaining clergy became more common. This was done in exchange for privileges,

57. Sanneh, *Disciples of All Nations*, 50.

58. Walls, *Missionary Movement in Christian History*, 74.

59. Walls, *Missionary Movement in Christian History*, 72.

60. Landon, *A Manual of Councils of the Holy Catholic Church*, 450.

foremost being that those "who built and endowed these private churches also wanted for themselves and their heirs the right to appoint the clergy."[61] Over time this church patronage system became part of the church's standardization for establishing new churches.

The patronage system furthered the intermingling of the church with governmental entities. Those outside the church hierarchy were appointing clergy to fill church positions. Furthermore, "the clergy thought themselves competent to deal just as well with the administration of just prices or the observance of treaties as with the sacraments."[62] The role of the clergy enlarged as power dynamics and wealth became obstacles to a life devoted to prayer and service. For a time, this changed the power structure of the church. Local territorial autonomy was emphasized, and the weakening of Rome's control reduced the centralization at the top of the hierarchical structure of the church.[63]

Specialization

Monasticism represented an increasing specialization of ministry, as well as the expansion of the church's territorial footprint and wealth. Monks transcribed Scripture, farmed the land, and devoted themselves to simplicity. Monasteries were widely regarded as centers of learning and havens for those who desired to devote themselves more fully to the Lord. They also served as mission stations and specialized in meeting the needs of the poor, the sick, and travelers. Yet Walls describes how this was difficult to sustain. "Long a potential sign of the kingdom, the monasteries over time became counter-sign of the kingdom. Within Anselm's old domain of England, following processes in themselves natural and intelligible, the corporate followers of the one who had nowhere to lay his head became over time collectively the major holders of real estate, the directors of the most profitable export business, and a comfortable class of rentiers."[64] As land holders, monasteries were a revenue generating source of tax-free wealth for the church. They began as a specialized subset of ministers, but the goals of monasticism were subverted by temptations of corruption and greed.

61. Sack, *Human Territoriality*, 115.

62. Sanneh, *Encountering the West*, 188.

63. Sack, *Human Territoriality*, 116.

64. Walls, *The Cross-cultural Process in Christian History*, 16.

Further Centralization

Toward the twelfth and thirteenth centuries, the church used territoriality as a strategy to further increase centralization. The right to erect any new diocese within Christendom was a right reserved solely for the Pope.[65] There was also concern that the church's growing territorial footprint, and corresponding wealth, needed to be protected from local authorities who may have wanted to seize it for their own purposes. Bishops reasserted their territorial rights based on earlier canons. As a result, this clarified the roles of church and state.

> The King became less of an anointed person and more of a secular ruler. In many respects, society in general was more willing to have the Church manage religious functions, and the Church actively sought this role . . . The Church's attempt to reestablish Church control over its own hierarchy led to a narrowing of the religious domain. Ecumenical councils were convened, canon law became codified and extended. Church discipline for the most part increased, and the Pope became the undeniable focus of Church leadership.[66]

The result strengthened and weakened the role of the church.

Impersonalization

Consolidation made the church more visible but also more set apart. The combination of visibility and separation furthered the experience of impersonalization. Centralizing the church's power meant that the ultimate symbol of the church was the Pope, a figure far removed from the everyday lives of the vast proportion of Christians. More than ever, *the people of the church* referred to the professional clergy, not the collective body of believers. Decisions regarding church assets, discipline, and theology became the prerogative of the church hierarchy alone.[67] Sack states that "the princes found a centralized Church power in Rome easier to deal with (or ignore) than a multitude of different sources."[68] And yet making decisions from a distance meant that the Pope would need to rely on local leaders for

65. Millett, "Dioceses in Ireland Up to the 15th Century," 1.

66. Sack, *Human Territoriality*, 117.

67. Sanneh, *Encountering the West*, 214.

68. Sack, *Human Territoriality*, 118.

recommendations for filling vacant offices. Securing coveted positions of leadership in the church became an end in itself which increased corruption and inequality.

For many, distance from the religious center created differential access to resources. Renaissance building projects were costly and only experienced by a fraction of the total Christians in Christendom. Sanneh states that of all the shifts that occurred during Christendom, "none [was] more ominous than the eventual bourgeois transformation in which prayer served the ends of profit."[69] The church's hierarchical establishment failed to address increasing inequality and corruption, choosing to instead protect the status quo.

The increase of those professing the Christian faith within Christendom, due especially to the collective conversions of people in the north of Europe, led to further hierarchical developments of the church centered in Rome. There was also an increase in the building of physical structures (cathedrals, churches, monasteries, and nunneries) which increased the span of control and church leadership on various scales.

Enforcement

Defense of territory often stands as the defining feature for identifying instances of territoriality. The intensity of force that accompanies or sustains territoriality can exist on a spectrum ranging from influence to coercion, as addressed in chapter 2. Within Christendom, the entire spectrum was used to defend and advance Christian territory. The degree of force often makes visible the efforts to influence and control that might otherwise remain less apparent. Because of the way that the church and the state worked together to achieve goals, Christendom provides some convincing examples of defense of territory. These are but a few of them.

Christianizing Norway and Iceland

As Christianity moved into Northern Europe, it was more than privileged. The faith was becoming mandated through conquest, making it the only legitimized option. Olaf Tryggvason of Norway is said to have made full use of the wide spectrum of enforcement techniques from influence to coercion. His stated aim was to see the various Nordic territories become

69. Sanneh, *Encountering the West*, 188.

Christian. In the Orkneys and Southern Norway, Tryggvason's influence could take the form of preaching or threats to upend marriage alliances.[70] In Northern Norway, Tryggvason is said to have executed sorcerers "by burning or various tortures."[71] When he wanted Iceland to convert to Christianity, they were not initially willing. Sanneh describes how his response drew upon his past experience, "old warrior that he was, [Tryggvason] threatened to kill the people for their recalcitrance."[72] The ends seemed to justify the means.

Conversion by conquest could yield compliance, but also superficial acceptance of the faith. Walls comments that "because Christianity was the pledge of loyalty to Olaf of Norway . . . the Orcadians rejected it as soon as they safely could, and waited until they were ready to receive it for their own reasons, not someone else's."[73] Walls underscores the way that intense means of force can be counterproductive, but external compliance was understood to be sufficient.

Christianizing the Baltics

Tryggvason's efforts to Christianize the Nordic regions were not directed or organized by Rome. But by the thirteenth century papal leadership was more active in advocating for the extension of the territory of Christendom. According to Nora Berend, the upper leadership of the church believed that "potentially, this territory could be extended to the entire world."[74] The boundary lines of Christendom were not fixed, it could be enlarged by conquest. And as the church centralized its leadership, the power of the church to support such efforts was greater than ever before. Sack describes how "bishops and archbishops . . .were capable of raising armies and maintaining law and order."[75] Territorial strategies to advance one's objective were made easier by leaning on such enforcement capacities, but uncomfortable situations arose.

After the east Baltic lands were conquered, missionaries were supposed to baptize those who had not been killed. This was in accordance

70. Bagge, "The Making of a Missionary King," 478.
71. Bagge, "The Making of a Missionary King," 478.
72. Sanneh, *Disciples of All Nations*, 42.
73. Walls, *Missionary Movement in Christian History*, 72.
74. Berend, *At the Gate of Christendom*, 43.
75. Sack, *Human Territoriality*, 116.

with cannon law, which "granted full membership in Christendom to the baptized."[76] However, the situation created a dilemma.

> The knights who carried out these conquests, even though designated agents of the propagation of the Christian faith, were not ready to give up acquiring territories and wealth in order to satisfy ecclesiastical ideals. In Livonia, for example, the Sword-Brothers killed converts and prevented others from receiving baptism in order to retain their power over newly conquered lands. They confronted the papacy over what procedures to follow. The popes wished the territory to be transformed into a state under papal power. The Sword-Brothers would have lost much of the territory and would have had to give equal rights to converts.[77]

As Berend describes, the expansion of Christendom often reflected a complex mixture of spiritual and territorial motives. The pursuit of conversion was entangled with the desire for land, wealth, and influence, making it difficult to discern whether the goal was truly evangelization or domination. Under Sack's theory of territoriality, this is also an example of how territory becomes an end rather than a means, an effect of increasing territoriality made possible by a powerful capacity for enforcement.

Reclaiming Lost Land

The land of Islam presented an almost impenetrable physical and ideological boundary to Christendom. And yet, Christendom fostered habits of the mind regarding the relationship between religion and land that were comparable to Islam's understanding of the world. The idea of religious conquest and crusade became "the natural model for encounter."[78]

Land could be claimed (classified and communicated) and these claims would be defended (enforcement). All of this was intended to enlarge the kingdom. Berend explains that "the papacy increasingly came to see non-Christians as internal and external enemies of Christendom, and Jews and Muslims as a spiritual and temporal threat."[79] These ideas together motivated the ethos of the Crusades and approval from the Pope gave the illusion that Christendom was the kingdom of God. "A territorial

76. Berend, *At the Gate of Christendom*, 49.

77. Berend, *At the Gate of Christendom*, 49.

78. Walls, *The Cross-cultural Process in Christian History*, 220.

79. Berend, *At the Gate of Christendom*, 51.

Christendom, along with the enemies of this territory, became the focus of attention during the crusades . . . the role of Christian kings was equated with that of defenders of Christendom. By the thirteenth century the idea of *Christianitas* was fully developed, together with its political and juridical overtones: a territorial unit to be defended and enlarged, under the leadership of the pope."[80] Failure to extend the borders, and to capture the so-called *Holy Land*, led to what Berend calls "a crisis of Christian consciousness."[81]

The people of Christendom turned their attention to recapturing the Iberian Peninsula with much success. The end of Islamic rule in that place came as Granada was restored to the territory of Christendom. In Walls's estimation, the reclaiming of this land "seemed to authorize the use of the sword" to further extend the domain of Christendom.[82] He expounds on this rationale, "the fact that God had so significantly and recently blessed the use of the sword in reclaiming Granada could only reinforce the conviction. Conquest and conversion belonged naturally together."[83] In time, the success of reclaiming lost land by the sword and Europe's growing nautical capability was enough to convince the pope of a different territorial strategy than had been endeavored before.

Counter Examples of Significance

It is important to note that such conquest and conversion approaches were typical of the time but there were voices pointing to alternatives. The mendicant orders of the Dominicans and the Franciscans were a counter narrative to the fixity of monasteries and stationary parish ministry. At a time when the church was the largest land holder in Europe, these orders emphasized poverty and itinerancy. Ramon Lull is one such example that Sanneh commends. Quoting Lull, "it is my belief, O Christ! That the conquest of the Holy Land should be attempted in no other way than as Thou and Thy apostles undertook to accomplish it–by love and prayer, by the shedding of tears and blood."[84] Yet the gains made by conquest seemed all

80. Berend, *At the Gate of Christendom*, 43.

81. Berend, *At the Gate of Christendom*, 51.

82. Walls, *The Cross-cultural Process in Christian History*, 38.

83. Walls, *The Cross-cultural Process in Christian History*, 199.

84. Sanneh, *Summoned from the Margin*, 188.

too tempting. The voice of Lull echoes as a sad reminder of what could have been if such a malevolent territoriality had not been attempted.

The Extent of Territoriality Within Christendom

The use of territoriality as a strategy within the territory and time period of Christendom was pronounced. A significant proportion of the population claimed the Christian faith merely by being born in the Christian land. While there was a diversity of Christian expressions, the European landmass served as a conceptual container that reinforced and maintained broadly held Christian beliefs and behaviors. As the proportion of the population became Christian, an increasing number of physical structures and religious workers were brought into the hierarchy of the church. This enlarged the span of control as well as the wealth of the church. For the purpose of defense and enlargement of Christian territory, strategies that were employed made use of the full spectrum of force available. In terms of identifiable instances of territoriality, Christendom is the exemplar.

THE SPLINTERING OF CHRISTENDOM

Christendom's territoriality increased until it became overburdened by inefficiency and inequality, making it vulnerable to division and secession. As Christendom begins to splinter and divide, territoriality continues to be present. Innovation brings out new forms of this strategy on various scales and within new organizational structures.

In the remainder of this chapter, the splintering of Christendom will be presented as the result of two clusters of roughly contemporaneous events—the Spanish colonization of the Americas and the Protestant Reformation. Both events influenced Christendom: the former stretched the concept beyond what it could sustain, while the latter divided it from within. In both cases, evidence of territoriality appears in forms that are both similar and new.

Spanish Territoriality

The decline of Christianity in other parts of the world between the seventh century and the thirteenth century reinforced the faith's association with European land and people. By the fifteenth century, "Christianity was geographically more concentrated on Europe than at any time before or since."[85] The faith was contained, and consequently limited, to a territorial block. But as Walls points out, "the way to propagate an essentially territorial faith was to expand Christian territory."[86]

To the south and east, the boundary of Christendom was marked by its frontier with the world of Islam. This boundary seemed immovable. Attempts to expand into this territory—to reclaim what was once understood as Christian land—led to a frustrating, centuries-long deadlock. The Crusades were an efficient means of unifying Europe under a supposed Christian cause, but the campaigns failed to retain any land they conquered. This further underscored the fact that Islam would not be moved from its original geopolitical position in the way Christianity had done so many years earlier.[87] While the *Reconquista* on the Iberian Peninsula fared better, "Islam's unwavering repudiation of the gospel" was frustrating to Christian morale.[88] If territoriality has a tendency to perpetuate and expand territorial holdings, the situation would necessitate a different approach.

The Inter Caetera

To the west of the European Christian container was the boundary of the Atlantic Ocean. With advances in maritime technology, opportunity arose to push back this boundary and explore a vast ocean of unfamiliar land. In so doing, "the first instinct of Western Christians was to seek to incorporate the lands they now came upon into Christendom."[89] It was assumed that the territoriality of the Crusades could conceivably be fitted to these new environments. Sanneh observes that Columbus understood his 1492 voyage in continuity with this Crusading vision, seeing it as part of a Christian mission endorsed by the Spanish crown.[90] Columbus himself reflected this mindset when he wrote: "Your Highness, as good Christian and Catholic princes, devout and propagators of the Christian faith, as well as enemies of the sect of Mahomet . . . conceived the plan of sending me, Christopher Columbus, to this country of the Indies, there to see the princes, the peoples, the territory, their disposition and all things else, and the way in which one

85. Walls, *Missionary Movement in Christian History*, 174.

86. Walls, "Ecumenical Missiology in Anabaptist Perspective," 194.

87. Sanneh, *Disciples of All Nations*, 86.

88. Sanneh, *Disciples of All Nations*, 87.

89. Walls, *Crossing Cultural Frontiers*, 185.

90. Sanneh, *Disciples of All Nations*, 87.

might proceed to convert these regions to our holy faith."[91] As Christendom seemed poised to have a significant increase in territory, Islam was not far from its mind.

As a result of Columbus' exploration, in 1493 Pope Alexander the VI issued a papal bull dividing, at least on paper, the unknown world between two European powers. The bull was issued in response to a dispute between the King of Spain and Portugal. At the request of King Ferdinand of Spain, the Pope issued the *Inter Caetera*. It was a profound act of classification of space by the leader of the church who was far from the location of the land in question. Making use of navigational technology, he selected a particular line of longitude and classified all non-Christian land west of this line as the responsibility of Spain, while all non-Christian lands to the East would belong to Portugal. Sack notes the significance of the Pope's methodology as "the first time in history an abstract geometric system had been used to define a vast–global–area of control."[92]

The papal bull demonstrated the immense power held by the Pope to make decisions regarding such large amounts of territory. Yet at the time it may not have been thought of as quite so vast because "the discoveries of Columbus and his immediate successors were not thought to be continents but rather numerous islands off the coast of Asia."[93] These new lands were classified similarly to Cape Verde's cluster of islands. Per the *Donation of Constantine*, such islands were claimed to be the Popes' territorial dominion to do with as he pleased. Consequently, Pope Alexander used the opportunity to grant his home country's request and Spanish colonialization quickly followed.

The bull was an imposition of a different kind of conceptual framework to divide unknown space, but in retrospect, the *Inter Caetera* illuminates how little the people of Europe understood of the new land. Sack explains that letters by European rulers initially underestimated the difference between places. Instead, they assumed similar political organizations and territorial establishments including towns, cities and, castles.[94] There were social and political organizations and territorial boundaries, but they were dissimilar to what could be found in Europe. Without the forms to which they were accustomed, it was possible for Europeans to view the land

91. Sanneh, *Disciples of All Nations*, 87.

92. Sack, *Human Territoriality*, 132.

93. Sack, *Human Territoriality*, 132.

94. Sack, *Human Territoriality*, 132.

as conceptually empty of the meaningful structures of society. What was unknown or misunderstood was declared empty, seemingly legitimizing their classifications and the use of abstract systemization.

While many European powers eventually disregarded the Pope's classifications, the use of longitude and latitude to classify and structure unknown spaces became common practice. Alongside such abstract systems of classification, the notion of conceptually empty land emerged as an increasingly useful form of territoriality. In this way, the use of abstract classification and conceptually empty space exemplified a new kind of territorial innovation.

Patronato and Padroado

Expanding Christian territory was not the only goal being pursued. This period also fostered a new mercantile class that recognized the potential of territorial expansion for accumulating wealth. Sanneh highlights the mixed motivation by incorporating the words of one adventurer, "they crossed the seas 'to serve God and His majesty, to give light to those who were in darkness,' but most emphatically 'to grow rich, as all men desire to do.'"[95] It may be reasonable to dismiss the stated importance of Christianizing as merely a pretext for financial gains but Walls believes both motives to be sincere. "There seemed every reason to believe that trade could be developed, territory acquired, and Christian worship and doctrine enforced at the same time."[96] Several hundred years of Christendom's military experience demonstrated that these were compatible aims. In the long struggle against Islam, Europe would surpass their rival "by colonizing distant societies in pursuit of global economic supremacy."[97]

Spain had the capacity to enforce the classification outlined in the *Inter Caetera*. They used territoriality to assert dominant control over the people and the land. Compulsion was used to bring all the occupants within the classified area into the sphere of Christendom. As a result of the church's ignorance the responsibility of church oversight was granted to the monarchs of Spain and Portugal under the system of *Patronato* and *Padroado*, respectively. Sanneh states that "Philip II's interpretation of the papal bulls had the popes implausibly abdicating to him in ecclesiastical

95. Sanneh, *Disciples of All Nations*, 107.

96. Walls, *The Cross-Cultural Process in Christian History*, 92.

97. Sanneh, *Disciples of All Nations*, 89.

affairs, and so he buttressed the power of the crown over the church with administrative sanctions to secure Christendom abroad."[98] No churches, monasteries, hospitals or religious establishments could be built without the consent of Spain. Spain's powers appeared unlimited, but its interests were soon divided. With religious conversion and economic prosperity under the State's responsibility, they were bound to get in each other's way.

The religious motivation of converting non-Christians became subsidiary to the vastly more promising economic opportunities. Compulsion could be used not just for religious conversion, but for labor as well, which provided a clear economic benefit. Compliance was demanded from the subjects "without regard for local interests, and without the papacy to create moral obstacles."[99] Walls states that "the brutality and rapacity of the representatives of Christendom, taken as a whole, called into question the moral, and thus the Christian, status of the Spanish mission."[100]

The inadequacy of using compulsion for religious conversion and the cruelty of forced labor became evident at the pastoral level. Priests such as Antonio de Montesinos and Bartolome de Las Casas sided with a portion of the enslaved population against the practices of the Spanish.[101] Yet, in the case of Las Casas, he argued inconsistently for the continuation of enslaving Africans even as he pleaded for the humane treatment of those understood to be indigenous.

Despite efforts by some priests to advocate for the inhabitants of the new land, the church by the mid 1550s was marked by infighting over territorial resources. Sanneh provides evidence of rivalry among different monastic orders as described by the archbishop of Mexico written to Seville and reminiscent of the challenges in earlier eras of the church:

> Each defends its territory as if the villages were its own property. There has been and is great feeling between the Orders, not about which can best care for the flock, but which can have the greatest number of places and provinces in its hands; and so they go, occupying the best centers, building monasteries close together . . .not wishing to live in the difficult and needy places . . .So great is the fear which the Indians have of the friars because of the severe punishment they practice upon them that they do not dare

98. Sanneh, *Disciples of All Nations*, 90.
99. Sanneh, *Disciples of All Nations*, 89.
100. Walls, *The Cross-Cultural Process in Christian History*, 39.
101. Terry and Gallagher, *Encountering the History of Missions.*

> to complain. And if this is true of the province of Mexico, what of the mountains? [On account of this,] very little fruit, it may be suspected, has come of the gospel among the people.[102]

Such passages suggest the outgrowth of a malevolent territoriality occurring at this time and in this location. Places were becoming ends rather than means further exacerbating inequalities in access to resources and authority. If there was ever a fervor for the salvation of souls, it was replaced with a disdain for local populations and a kind of greed which took a territorial form.

The goal of Pope Alexander was to extend Christendom's footprint, to bring the nations of the world into submission to Christ and his church. The Spanish attempted to do this by merging the state and church, but colonialism presented a "choice between the political and economic interests of the European powers and their religious profession."[103] Unsurprisingly, the economic interests won out, the violence continued, and all the while Christianity looked culpable.

Persuasion Over Compulsion

The Spanish style mission was the primary way Christianity spread in the southern part of North America and the northern part of South America. Yet for much of Asia and Africa "conversion was at best a distant dream, and conquest an impossibility."[104] The classifications delineated in the *Inter Caetera,* and ratified in the Treaty of Tordesillas, assigned to Portugal a significant portion of land far beyond the ability of that nation to take by the sword. There was no theological difference that separated the Portuguese from the Spanish, but merely the impossibility of applying the same kind of force. Territoriality would need to adapt to the circumstances or as Walls states, "it was necessary to accommodate the Christendom idea to political and military reality."[105] Consequently, the impracticality of the so-called crusading model, at least in some locations, led to new methods and models for commending the Christian faith.

102. Sanneh, *Disciples of All Nations*, 90.
103. Walls, *Crossing Cultural Frontiers*, 51.
104. Walls, *Crossing Cultural Frontiers*, 185.
105. Walls, *The Cross-Cultural Process in Christian History*, 199.

The third requirement of territoriality is enforcement, but that enforcement can be on a spectrum ranging from coercion to persuasion. The Spanish and Portuguese mission efforts embodied the opposing sides of this spectrum.

> It was a situation in which the crusade model was not only inappropriate but impossible to apply that forced the creation of a new model for the spread of Christian allegiance.In this model the representatives of Christendom were to commend, demonstrate, and illustrate the gospel; to persuade without the instruments to coerce. To undertake this task implied a readiness to enter someone else's world instead of imposing the standards of one's own. It meant learning another's language, seeking a niche within another's society, perhaps accepting a situation of dependence.[106]

The new model, built on persuasion, set in motion a different way of doing mission. It also further separated the spiritual from the economical and the church from the state.

Slowly, the thrones of Europe showed that they were more interested in the accumulation of wealth than the advancement of Christianity. The Portuguese also found means of extracting wealth without controlling area and this relieved them of the responsibility of the more custodial role of territoriality. As a result, "the missionary principle . . .did not in itself extend Christendom (though for a long time, many, perhaps most, missionaries hoped that it eventually would do so)."[107] When the colonial powers of Portugal were capable of religious compulsion, they were no longer interested in such efforts to extend Christendom.[108]

What transformed Christianity was not Spain's methods of compulsion but the work of the radicals within Christendom. As Walls notes, "it was the radicals of Christendom . . . the missionary movement, foreshadowed by Ramon Lull and by Francis . . . a model that differed in concept from the crusading, in that it depended on persuasion and demonstration."[109] The distinction lay in the intensity of force—replacing coercion with influence. This shift necessarily required abandoning political domination and the vast span of control that Christendom had once enjoyed. The church's use of territoriality would therefore take on a new form, and Christianity

106. Walls, *The Cross-Cultural Process in Christian History*, 220.

107. Walls, *Crossing Cultural Frontiers*, 186.

108. Walls, *Crossing Cultural Frontiers*, 51.

109. Walls, *Crossing Cultural Frontiers*, 51.

would once again become something more than a European religion. If the missionary movement represented "the last flourish of the Christendom idea" it was not the end of territoriality but rather the beginning of a new territorial strategy.[110]

The tendency of territoriality to expand by its own momentum often leads to greater inefficiency and inequality. This, in turn, creates vulnerability to division and secession. In the case of the Spanish territoriality, the increase of territory separated the centralized decision makers in Europe from the situation on the ground in the areas of Spanish conquest. This created, among other issues, inefficiency. The solution may have been caused by inequality (namely the perspective that those people over there were of lesser significance), but it also had the effect of inequality. The church abdicated moral responsibility leaving those few priests bothered by the enslavement and oppression of others with little power to affect change through the hierarchical channels familiar to them. As a result, the authority of the church was marginalized and diminished.

The attempt of expanding Christendom outward through Spanish Colonization was somewhat successful. But it was, among other things, an overextension of territoriality beyond the church's capacity to maintain authoritative control. The other challenge to Christendom came at a similar time, dividing the unified cohesion of the church.

The Protestant Reformation

At the time of the *Inter Caetera*, Martin Luther was a ten-year-old boy in what was to become Germany. Twenty-four years later, hoping merely to spark a debate, Luther posted his ninety-five theses. This would set off a chain reaction that would lead to the most significant division within the church under Rome. The Protestant Reformation would have implications for the territorial expression of Christendom and challenge the Pope's authority.

Andrew Walls states that "the Protestant Reformation left the territorial principle intact."[111] The context of this claim is one where Walls closely

110. Walls, *Missionary Movement in Christian History*, 258.

111. Walls, *Missionary Movement in Christian History*, 82. In several other passages he describes the effect of the Reformation on Christendom somewhat differently. The references are all from his 2002 compilation *The Cross-Cultural Process in Christian History*. In the first passage he states that "the Protestant Reformation resulted in the division of Christendom, but not in the abandonment of the idea" (36–37). In the other passage Walls seems to acknowledge that "the underlying principle of Christendom was

links the idea of Christendom to "the territorial conception of the Christian faith that brought about the integration of throne and altar."[112] I would like to use Sack's theory of territoriality and Walls claim to understand the territorial dynamics of the Reformation.

To begin, it is appropriate to acknowledge that Walls's statement implies a particular scale of territoriality. Yet if one considers territoriality on multiple scales a more complex picture emerges. To understand the relationship between territoriality in Christendom requires this level of nuance. The question should be, "What is the influence of the Protestant Reformation on the use of territoriality as it existed on multiple scales?" This section shows how Christendom began to splinter, resulting in, not the end of territoriality, but the development of different territorial arrangements.

Territorial Christendom and the State

On the largest scale, the Reformation changed the religious territorial landscape by dividing the once unified European landmass into Catholic and Protestant places. The division was conceived of in territorial expression. For example, the Peace of Augsburg gave freedom to the German princes to decide whether their territory would be Lutheran or Catholic. The territories were classified and enforced. Those who did not align could sell property and move to another region. In other words, one's domicile was still the greatest factor for determining one's religious commitment. The united Christian land would now be broken into either Protestant or Catholic territorial containers. A similar arrangement at the Treaty of Westphalia, with some added tolerance of religious minorities, continued the pattern of state leaders choosing the religion for their people and land.

---

initially breached by the Protestant Reformation itself, which replaced the thought of a universal territorial church by mutual recognition of national churches" (211). His reason for doing so was related to emphasizing the Pietists and Evangelicals that would follow and their own identification with the Reformation. Furthermore, Walls recognizes the territorial challenge to the monastic traditions as complicating the structures of mission. "Protestant concepts of Christendom were not basically different from Catholic, and the sixteenth-century Reformation left the foundational assumptions of European Christianity essentially untouched. But the structures to give effect to the missionary movement took much longer to develop. The Catholic movement had been able to develop on the basis of the religious orders, but the Reformation had slain the goose that laid that particular golden egg" (220). These statements seem to further the argument that clarity is needed to understand the role of the Reformation and the territorial principle.

112. Walls, *Missionary Movement in Christian History*, 81.

The demarcation between Protestant and Catholic territory was not random. There may have been perspectives (both cultural and physical) that shaped these changes of territorial classifications. The division is often understood on religious grounds, but following Fernand Braudel, Walls believes it also needs to be understood culturally.[113] The delineation between Protestant and Catholic followed that of the old Roman Empire with few exceptions. "The line between Catholic and Protestant Europe so closely follows the line between the true provinces of the Roman Empire and the areas in which Roman rule was temporary, peripheral, or absent."[114]

Recognizing the status of Rome as the *center* of the church in this era helps to tease out some of the geographic dynamics of Walls's observation. The inequality created by the center-periphery dynamic encouraged reform for those far from the center. Just as Jerusalem was once abandoned, the Protestants were able to redefine their religious life apart from Rome. Walls states that the division "marked a growing cultural divergence between the north and the south of the area" and the best way to understand Protestantism is as "essentially Northern vernacular Christianity."[115]

The Reformer's desire for church purification was now aimed at "the whole church within each nation."[116] The early Protestant movement did not challenge the idea that there should be a close relationship between the church and the government. Now more empowered, state leaders took the opportunity to claim land once owned by the Catholic church. However revolutionary the new territorial arrangements were, they served to strengthen the relationship between the throne and altar on a more local level.

At the largest scale, the Reformation redrew the lines of religious classification dividing Christendom. The Protestants abandoned the notion of Rome as their religious *center* and in the void once filled by religious authority, the power of state and local provinces increased. The territorial dynamics changed but the view of land as a container for particular beliefs was reaffirmed.

113. Braudel, *The Mediterranean and the Mediterranean World.*

114. Walls, *Missionary Movement in Christian History*, 41.

115. Walls, *Missionary Movement in Christian History*, 20–21, and 41.

116. Walls, *Crossing Cultural Frontiers*, 74.

The Parish

How did the Reformation influence the territorial principle on the scale of the parish? During the earlier period of the Reformation the parish was not the focus of critique. Beyond its importance to the church's territorial self-understanding, the parish, and the larger dioceses were also the units of administration used by the state. Without the authority of the pope, the local government and parish were by necessity empowered. Sack argues that, "Luther accepted, without question, the use of the parish and diocese."[117] He would "insist on mandatory church attendance within the parish even for unbelievers, to be enforced by the local secular authorities."[118] For Luther the parish was still the most effective means of organizing groups of people into worshiping communities.

John Calvin's perspective was similar to that of Luther. Sack states that "Calvin's Church government was designed to work with secular government, and in particular the government of the city of Geneva . . .Church government and discipline [were] to be applied territorially."[119] Calvin upheld the parish system for the spiritual training and discipline of the community. The church and the government could strive together toward these outcomes.

John Smythe is an example of a voice in the early Reformation period that called the parish into question, but in time those with a similar reforming spirit would challenge the parish system more directly. Walls states in John Wesley's day religious plurality was increasing but that the parish and the parish minister were still the default forms.[120] Wesley's itinerant preaching in the open fields trespassed upon the clergyman's parish, creating a territorial challenge. But Wesley was adamant. "You think I ought to sit still; because otherwise I should invade another's office if I interfered with other people's business, and intermeddled with souls that did not belong to me. You accordingly ask, 'How is it that I assemble Christians, who are none of my charge, to sing psalms, and pray, and hear the Scriptures expounded?' and think it hard to justify doing this in other men's parishes . . ."[121] In light of his duty to share the glad tidings of salvation wherever

117. Sack, *Human Territoriality*, 122.

118. Sack, *Human Territoriality*, 122.

119. Sack, *Human Territoriality*, 123.

120. Walls, *Crossing Cultural Frontiers*, 175.

121. Wesley, *Works: Journal*, 138.

he was, Wesley defiantly stated, "I look upon all the world as my parish."[122] The unwillingness of Wesley and the Methodists to conform to the parish container model was a challenge to the hierarchical authority that was built on the territorial divisions of the church. It was also an evangelistic and pastoral innovation that would carry over into other places.[123]

Innovation is an appropriate way to understand the changes that Wesley initiated. The reason for this is that the parish system is but one kind of territorial arrangement at this scale. It was however a significant part of Christendom's territoriality. So significant that it was likely difficult for early Reformers to think outside of this frame. Luther and Calvin left the parish system intact, building their new ecclesial structure on the basis of the prior territoriality and in coordination with state authority. Later reformers like Wesley challenged the limitations this arrangement presented.

Church Buildings and Monasteries

The Basilica of St. Peter is mentioned prominently in Luther's Ninety-five Theses. The indulgences seemed to set up a contrast between poor believers and "miserable money with which to build a church."[124] Ideally for Luther, Christians would be so convinced of the Popes care for souls that "he would rather that the Basilica of St. Peter were burned to ashes than built up with the skin, flesh, and bones of his sheep."[125] Much of what one could call Luther's territorial critique was focused on this smaller scale where, "the major objectionable territorial entity" was the church building.[126]

His frustration with the Basilica and all that it represented led Luther to specific convictions regarding church buildings and monasteries. In contradiction to prior models where reification was expressed in ornate church buildings, Luther wanted to reinvigorate the idea that the church was the people of God. This was a clear expression of low territoriality, a return to some of the earliest convictions of the church as a social definition of territory. The emphasis was also on the local congregation, a flattening of the hierarchy in line with the principle of the priesthood of all believers. In Sack's perspective, "Luther was either against church buildings entirely or

122. Wesley, *Works: Journal*, 138.

123. Walls, *Crossing Cultural Frontiers*, 174.

124. Luther, *95 Theses, 61*.

125. Luther, *95 Theses, 59*.

126. Sack, *Human Territoriality*, 120.

tolerated them as convenient, but unconsecrated places for assembly and worship."[127] A significant concern for Luther was that the physical structures of the church were diverting or displacing attention from what should be the true focus of worship.

Calvin's view of the church building was also similar to that of Luther. Meeting together required some structure for the purpose, but this did not make the space uniquely holy. This too was a return to the earlier understandings of the church. To underscore this point, Calvin quotes fourth-century Hilary of Poitiers, "We do wrong in venerating the Church of God in Roofs and Edifices. Is it doubtful that in these Antichrist will sit? Safer to me are mountains, and woods, and lakes, and dungeons, and whirlpools; for in these, either hidden or immersed, did prophets prophesy."[128] This broadening of where one could worship God diminished the perceived power of Christendom's basilicas and cathedrals. It reasserted the truth that they had no real power, it belonged to God.

The Reformers also abandoned the monastery system. Their argument was that "family life and active participation in society could be just as holy as life within the monastery walls, and life within them as sinful and self-centered as life outside."[129] Smythe argued against any religious institution apart from the church. He stated, "All religious societies except that of a visible church are unlawful [and among the more notorious of these are]: Abbeyes, monasteries, Nunries, Cathedrals, Collegiats, [and] parishes."[130] The abandonment of the monastery system may have worked well for state leadership who found opportunities in this new arrangement. Under his countries reform movement, Henry VIII of England took possession of the monasteries and distributed the property to friends of the crown.

Of all the territorial scales, church buildings and monasteries were the focus of the early Reformers' critique. Luther's ambivalence regarding church buildings would be an important part of the Reformation's challenge to one particular scale of territoriality within Christendom.

The use of church buildings continued but there was a greater value for simplicity and an emphasis on the body of believers as the church. The church building was not to be understood as a reification of God's power but a building of practical purpose for gathering the true church.

127. Sack, *Human Territoriality*, 122.

128. Calvin, *Tracts and Treatises of John Calvin*, 103.

129. Walls, *The Cross-Cultural Process in Christian History*, 16.

130. Smythe, *The Works of John Smythe*, 252.

The Extent of the Reformation's Influence on the Territorial Principle

In light of the evidence presented, it is necessary to revisit Walls's statement that "the Protestant Reformation left the territorial principle intact."[131] On the broadest scale, the Reformation divided the territory of Christendom but left many of the hallmarks in place. The idea of a united cohesive Christendom under a central authority was no more. Yet the authority of the individual states increased leaving the combination of throne and altar well intact. The proportion of those who claimed to be Christian and the idea of Christian land was not questioned. On this count Walls's statement rings true.

Many, but not all, of the early reformers left the parish territorial system in place. It was later reformers such as John Wesley who spoke out against the limits of the parish model for ministry and evangelism. One can say that at the parish level, the territorial principle was beginning to wobble. The Reformation was at least indirectly responsible for this. The greatest challenge to the territorial principle in the era of the Protestant Reformation was at the smaller scale of church buildings and monasteries. The idea of church as a group of people rather than a building was a significant challenge to Christendom's territorial model.

Three scales have been presented to consider the impact of the Reformation on the territorial principle. Yet these scales are not truly discreet and separate from each other. Inequality at a larger scale may be symbolized in a smaller scale. Convictions that encouraged reformulation at one scale could become the basis for another. Consider, for example that there was unequal distribution of resources within Christendom's broader territorial system. The Basilica of St. Peter was, if not a symbol, one significant example of this inequality. The indulgences sold in Luther's homeland were sent far away to pay for a basilica that was in Rome. The indulgences were theologically wrong, but they also revealed the church's territorial inequality. Luther's criticism was made concrete at the smaller scale, but the system as a whole had problems. In time, the territoriality present at all of the scales would be examined and found wanting. The implications would continue long after Luther.

Throughout Christendom there were those that sought to express their sincere commitment to God beyond the standard forms. At times monasticism provided this outlet as well as the reform movements of the

131. Walls, *Missionary Movement in Christian History*, 82.

Waldensians, Lollards, and Hussites. For the most part, prior to the Reformation the church was able to restrain these movements so as to not impinge upon Christendom's more tame religious expression and territorial unity.

The Reformation began with the voicing of legitimate ethical concerns out of a desire for the church's improvement. When it was clear that there was no way of addressing the underlying inequality and corruption, movements of secession arose. Among other things, the Reformation created space for creative territorial and organizational innovation without the threat of excommunication. Sincere Christians could develop new ways of relating to territory, government, and each other. Some stayed close to the tradition they knew. Others saw opportunity for different arrangements that they understood as a return to the earliest models of the church. Walls is right that "the Protestant Reformation left the territorial principle intact" in the sense that the Reformation was not the elimination of territoriality.[132] Yet if the various scales can be taken together as a fuller picture, one can see that the Protestant Reformation was the beginning of significant changes in how the church, in its increasingly varied forms, expressed territoriality.

The various Protestant movements that seceded from the Roman Catholic Church made use of territoriality because as organizations that exist in space and time this is a very human thing to do. Organizations require discipline and territoriality is used to meet this need with efficiency and clarity. Yet one can expect that in time these same denominations and movements can also run the risk of the more negative aspects of territoriality–the inequality, the tendency toward greater territoriality, and the tipping point where efficiency is lost and bureaucracy impedes.

In both the Spanish colonialization of the Americas and the Reformation, the form and structure of the territoriality of European Christendom could not be maintained. In the case of the Spanish colonization, through a series of choices the authority of the church diminished while that of the state increased. Greater still, the oppressive treatment by those who were supposedly extending Christendom damaged the witness of the church. In the case of the Reformation, Christendom's territoriality was divided as the Protestants seceded. In both cases the form of territoriality under Christendom was significantly changed.

132. Walls, *Missionary Movement in Christian History*, 82.

THE END OF CHRISTENDOM, BUT NOT TERRITORIALITY

Christendom's Epilogue

After the Thirty-Years War, Christendom's "universal territorial church" was replaced by a "mutual recognition of national churches."[133] Though divided and far less stable, elements of Christendom lived on in what was understood to be Christian nations. Initially, the leader of the state decided how the people of the territory would express their Christian worship. This approach toward national religious uniformity did not last long. Sanneh writes that "rather than as a matter of birth right, being Christian would be a matter of voluntary choice–first by the state and then the people."[134]

The Reformation and the development of national states was part of a move toward what Sanneh calls "the radical secularization of life."[135] The belonging once central to the idea of Christendom was replaced by commitments to one's language and one's country. The edict of national religious uniformity was in time replaced by forms of religious toleration and the expectation of more religiously plural societies. Sanneh concludes that the state became "the carrier of the doctrine of birth and soil."[136] The singular code of custom continued without Christianity as its cornerstone. In its place, as a kind of "secularized survival of the Christendom ideal" was the notion that "faith in democracy and in elections [was the] cure to human misery."[137]

Intellectual movements arose stressing autonomy, individualism, and responsibility. Walls states that while these "posed a direct threat to the idea of the territorial Christian realm" out of them "developed the principles of contract and association as the modes by which this responsibility could be collectively expressed."[138] The Enlightenment, in Walls's perspective, "had the effect of moving religion from the sphere of the public and communal to the sphere of the private and personal, and thus to the sphere of group and family, and ultimately to individual responsibility and choice."[139] The illusion that all within the land are Christian was broken. Where once being

133. Walls, *The Cross-Cultural Process in Christian History*, 211.

134. Sanneh, *Encountering the West*, 188.

135. Sanneh, *Encountering the West*, 186.

136. Sanneh, *Encountering the West*, 189.

137. Walls, *The Cross-Cultural Process in Christian History*, 194.

138. Walls, *The Cross-Cultural Process in Christian History*, 212.

139. Walls, *The Cross-Cultural Process in Christian History*, 212.

a Christian was taken for granted, now being a Christian was a matter of voluntary self-determination or merely the private default religion of Europe. Was Christendom over?

Understanding Christendom as a complex multifaceted development makes it difficult to determine a precise end date. Sanneh highlights 1571 Battle of Lepanto as one of the "last gasps of Christendom."[140] Likewise, Carroll and Lechner place the end of Christendom in the sixteenth century tied to changes brought by the Reformation.[141] While the use of the term continued well into the twentieth century, Walls notes that by the late 1700s and early 1800s the Christendom concept "was increasingly ambiguous."[142] Hanciles, following Walls, argues that Christendom was a particularly European expression that Christianity has moved beyond,[143] while Jenkins argues (seconded by Leithart) that Christianity may just be moving to the next phase of Christendom.[144] One wonders if such efforts to reframe Christendom are, in effect, attempts to pour new wine into old wineskins. Perhaps the real challenge is that we need to think in categories other than Christendom.

Within Protestantism

The focus on voluntary association and privatization also contributed to increasing division within Protestantism. Some associations were made on linguistic, national, or theological grounds but in time, according to Walls, they "became routine until it became a matter of convenience."[145] The "principles of contract and association" as novel modes for Christian collectivity stood in stark contrast to the territorial hierarchy that had formed the church for so many years.[146]

The proliferation of Christian organizations ushered in by Protestantism and marked by voluntary membership and privatization, also had implications for territoriality. As opposed to previous arrangements that closely linked belonging to domicile, "common purpose could link groups

140. Sanneh, *Encountering the West*, 186.

141. Carroll, *The Founding of Christendom*. Lechner, "Sovereignty and Territoriality."

142. Walls, *The Missionary movement in Christian history*, 83.

143. Hanciles, *Beyond Christendom*, 3.

144. Jenkins, *The Next Christendom*; and Leithart, *Defending Constantine*.

145. Walls, *Crossing Cultural Frontiers*, 15.

146. Walls, *The Cross-Cultural Process in Christian History*, 212.

in different countries who stood for 'real' Christianity." Walls called them "Pietist Evangelical islands" in a supposed "sea of Christendom."[147] In this metaphor, Walls hints at the reality of a new religious territorial order. There was no longer one territorial block, one church organization, and one body of people. There was now a multiplicity of churches in a variety of locations. While the proportion of those who would claim to be a Christian may have remained high for some time, one's religious identity was coalescing around one's specific denomination or organization. For any one denomination or organization, voluntary association dramatically decreased the span of control relative to the proportion of the population. Accordingly, the intensity of force available lessened and territoriality was relegated to smaller geographical scales.

On these smaller scales, prior approaches were reconsidered and territorial innovation flourished. Migration to new lands also helped to reset the territorial mindset. Even today, church membership is driven by personal choice and convenience, as opposed to being strictly related to one's domicile. Additionally, Sack notes that, "with the exception of Episcopalians and some Methodist denominations, twentieth-century American Protestant faiths do not refer to parishes or dioceses in describing their structures."[148] In the absence of parishes, US denominations have often found it helpful to subdivide the country and classify territories based on their congregant population and organizational needs. Churches are grouped and may even send delegates to represent their territory at higher church councils.[149] The decreased denominationalism in the US has also spurred new forms of territorial church organization, such as megachurches with satellite configurations.[150] These novel forms of territorial structure can facilitate different manifestations of the effects of territoriality.

147. Walls, *The Cross-Cultural Process in Christian History*, 212.

148. Sack, *Human Territoriality*, 124.

149. For example, in the Reformed Church of American (RCA), churches are grouped into Classes that in turn are grouped into Regional Synods. Every Classis sends pastor and elder delegates to the General Synod. The number of delegates is determined by the number of churches in each Classis.

150. Smietana, "High-Tech Circuit Riders."

Attempts to Reconstruct Christendom

Once privileged by Christendom, some Christians found themselves increasingly on the outside looking in. Sanneh is somewhat sympathetic, the loss of Christendom likely felt like weakness and defeat.[151] There were clear advantages Christians experienced under Christendom. It provided protection and security. The singular code of custom meant that residents of Christendom had the advantage of knowing that wherever they went across their land the religious forms remained the same. It relieved Christians of the need for religious choice or the responsibility for intellectual defense.[152] The advantage of territorial mass meant that one's beliefs were upheld by those around them, a kind of sacred canopy.[153] Christendom, as a place, assembled a collective echo that reinforced their confidence in the truth of their perspectives.

The lack of Christendom has given rise to, what Sanneh calls "retrieval projects."[154] He explores where such impulses lead. "Thus disinherited, believers indulged a fond, illusory nostalgia for a Christendom in which kings and rulers had been sacred messengers, with Christian society predicated on a model political head cast in the profile of Constantine on the principle of *cuius region eius religio*. That notion had been so deeply inscribed in the collective Christian memory that believers deluded themselves by finding common cause with jingoist national policies."[155] These attempts to reinvigorate the prior protections and privileges have generally underscored Christianity's division and its more limited capacity for influence.

151. Sanneh was also aware that Christianity had been critiqued by theologians of Islam, such as tenth-century Al-Jabbar, for abandoning its "founding territorial warrant." The loss of Christianity's religious territorial "birthright" in their perspective, "condemned Christians to dealing with religion as social construction rather than a divine command." By contrast Islam maintained an "unbroken legacy of devotion and veneration" in its territorial core of Mecca and Medina. These quotes are all from Sanneh, *Disciples of All Nations*, 79. Such arguments could be made by other religions as well. Christianity is unique among major world religions in its experience of being a religious land orphan. It cannot claim to possess the land where Christ had walked and the breakdown of Christendom was perhaps just a further humiliation.

152. Sanneh, *Encountering the West*, 214.

153. Berger, *The Sacred Canopy*.

154. Sanneh, *Encountering the West*, 189.

155. Sanneh, *Encountering the West*, 189.

Christendom "remains only a dream and a fascination, not the workable arrangement it once was."[156]

Sanneh wonders if the slowness of Christianity to conform to its lack of supremacy is rooted in an unwillingness to "deal with the fundamental issues of the many idolatries of tribe, nation, power, and success."[157] A Christianity without Christendom may reveal where a Christian's true allegiance lies. Is their commitment first to their national political agenda which claims to secure power and privilege, or to their faith, which is no longer contained in the territorial borders of Christendom. Against the backdrop of this temptation to retain power at all costs, Walls holds that "the new situation requires Western Christians to find a joyful place in a predominately non-Western church."[158]

CONCLUSION

Christendom was powerful and this power was expressed in territorial forms. The extent of that power was in terms of proportion, scale, and intensity of force. The leaders of Christendom had once sought to expand their territory, believing in the potential for their kingdom to spread out and encompass the whole world. The problems associated with attempting to extend their reach, matched with the breakdown of the cohesive unity meant that Christendom was diminished on both fronts. But territoriality existed prior to Christendom and continues on after Christendom. The end of Christendom does not imply the end of territoriality. It takes different forms, and exists more commonly on smaller scales of territory. Nonetheless, it continues on because it is not merely a feature of Christendom, but a tendency of human behavior.

The Reformation helped to develop new forms of territorial expression within the Christian faith. Some of those territorial expressions were related to mission. The next chapter will explore several examples of continued territoriality associated with Christian mission.

156. Sanneh, *Encountering the West*, 186.

157. Sanneh, *Encountering the West*, 225.

158. Walls, *The Missionary Movement in Christian History*, 196.

6

Examples of Territoriality in Mission

THE ARGUMENT

THIS CHAPTER ARGUES THAT even as Christendom had come to an end, territoriality continued. To show the continuation of territoriality after Christendom several examples from Protestant missionary activity will be considered. The first example looks at how Christians organized themselves into voluntary societies, separate from the formal church structures, to meet their evangelistic goals. Three other examples will consider the missionary strategies they implemented as demonstrations of ongoing territoriality. The chapter concludes by looking at contemporary expressions of territorial structure that show ongoing territoriality.

CLARIFYING PRIMARY AND SECONDARY TERRITORIALITIES

To begin this chapter, it will be helpful to distinguish between a primary and secondary territoriality. This distinction was addressed in chapter 2, but it is worth tracing the specifics in this chapter because of how it begins to manifest particularly in this time period. For example, voluntary associations existed in the Greco-Roman world at the time Christianity began to take shape.[1] But after Christendom, voluntary associations among Christians emerged with renewed energy, becoming a powerful force for change.

As the sun set on Christendom, different kinds of territoriality came to prominence impacting power dynamics. When the Spanish conquistadors

1. Banks, *Paul's Idea of Community*, 7.

took Central America, it was nearly an absolute territorial conquest with intended implications on almost all territorial scales of life. It is helpful to set this type of territoriality, which continued to exist long after the conquistadors, in contrast to a type of territoriality that is less absolute. To clarify this contrast, one could refer to the government's control of area as a primary territoriality. But there are other influential organizations that function with various degrees of autonomy from state control that also make use of territoriality. These are referred to here as secondary territorialities. In the 1600s and 1700s onward, European organizations such as trade companies, religious groups, and other voluntary societies formed a plurality of secondary territorialities which were conceptually layered on top of the primary. It was the structure (or perhaps context) of the primary territorialities that allowed the secondary territorialities to thrive. This was the case whether the secondary territorialities were sanctioned by the primary or not.

Organizations in the category of secondary territoriality were more limited in terms of the force they could use. They could not directly martial armies for assisting their cause in the way the primary territoriality could. Additionally, because there was a plurality of organizations in this category, there was competition that could further limit the scope of their power. This required skills of negotiation and collaboration that were typically less necessary in situations of primary territoriality where power was generally thought of as zero sum.

While limited in force, secondary territorialities provided the opportunity for choice. Walls describes how voluntary societies needed "a social system that allows for plurality and choice," one where "people are not required or prepared to act in the same way as all their neighbours, in which there is a highly developed sense of the individual and of individual autonomy."[2] Free association provided the opportunity to express individual convictions within a collective frame. Such values were characteristic of most secondary territorialities. This aligns with the way Sack describes organizations with lesser territoriality by highlighting the voluntary nature of their association.[3] The rise of voluntary societies was a shift toward a social definition of territory. This was a step back from a society mostly governed by territorial definitions of social relationships where individuals

2. Walls, *The Missionary Movement in Christian History*, 225.

3. Sack, *Human Territoriality*, 7.

are mostly defined by their domicile. Such social definitions of territory are a hallmark of a more decreased territoriality.

The voluntary makeup of secondary territorialities generally meant that they were understood to be less influential than a primary territoriality. This difference can be observed when one compares the proportion of the population each territoriality influences. In the case of the primary, their influence was on the entirety of the population within their borders. A secondary territoriality influences a lower proportion of the total population within any one particular place. But, in ways distinct from a primary, they also have the potential to reach farther than the fixed borders of a nation-state. This gives them the opportunity for a larger span of control. For example, trading companies may have networks of ports and trade routes, and religious communities might have establishments on either side of the Atlantic.

These organizations created their own territorial classifications, such as maps of territorial subdivisions. Such subdivisions may conform to political jurisdictions already in use (defined by the primary territoriality), or they may be created with the organization's particular needs in mind. Regions may be classified based on the location of members, but there is no expectation that all that reside in the area are members. Furthermore, the classifications may not be understood as significant to those outside the organization but can be very important to those within. And within this created territorial structure, territoriality can be present along with the cause and effects that tend to accompany it.

Clarifying the contrast between a primary territoriality and a secondary territoriality is important for this chapter because missionary societies and organizations are examples of secondary territoriality. Their use of territoriality was different from those in Christendom and reflected their own changing world and various churches' changing relationship to the state. Their ability to influence and their capacity to enforce their territoriality was limited. There was also competition with other secondary territorialities, including between different trading companies, organizations, or mission societies. Even with these limits, they had the potential for a broader geographical range that previously may have been restricted to only state entities. They made use of territoriality in a more limited form to achieve their desired purposes and were nonetheless influential. Missionary societies and organizations were not formally part of the primary territoriality, as the church had been during Christendom. Yet they were still territorial, strategically using their more limited power to bring about change.

As layers of different companies, religious groups, and organizations developed, territoriality increased and took different forms with different effects. The increase of territoriality can take shape in expansion outward or subdivision inward. An organization may seek to acquire more land or property, expanding operations, and establishing new routes, settlements, or stations. In this way territoriality moves out, adding more area to control. Or established stations, property, or routes may become more complex and require subdivision and stratified hierarchy to better organize the interior territory.

As layers of companies, religious groups, and organizations developed, territoriality expanded, assuming new forms and producing varied effects. This increase in territoriality could manifest as either outward expansion or inward subdivision. An organization might seek to acquire additional land or property, extend its operations, and establish new routes, settlements, or stations. All are examples of territoriality moving outward to encompass greater area. Alternatively, established stations, properties, or routes could become more complex, prompting subdivision and hierarchical stratification to better organize the interior territory.

With these changing dynamics in mind, the remainder of the chapter will consider the rise of the missionary society as it deconstructed the prior territoriality of the European context and the missionary strategies that followed this. Territoriality continues to play a role in how groups of Christians engage land, organize hierarchy, and achieve their goals.

EXAMPLE: THE MISSIONARY SOCIETY

In his chapter "Missionary Societies and the Fortunate Subversion of the Church," Andrew Walls explains how voluntary societies provided a space for like-minded Christians to pursue evangelistic goals. The rise of the voluntary society illustrates how territoriality was shifting in relation to the church. At that time, the structures of most Protestant churches were unable to achieve these aims on their own. As Walls observes, "in Europe and America alike, effective overseas missions began not with the official machinery of the churches, but with voluntary societies."[4] As missionary efforts expanded, these societies contributed to new ways of classifying land,

4. Walls, *The Missionary Movement in Christian History*, 229.

constructed new forms of church hierarchy, and articulated fresh expressions of custodial responsibility for lands beyond Europe.

Walls traces the beginnings of the missionary societies in London to the late 1600s, when a group of earnest Christians sought to live out their faith with greater devotion. During this period, awareness of and engagement with the world beyond Europe were increasing. Earlier theological objections to mission activity were countered by others who argued that evangelization was a goal worth pursuing. Even so, the idea of mission remained a marginal concern within the church. Walls states that, "the missionary movement was rarely a primary concern of the official Western church, and usually involved the energies of only a minority among those in Europe who professed and called themselves Christians."[5] The shift toward free association in format of the voluntary society had significant implications for the church and contrasted with prior dominant territorial models of Christendom.

During and within Christendom, where a person lived, their domicile, substantially determined their religious affiliation. After the Protestant Reformation, a variety of ecclesiastical organizations took shape. Many continued to link land with particular Christian expressions and subdivide the broader territorial container of Christianity into parcels of parish land for the purpose of ministry. This link between land and faith also perpetuated the close relationships between religious and state powers. Those that did not conform to the system were religiously and politically marginalized. Some chose to leave as refugees in search of religious freedom. That this choice was their best option demonstrated the effectiveness of religious territoriality in these areas.

Even as domicile continued to be important, the growth of voluntary societies offered an alternative. The Methodists are an example of this shift. Initially they saw themselves as a reform movement within the Anglican church. In time they developed their own leadership structure, networks for enforcing discipline, and classification of territory for ministerial responsibility.[6] Wesley, who once stated that "all the world" is his parish, also intensely subdivided adherents into small groups by age, gender, and marital status.[7] His preference was strongly in favor of social definitions of territory rather than domicile. The initial formation as a voluntary society

5. Walls, *Crossing Cultural Frontiers*, 186.

6. Terry and Gallagher, *Encountering the History of Missions*.

7. Wesley, *Works: Journal*, 138.

was the half step that allowed the Methodists to ultimately secede from the church of England and flourish as their own church structure.

New Organizational Structures

The example of the Methodists showed why these societies may have been viewed with suspicion by the established church hierarchy. The "'instrumental' society," as Walls alternatively refers to it, was an "association of Christians banding together to achieve a defined object."[8] Yet the objective, in this case, was fulfilling the church's responsibility of evangelism and to extend "the geographic scope of missions."[9] Pursuing this end required navigating accusations of being ecclesiastically subversive, particularly within the Anglican church. Of the Society of Providing Christian Knowledge and the Society for the Propagation of the Gospel, Walls states that "care was taken to link their management with the bishops of the Church of England" so as not to appear as agitators.[10] Yet, in an example of how missionary societies were not well fitted to the hierarchical establishment of the Anglican church, it was often the aristocratic lay members of the societies who had the social prestige necessary to approach a bishop directly.[11]

A voluntary society composed of lay church members and lower clergy who sought to fulfill a ministry function of the church was, at the very least, hierarchically awkward. As Walls observes, this produced "a new type of church government . . . growing up alongside the old, parasitically attached to forms that had seemed permanent, argued over till there was no more to say."[12] Such developments illustrate what Sack describes as *territorial secession*—"the condition wherein an individual or group uses territorial tendencies to lessen or remove the authority of others."[13] While these societies did not fully reject ecclesiastical authority, they did effectively diminish it, operating according to their own rules and values. In this way, missionary societies dangled between reform and secession, setting up a nimble parallel structure. They served at the margins, expanding the territoriality of the church but in ways so far removed from the centers of power as to seem nearly autonomous. The structural changes they introduced

8. Walls, *The Missionary Movement in Christian History*, 246.

9. Walls, *The Cross-Cultural Process in Christian History*, 206.

10. Walls, *The Missionary Movement in Christian History*, 243.

11. Walls, *The Missionary Movement in Christian History*, 249.

12. Walls, *The Missionary Movement in Christian History*, 249.

13. Sack, *Human Territoriality*, 40.

through their organizations amounted to a kind of deconstruction of what was present. Their desire was to influence the world beyond them, but the territorial systems they inherited had been designed primarily to perpetuate the maintenance of Christendom.

Some autonomy was necessary for the missionary societies to organize effectively to pursue their goals. Their structure flourished as a result of what Walls describes as "decentralization and dispersal of its organization."[14] The missionary society was able to singularly focus on their goal of equipping and sending out missionaries. Their energy, finances, and prayers were directed toward this end.[15] The logistics and technology required for this initiative led early advocates such as William Carey to draw comparisons to maritime trading companies.[16] As secondary territorialities both required voluntary investors, recruitment, particular training, and overseas travel. They also both had the capacity to influence beyond their nation-state borders and beyond their own expectations.

According to Walls, the voluntary society is "the main organizational engine of the Protestant movement."[17] Its significance is highlighted repeatedly in Walls's work as subverting "the traditional European forms of church government" which, "had arisen in the setting of territorial Christianity."[18] The structures of the traditional church government were well suited for parish ministry, not for expanding beyond the territorial context where they were already in place. A new organizational engine was needed. "The Protestant missionary movement that arose became possible only by means of these new structures. Small groups of people-lay people, very often, and when clergy, not generally the most significant leaders of their denomination-made their own arrangements for preaching the gospel and establishing churches overseas."[19] The new structures were agile, responding quickly to the changing world around them. But while most new institutions and organizations begin with the privilege of such virtues, these ideals are difficult to maintain over time.

14. Walls, *The Missionary Movement in Christian History*, 225.
15. Walls, *The Missionary Movement in Christian History*, 257.
16. Walls, *The Missionary Movement in Christian History*, 246.
17. Walls, *The Cross-Cultural Process in Christian History*, 232.
18. Walls, *The Cross-Cultural Process in Christian History*, 232.
19. Walls, *The Cross-Cultural Process in Christian History*, 17.

New Territorial Structures

Even as missionary societies were able to successfully partner with the religious hierarchical structure, they would face several other obstacles related to territoriality. Christendom ended, but the perspectives that it fostered influenced Christians and missionaries for a much longer time. Of specific interest to the present exploration is the way in which the territorial aspects of Christendom shaped the missionary movement.

Walls highlights the territorial mentality which continued to classify land with religious belief and to inevitably define the missionary task. Christians were in Europe and the rest of the world was non-Christian and so the initial missionary impulse was to extend Christendom.[20] This territorial division meant that going overseas was a necessity for promoting the faith. Consequently, "the missionary movement as it developed was essentially maritime in its thinking."[21] These classifications display a continuity with Christendom ideas even as the full structure could not be replicated.

The parish represented another territorial pattern that the missionary society had to reimagine for a different context. While the mendicant orders of the Catholic Church were more readily adaptable to cross-cultural ministry, the Protestant world continued to think largely in terms of the parish. Walls observes that "the very concept of a missionary had to be built from European patterns of Christian ministry; and those patterns were conditioned by territorial concepts, such as the parish."[22] On the *who-will-go* side of the missionary equation, mission societies had to find ways to overcome the prevailing view of ministry as "the ordained pastor in his parish."[23] This made it difficult for those in ministry or ministry preparation to think beyond the parish framework. Walls notes that evangelical Anglicans in particular "were pledged to honour the monarchical ordained parish ministry, and were sensitive to accusations of Methodist freewheeling."[24] Such perspectives, for a time, delayed missionary recruitment and shaped the strategy of the missionary task. When the goal was conceived as establishing new parishes in places far from centers of power and resources, the proposal was not especially compelling.

20. Walls, *Crossing Cultural Frontiers*, 186.

21. Walls, *Crossing Cultural Frontiers*, 190.

22. Walls, *Crossing Cultural Frontiers*, 186–87.

23. Walls, *The Cross-Cultural Process in Christian History*, 222.

24. Walls, *The Cross-Cultural Process in Christian History*, 222–32.

The other complication presented by the parish subdivision was that it implied the need for a primary territoriality to provide its structure–at least, that was how it had generally been done. In places where the British government had asserted a primary territoriality, even in small settlements such as in Sierra Leone, a parish could be established more easily. Accordingly, early missionary society efforts were mainly focused on the English colonists, only realizing "visions of a wider missionary sphere . . . [in] the nineteenth century."[25] In places without a British primary territoriality, a different approach was required. The parish needed to be reimagined in terms of the negotiated presence of a secondary territoriality with another country asserting primary territoriality. In such cases, the examples of "Catholic orders and societies, Protestant voluntary societies, Methodist itinerancy" were helpful for moving beyond the parish model According to Walls, such structures "had arisen where parochial and other territorial models had manifestly failed."[26]

Walls observation regarding "parochial and other territorial models" appears to set up a contrast. The Christendom model of parish ministry on one side, and monastic orders, itinerancy, and voluntary societies on the other. This could give the impression that the latter groups do not make use of territoriality in their ministerial activities. Yet using Sack's definition of territoriality broadens one's understanding and opens new opportunities for analysis. New structures may employ forms of territoriality distinct from the territoriality of Christendom but are nonetheless still territorial.

New Leadership Structures

While missionary societies operated at the margins of church life, their revolutionary effect was capable of altering existing religious power dynamics. As evidence of this, Walls points to the influence of one man in particular, asking rhetorically "in the whole of the nineteenth-century, did any archbishop hold a more extensive or more important *episcope* than Henry Venn?"[27] Venn, who held only small ministerial positions within England, resigned these to serve the Church Missionary Society (CMS) and as a result "no bishop had so wide a diocese."[28] That Venn was so influential to such a large territory indicates the kind of mismatch and spillover dynamics that

25. Walls, *Missionary Movement in Christian History*, 243.
26. Walls, *Crossing Cultural Frontiers*, 187.
27. Walls, *Missionary Movement in Christian History*, 249–50.
28. Walls, *Missionary Movement in Christian History*, 250.

the new territoriality could create. That one person was permitted to hold such a large territory demonstrates how the new power arrangements were occurring at the margins of church life.

In their beginning, Protestant forms of association, embodied in missionary societies, tended toward being "free, open, responsible, embracing all classes, both sexes, all ages, [and] the masses of the people." The same could not be said of "any of the classical forms of church government, whether Episcopal, Presbyterian, or Independent."[29] At their best, societies held a view of human depravity which put all people on level ground in need of salvation. This served to challenge some of the long-standing perspectives of superiority and elitism that could be held by the church.[30] The formal church structures also required forms of standardization, such as education and ordination. The societies could make rules outside these structures, allowing for the inclusion of women and lay leadership without fear of disrupting systems solidified by theological rationale. Within the sphere of the missionary society, "no one raised difficulties about the ordination of women, or even about their being silent in the church."[31] This provided new leadership opportunities for those who would have otherwise been considered unworthy.

The societies also challenged the necessity of having only ordained clerics performing ministry functions. Walls points to the happenstance that led to this arrangement within the CMS. Because of their close alignment with the Church of England, they had fully intended to send out educated ordained clergy as missionaries. According to Walls, "for a long time, episcopally ordained clergy simply did not offer for missionary service."[32] The CMS adjusted their expectations and looked to precedence in the early church. The standard for those entering missionary service was altered to allow for "pious laity whose social and educational background were obstacles to their ordination."[33] Several other missionary societies had to drop requirements of ordination when no one deemed qualified offered for service. In the Scottish missionary movement, "most of the early offers of service were from artisans, and few of the early missionaries completed the

29. Walls, *Missionary Movement in Christian History*, 225.

30. Walls, *Missionary Movement in Christian History*, 79.

31. Walls, *Missionary Movement in Christian History*, 250.

32. Walls, *Missionary Movement in Christian History*, 223.

33. Walls, *Missionary Movement in Christian History*, 223.

course of study for the ministry."[34] The standards and specialization of the clergy were set aside for the purpose of fulfilling the goals of the society.

The reduction of clerical standards by the CMS and others can be understood in various ways. Walls presents it as a win for pious laity, an example of changing leadership structures, and a providential act of God.[35] In terms of territoriality though, a reduction in standards in different territories can set up a kind of stratification with unequal access to resources. This does not mean that professional clergy would have been more successful as missionaries. Rather it is to point out how such reductions of standards could serve to reinforce perspectives of superiority in England. At the same time, the voluntary nature and more open approach to leadership may have made missionary societies more popular with those less elite. Walls states that missionary societies, "held seigneurial rights to a lay fiefdom; and its symbolic figure is a penny-a-week collector, reading a missionary magazine."[36]

Missionary Magazines

One of the ways the missionary society inspired lay involvement was through the use of missionary journals and magazines. The impact of the "penny-a-week" magazine was threefold. First, it created access to information that most ordinary congregants in the pew would not otherwise have encountered. Such publications drew broadly from Christian missionary activity across denominational and organizational lines. Shenk notes that there was "a climate of openness toward other societies and a free exchange of ideas within the missionary world, especially through journals and magazines."[37]

Beyond this circulation of information, a second impact lay in the way these periodicals expanded the horizons of their readers. Through their magazines, the missionary societies functioned as emissaries, connecting subscribers to the wider world. Those who may never have traveled beyond London could, through these publications, develop a global awareness. The magazines invited readers to imagine the world beyond their own context and to see themselves as participants in a global Christian story. In doing

34. Walls, *Missionary Movement in Christian History*, 225.

35. Walls, *The Missionary Movement in Christian history*, 246.

36. Walls, *The Cross-Cultural Process in Christian History*, 235.

37. Shenk, "Rufus Anderson and Henry Venn," 171.

so, they effectively shrank the distance between what was happening abroad and what was happening at home. At times, they even inspired political activism that pressured the British government on humanitarian grounds. Underscoring the significance of this influence, Walls observes, "But how many people in Britain in the 1850s would have heard of Abeokuta, or been able to distinguish the King of Dahomey from the Queen of Sheba? Most of those that could do so would have gained their knowledge from the window of the world provided by the missionary magazines."[38] This expanding knowledge helped to normalize the idea of mission at a time when it was difficult to imagine service beyond the parish context.

The third impact of these publications was the way they inspired investment from a broader base of support. For the price of a widow's mite, even those of modest means could participate in the work of mission, finding purpose and belonging in a cause far larger than themselves. In this way, the magazines cultivated a shared sense of responsibility for the spread of the gospel that extended well beyond the clergy and wealthy patrons.

Christian Unity

The openness and free exchange of ideas in the missionary magazines reflected a broader commitment to Christian unity. The impulse toward evangelizing the world was not confined to a single denomination, and this shared purpose created a unifying theme around which collaboration could develop. Individual societies had to discern how to respond to this growing sense of unity even as they remained connected to specific denominational organizations. Some chose to stay intentionally neutral, while others remained distinctly particular, yet a spirit of unity could be present in both approaches. Shenk identifies this ethos in Article XXXI of the *CMS Laws and Regulations*, adopted in 1799: "a friendly intercourse shall be maintained with other Protestant Societies engaged in the same benevolent design of propagating the Gospel of Jesus Christ."[39] The spirit of the age is also captured well by the Baptist missionary William Carey, who wrote,

> I wish with all my heart, that every one who loves our Lord Jesus Christ in sincerity, would in some way or other engage in it. But in

38. Walls, *Missionary Movement in Christian History*, 252.

39. Shenk, "Rufus Anderson and Henry Venn," 168.

> the present divided state of Christendom, it would be more likely for good to be done by each denomination engaging separately in the work, than if they were to embark in it conjointly. There is room enough for us all . . . and if no unfriendly interference took place, each denomination would bear good will to the other, and wish, and pray for its success . . . but if all were intermingled, it is likely that their private discords might . . . much retard their public usefulness.[40]

The overarching desire was to prevent denominational discord from overshadowing the greater work of mission.

A Reflection of Their Place

In chapter 3, it was argued that territoriality arises from one's perspectives, which develop from one's place. How one views the world is shaped by their place in the world. These perspectives manifest in organizational structures, strategies, and territoriality. Walls makes a similar point, noting that the missionary movement "was the product of a particular phase of Western political and economic development."[41] He attributes part of this structural change to the influence of North Americans. His description resonates with Sack's spatial analysis: "Nineteenth-century American Christianity developed in a setting of apparently limitless space. In these circumstances it could be expansive and effective only by being entrepreneurial. Ponderous strategies on a continued wide basis, tight control by hierarchical bodies, were likely to be as self-defeating as the European tendency to think in terms of the parish as 'territory.' North American Christianity became pluriform and diffuse."[42] The difference between Europe and America, as Walls describes it, lies not merely in culture but in what Sack would identify as the interaction between the physical and the social dimensions of geography. Here, the realm of the physical (specifically space) is intermixed with the realm of culture (mental and social) creating difference that effected the territoriality of the missionary movement. The North American encounter with vast, seemingly empty landscapes fostered a more diffuse and adaptive organizational outlook, yet it did not eliminate territorial thinking. The concept of *limitless space* is but another way of describing Sack's notion of

40. Walls, *Missionary Movement in Christian History*, 247.

41. Walls, *Missionary Movement in Christian History*, 226.

42. Walls, *Missionary Movement in Christian History*, 229.

empty space—a concept deeply rooted in the European imagination and carried forward by those who settled and dominated U.S. territory. Their experience of this new geography prompted new ways of conceiving land and space, which in turn influenced how they envisioned and enacted the missionary task.

Along with the geography of the US, the form of government is also noted by Walls as having an influence on missionary societies. He quotes Rufus Anderson as saying, "the voluntary society is peculiar to modern times, and almost to our age. Like our own form of government, working with perfect freedom over a broad continent, it is among the great results of the progress of Christian civilization."[43] Here Anderson draws a parallel between the perspectives that shaped the formation of the missionary society and the newly created governmental arrangements of the United States. Walls observes that Anderson "has no compunction in associating American governmental theory, American continental expansion, and the providential direction of the Holy Spirit."[44] Missionary societies and their efforts were shaped by the places that initiated these activities. Walls points to the role of governmental philosophies and the topography of the US as two examples of this influence.

Sanneh describes the situation in the US as dominated by "the voluntary association: lay-led, marker-researched, popularly supported, self-assured, self-funded, task-oriented, goal-driven, individually motivated, close-monitored and self-documented."[45] From this description, the kind of control that is established is of a secondary territoriality. Similar to other territorialities, or business. This dynamic unfolds spatially on a large scale, but it also shapes smaller scales—determining locations, influencing what is built, and deciding who goes where. Sanneh notes, "the same principle of machinery, of tool-making, of religion as a marketable commodity, applied as much to frontier evangelism on the home front as it did to mission in foreign parts. The whole enterprise separately and jointly rested on confidence in proven methods and achievable goals."[46] For those making decisions, their particular place impacted their perspectives on world evangelism and helped to form their methodology for approaching mission.

43. Walls, *Missionary Movement in Christian History*, 225–26.

44. Walls, *Missionary Movement in Christian History*, 226.

45. Sanneh, *Encountering the West*, 193.

46. Sanneh, *Encountering the West*, 193.

Territoriality as Subversive Subdivision and Outward Expansion

On a whole, the voluntary missionary societies "subverted all the classical forms of Church government, while fitting comfortably into none of them."[47] The established church structures were the fruit of an earlier secession movement, the Reformation. At that time, the forms and structures had been carefully crafted by theologians who wanted to get church polity right. They were quite certain they had. "People had spent themselves for the sake of the purity of these forms, had shed their blood for them, had been on occasion ready to shed the blood of others for them. And then it suddenly became clear that there were things–and not small things, but big things, things like the evangelization of the world–which were beyond the capacities of these splendid systems of gospel truth."[48] For all their theological capabilities their vision for Christianity's global range was limited. The inability of these structures to meet the needs of the missionary movement further necessitated the need for a new structure. Walls perceives the dynamic as "one of God's theological jokes, whereby he makes tender mockery of his people when they take themselves too seriously."[49]

As missionary societies were flattening the hierarchy of the establishment, they were also expanding their territory outward. Walls states that one of the "revolutionary effects of missionary societies on the Church was "adding an international dimension which hardly any of the churches, growing as they did within a national framework, had any means of expressing."[50] As long as the missionary societies were ostensibly partnering with the churches, their efforts were received as advancing the same Christian faith. They may be marginal to the primary ministerial work, but they were still of some value particularly as they underscored the superiority of Christianity over other religious systems.

In the example of missionary societies, territoriality is present prior to the formation of the societies, and territoriality is also used to reorganize these power arrangements. In a sense, this example picks up in the middle of one territoriality and the beginning of another. The subversive character of missionary societies allowed them to navigate a form of secession that kept them part of the church while lessening the church's functional control of their organization. This allowed them to extend their reach geographically

47. Walls, *Missionary Movement in Christian History*, 247.

48. Walls, *Missionary Movement in Christian History*, 247.

49. Walls, *The Missionary Movement in Christian History*, 246.

50. Walls, *The Missionary Movement in Christian History*, 253.

and beyond the prior models of territorial ministry familiar to Christians of Christendom. From the organizational structures of the missionary society emerged their spatial counterpart: the mission station.

EXAMPLE: MISSION STATIONS

Establishing a Foothold

Walls portrays early missionary societies as subversive, scrappy egalitarians who were often dismissed within their home circles. Sanneh highlights a different angle, that in many ways, "mission represented power."[51] Organized mission efforts were well-connected, well-funded, and had at their disposal a "network of economic contacts and global outreach far superior to the subsistence economies and sporadic tribal councils of pre-industrial, pre-literate societies." He concludes, "in terms of sheer power, missions were without rival in the field."[52] This power took spatial form in territorial strategies to influence on the world stage.

Initially, the close association with trading companies meant that the territorial strategies of mission organizations were closely linked with port cities. As they moved into *the interior* some mission organizations recommended intensive occupation of one region, while others took a linear expansion strategy, and various other strategies followed. Prioritization also bounced back and forth from the city to the interior. The variety of territorial strategies suggests the tendency toward "innovation and adaptation" to meet the needs of a particular place.[53] This chapter will focus on three examples of different physical expressions of outward territorial expansion. The first of those strategies to be considered is the mission station.

To understand how mission stations were able to establish a foothold in a location requires further consideration of the dynamics that existed between primary and secondary territorialities. Walls and Sanneh highlight how the agents of mission organizations and European states tended to be parallel actors within territorial locations. Their proximity and familiarity produced both collaboration and conflict. While many European nations would still claim to be a Christian country the intentional promotion of the faith was mainly the church's responsibility. Public policy no longer included extending Christendom. At the same time, "the logistics of the

51. Sanneh, *Disciples of All Nations*, 210.

52. Sanneh, *Disciples of All Nations*, 210.

53. Walls, *Missionary Movement in Christian History*, 229.

missionary movement, the business of getting its personnel to viable overseas stations, still depended very much on the use of British facilities."[54] While the overt policy of throne and altar partnership was no longer in place, the loyalty to one's countrymen created instances that continued to mirror the prior arrangement.

Mission organizations differ from a primary territoriality, which possesses the capacity to direct military force to achieve its aims. As a secondary territoriality, mission organizations were not seeking this level of control over an area. Missionaries thought in terms of spiritual warfare where the spiritual possession or spiritual occupation of territory was the aim. In a sermon published around 1837, Rufus Anderson stated, "Never, till now, did the social condition of mankind render it possible to organize the armies requisite for the world's spiritual conquest."[55] The territoriality expressed by mission organizations relied less on force, while still exerting substantial influence. When necessary, however, those operating under a secondary territoriality could appeal to the power of a primary territoriality to supply the force they themselves lacked. Nigeria in the mid-nineteenth century provides one such example. Missionaries had seized sacred meeting spaces for their own Sunday services without permission or invitation. When the Efik population became angry, the missionaries requested military support from the British. "For their recalcitrance," the naval gunners of the *HMS Antelope* "razed the town."[56] It was not an isolated incident. When missionaries encountered resistance or mistreatment, local populations were reminded that they "would incur the extreme displeasure of the Queen of England" if harm came to her citizens. Sanneh concludes, "in a relatively short space of time, missionaries completely subdued Creek Town and the adjoining country."[57] Even as a secondary territoriality, the spiritual aims of a mission organization were never entirely disentangled from the political mechanisms of empire.

Sanneh uses these examples to illustrate how the British government and missionaries collaborated in places like Nigeria. Yet he also points out that the opposite was sometimes true, such as when the British supported the flourishing of Islam within Her Majesty's territories. Such decisions revealed that the two entities pursued distinctly different aims. Sanneh

54. Walls, *The Cross-Cultural Process in Christian History*, 200.

55. Walls, *Missionary Movement in Christian History*, 223.

56. Sanneh, *Disciples of All Nations*, 132.

57. Sanneh, *Disciples of All Nations*, 133.

describes how J. Spencer Trimingham was frustrated—not because Britain, as a Christian nation, was failing to give missionaries the advantage, but because British policy appeared to privilege Muslims over Christians in regions far from home.[58] As a result, "the differential outcome of colonial rule was that Islam prospered while Christianity faltered. Christianity was quarantined."[59]

Missionaries entered places like Africa seeking to have a profound influence. As they sought to establish a foothold in the location they were not alone. While independent they had a safety net of military force that often was there when things went wrong. The missionary enterprise was thus never an entirely independent endeavor. Even as it sought spiritual transformation, it operated within the gravitational pull of empire—sometimes protected by it, sometimes constrained by it. The missionary station exemplified this entanglement, serving as both a spiritual outpost and an instrument of territorial control.

Station Strategy

Within the broader framework of missionary territoriality, the station represented a concrete and enduring strategy for establishing presence. Sanneh states that "the stationary mission station" was "the model structure for establishing Christianity in foreign lands."[60] Though missionary stations are a small-scale territorial strategy, scales can be linked and decisions and actions on one level can reverberate in scales above or below. In the last chapter, it was shown that small scale reform efforts in time came to influence larger scales. Ingie Hovland in her *Mission Station Christianity: Norwegian Missionaries in Colonial Natal and Zululand, Southern Africa 1850–1890*, found something similar with mission stations. She argues that "the plots of land that they had taken hold of–the mission stations–soon came to 'take hold' of them . . . the spaces that they carefully fashioned, in turn came to fashion them."[61] The creation and maintenance of mission stations influenced how missionaries thought about themselves and the people they intended to convert. Hovland identifies a connection between mission stations and the furthering of colonial rule. In this way, there was a reciprocal relationship between smaller and larger scales.

58. Sanneh, *Summoned from the Margin*, 186.
59. Sanneh, *Summoned from the Margin*, 187.
60. Sanneh, *Disciples of All Nations*, 230.
61. Hovland, *Mission Station Christianity*, 20.

The missionaries who were the subject of Hovland's research chose to set up their "material existence" in fixed structures, distinct and separate from the Zulus, on land granted by colonial administration.[62] While mission stations seem ubiquitous for the era, Hovland lays out alternatives that were considered. Missionary conferences from the period reveal that initially the prospect of itinerancy was held in high regard among the Norwegian missionaries.[63] Establishing one base of operations along the coast would by far have been the most economical option. From there traveling missionaries could be sent out to teach, preach, and evangelize. Alternatively, they could have abandoned itinerancy and chosen to become more rooted among the Zulus.[64] The missionaries could live among the people adopting manners of dress, lifestyle, and eating habits. At a minimum, the missionaries could have built a sufficient relationship with locational leaders to allow them to live among them, even if they refrained from adopting cultural symbols. These options were all rejected.

The clear preference for permanent mission stations became a pattern. Hovland states that while missionaries from the US and Europe came to South Africa with a variety of strategies in mind, "by 1880 they had all, without exception, chosen to concentrate primarily on the work of their mission stations."[65] When there was itinerancy "the primary purpose of these expeditions was to assess the feasibility of establishing a new station in the area that the missionary traveled to."[66] Stations were intentionally Christianized space, on which the missionaries deeply depended.

The construction of mission stations had the symbolic effect of reification or "making the Christian God's presence visible."[67] Yet with this visibility, the physical expression also symbolized an otherness that stressed the distance between the people and God. For example, Hovland notes that while homes nearby were built in a round shape, the missionaries built rectangular buildings. "This difference was clearly desired by the missionaries in Southern Africa, who took rectilinearity to be a structuring principle in general–as they emphasized not just straight buildings but also straight pews, classroom seating, hemlines, and lines of print, not to

62. Hovland, *Mission Station Christianity*, 35.
63. Hovland, *Mission Station Christianity*, 6.
64. Hovland, *Mission Station Christianity*, 29.
65. Hovland, *Mission Station Christianity*, 6–7.
66. Hovland, *Mission Station Christianity*, 6.
67. Hovland, *Mission Station Christianity*, 39.

mention bearing and gaze."[68] By reinforcing their foreignness, the missionaries socially distanced themselves, and by extension their God, from the Zulus they hoped to convert.

Hovland's observations align with Sanneh's general description that mission stations were, "little bits of Europe rolled up and transplanted to a foreign country."[69] Sanneh remarks that for many missionaries, living among the people was understood to be "impossible."[70] As a consequence, the missionaries isolated themselves from being influenced by the place. Of the three forces that contribute to the uniqueness of a place, the missionaries had minimized the interaction with the social and mental realms and focused on adapting to the physical realm by forms and structures familiar to them. They only imagined influence flowing in one direction but failed to realize how this choice even inhibited that possibility. It is for this reason that Sanneh states, "geographical range affected little of the imaginative capacity for intercultural exchange or the willingness for equality."[71]

The establishment of these highly separate spaces for missionaries created a significant and physical contrast that served as a metaphor for conversion. Sanneh describes how stations further emphasized the foreignness of God, salvation, and heaven. Conversion was communicated as a "call to renounce non-Western customs" while "the kingdom of heaven fetched pictures in the mind stirringly reminiscent of the prime real estate known as the Home countries."[72] Consequently, "missions subordinated Christ to their social preconditions, conditions that favored stationary centers built under European direction . . ."[73]

68. Hovland, *Mission Station Christianity*, 43.

69. Sanneh, *Disciples of All Nations*, 220.

70. Sanneh, *Disciples of All Nations*, 219.

71. Sanneh, *Disciples of All Nations*, 139.

72. Sanneh, *Disciples of All Nations*, 220.

73. Sanneh, *Disciples of All Nations*, 228. There are examples of structures created by Christians that were built intentionally to downplay foreignness. The All Saints Church in Peshawar, built in coordination with the Church Missionary Society in 1883, had architecture that folded in Islam and Hindu notions of religious spatial construction. Walls summarizes this approach saying, "the less the effect of foreignness is paraded before them . . .the more likely are they to reflect on the central concerns which are the reason for the Christian buildings' existence" (182). All Saints Church was not a citadel of separation, but a space created to communicate belonging in a larger scale of context. Walls, *Missionary Movement in Christian History*, 177.

Territoriality in Christian Faith and Mission

Territoriality Begets Territoriality

The physical structures associated with missionary activity were initially multipurpose spaces—a home for the missionary, a worship space, a hospital, and a school. In time these spaces were *thinned out*, to use Sack's language. This is to say, they were physically separated into places with their own particular functions. Buildings became compounds with structures for all the different initiatives under way. This tendency was mirrored in personnel, who were increasingly specialized workers. Walls notes that "missions had become a means not only of planting churches but of servicing a huge international network with educational, medical, social, industrial, translational, and many other branches."[74] Mission organizations had begun as relatively flat hierarchical structures compared to the church. Now they were becoming increasingly stratified and hierarchically complex. The need for more organization and discipline led to increased need for territoriality to structure their efforts. As territoriality begat more territoriality the momentum changed the organizations.

There was a rapid increase in the purview of the missionary's role and the enlargement of the missionary enterprise into separate branches which further weighed down missionary organizations. Sanneh writes,

> Large institutions, guilds, clubs, halls, and structures were created and staffed with an army of expensive recruits. Heavy machinery was purchased, transported, and, at great cost, maintained by skilled expatriate specialists who were brought into remote areas that had scarcely the means to inherit or to perpetuate such top-heavy elaborate infrastructure. Missions were consumed in the creation of offices and departments, with directors, clerks, and accountants, divided and subdivided. Organization was an end in itself by overshadowing the end for which it existed.[75]

More always seemed necessary, and as the physical imprint grew so did the organizational hierarchy.

Consider, as an example, missionary medical activity. The first hospitals began in the missionary's home but "rapidly developed into large and ambitious institutions."[76] Specialized medical professionals were brought to work alongside trained clergy and the number of staff grew

74. Walls, *The Missionary Movement in Christian History*, 257–58.

75. Sanneh, *Disciples of All Nations*, 226.

76. Walls, *The Cross-Cultural Process in Christian History*, 229.

exponentially. With increased specialization of professionals came increased standardization of facilities and equipment. Furthermore, sending medical professionals without hospitals seemed to be "an inefficient use of medical personnel." Yet this could increase the size of the operation as "a hospital implied building, equipment, qualified nursing staff, [and] training facilities for local staff."[77] Younger medical professionals also wanted to use the newer technology on which they had been trained.[78]

The descriptions that both Walls and Sanneh provide demonstrate how territoriality has a tendency to multiply and complexify to the point of exhaustion. Organization became an end rather than a means to an end. Increasing specialization, standardization, formalization, and hierarchy occurred. This momentum, once started, is hard to slow. Sanneh states that "missionaries' love of organization" meant that "the effectiveness and continuity of missionary work depended on the strength and continuity of organization."[79] They expected that all of their programs, buildings, institutions, and organization would lead to spiritual results. At a certain point the increasing territoriality undercuts the organization's aims, it becomes inefficient and encourages secession or reorganization.

Henry Venn noticed this tendency toward increased organizational expansion and feared the lack of sustainability. Increased territoriality was shifting the priority away from evangelism and toward programmatic pastoral care. The growing responsibility for managing all this increase, inhibited progress toward "the regions beyond."[80] Venn was concerned that this was the parish model imported unnecessarily.[81] His desire was to see converts create their own ecclesiastical structure rather than have one imposed by external agents. They would know the best way, through "the operation of the Holy Spirit" to organize themselves based on their own resources.[82] Doing otherwise failed to allow converts the opportunity to construct their own ecclesiastical structure. Sanneh shares this misgiving, "It was the diocesan structure transferred root and branch to conditions unlike anything in Europe. In a nominally Christian society, such as Europe, synods, church councils, committees, schools, halls, and bureaucratic organizations were what you needed to shepherd a flock largely anonymous

77. Walls, *The Cross-Cultural Process in Christian History*, 215.

78. Walls, *The Cross-Cultural Process in Christian History*, 229.

79. Sanneh, *Disciples of All Nations*, 226.

80. Shenk, *Henry Venn: Missionary Statesman*, 46.

81. Shenk, "The Contribution of Henry Venn to Mission Thought," 38–39.

82. Shenk, "The Contribution of Henry Venn to Mission Thought," 38–39.

and largely irregular in its religious habits."[83] It is for this reason that Venn "attacked the dangers of the mission-station approach" and formulated his convictions of the self-supporting, self-governing, and self-propagating church.[84]

One way to look at Venn's advocation for self-supporting, self-governing, and self-propagating is as a means of limiting custodial territoriality for the purpose of territorial advancement in another location. These principles were an expression of an awareness of limitations. Mission organizations were not to be building Christian empires, even as they likely imagined that Christianity would have significant political influence. Venn's intention was to relieve the societies of the ongoing custodial control and responsibility for the churches established by missionaries. It is to Venn's credit that he kept himself from attempting to do what was so common among Europeans of this era—making unilateral decisions at a distance about how to divide space, group people, and define places.

While Venn had his doubts, others doubled down on the mission station approach but took the idea in a new direction. They felt that mission stations could be a means of reaching further into the interior.

Chain of Stations

In "The Location of Christian Missions in Africa" published in the *Geographical Review*, Hildegard Binder Johnson points to a shift in how collections of mission stations were arranged.[85] Where once there was a preference for a concentration of stations in a single location, increasingly mission stations were being arranged in a strategic linear expansion or chain approach. While mission stations were a smaller-scale physical structure, the move toward a linear strategy to penetrate a larger region shows how scales are not isolated but linked. A smaller-scale strategy can move up scales to influence a larger area, as was the case here.

The arrangement of stations into a linear formation served different strategic purposes. Some lines envisioned connecting pilgrims to Jerusalem; some served to advance to the unknown interior bringing Christian civilization and hindering the slave trade; still others were part of a competitive scheme to stop the influence of other religious groups. In each case,

83. Sanneh, *Disciples of All Nations*, 230.

84. Shenk, "Rufus Anderson and Henry Venn," 171.

85. Johnson, "The Location of Christian Missions in Africa."

chains of stations were understood to be an important strategy for promoting and protecting one's religious interests.

In the 1836 Annual Report of the American Mission Board, a very early rendering of this idea begins to take form. Several lines of advance to the interior were proposed. With respect to Africa the author writes, "the Board propose, the Lord granting permission, to advance northward till our line of missions from the west and south shall meet . . .the proposed line of operations from Cape Palmas to Port Natal is about 4,500 miles."[86] So limited was their geographic understanding at this point that they imagined the potential to run into "a great southern Sahara" in the Congo basin.[87] The rationale for this chain of stations was to reach the center of the continent. There were also several lines proposed for Asia.[88] R. Pierce Beaver, writing in 1962, notes these early plans, but Klaus Fielder points to another as the first to make progress on this strategic territorial approach.[89]

Christian Friedrich Spittler has been identified as one of the earliest proponents of this kind of strategic linear expansion.[90] In 1840, he founded the Pilgrim Mission of St. Chrischona in Switzerland around the idea of "Christian journeymen" going out into the world as itinerant evangelists.[91] Many of those trained went to work among the migrant laborers of North America but increasingly attention was turned toward Palestine.[92] Chris-

86. American Board of Commissioners for Foreign Missions, "Meeting," 110.

87. American Board of Commissioners for Foreign Missions, "Meeting," 110.

88. The annual report reads, "In Asia, the Board have another great line of missions marked out for the enterprise of the churches. The line begins at Constantinople, or rather in Macedonia; runs through the northern districts of Asia Minor, through Persia and Afghanistan, down through western and southern India to Ceylon. On this line we have stations already at Constantinople, two in Asia Minor, one or two in Persia, three in western India, one in southern India, and a number in Ceylon; and a missionary has been appointed to Rajpootana, higher up the line in western India . . . Another line commerce in Greece, passes through the southern districts of Asia Minor, through Syria and Palestine to Mesopotamia. On this line three stations have been formed among Greeks, one in Asia Minor, and two in Syria and Palestine . . . Another series of missions has been projected and commenced in eastern Asia and the neighboring archipelago. The central point is Singapore, at which a station has been formed. The plans of the Committee, however, concerning the vast field of which this is at present the geographical, commercial, and religious centre, are not matured, and cannot be without more facts," "American Board of Commissioners for Foreign Missions, Meeting," 110.

89. Beaver, *Ecumenical Beginnings in Protestant World Mission*, 52.

90. Fielder, *The Story of Faith Missions*, 73.

91. Lehmann, "The Mobilization of God's Pious Children," 195.

92. Lehmann, "The Mobilization of God's Pious Children," 195.

tians were interested in evangelizing the Jewish inhabitants, and Spittler established a missionary society toward this aim.[93] Around the 1840s, the entrepreneurial Spittler conceived "a series of twelve safe places for pilgrims on the road" running from Abyssinia to Jerusalem.[94] The stations of the *Apostles Street*, as he called it, would be maintained by evangelists from St. Chrischona who would witness to and provide care for pilgrims along their journey. This orientation toward Jerusalem reflected Spittler's belief "that the Second Coming was imminent and that the returning Christ would make his first appearance in Jerusalem."[95]

Lehmann notes that some rivalry existed between Spittler's Pilgrim mission school and the older Basel Mission Society.[96] While the schools were located near each other, they represented very different spatial approaches. Johnson describes how the Basel Mission preferred "intensive occupation of small regions" while Spittler's linear strategy was set in contrast to this norm.[97]

Spittler's chain, smaller in scale and oriented toward Jerusalem, contrasted with Johann Ludwig Krapf's vision. Krapf saw mission stations as part of a large-scale means of evangelizing Africa.[98] Around 1850 he began to imagine the potential for a chain of stations running east to west across the continent. His hope was to have nine stations with fifty-mile intervals between them stretching from Rabai near Mombasa to Gabon.[99]

The purpose Krapf gave for this strategic linear expansion was to offer "the blessing of Christian civilization" and to inhibit the slave trade.[100] His

93. Schlienz, *The Pilgrim Missionary Institution of St. Chrischona*, 21. Lehmann, "The Mobilization of God's Pious Children," 195.

94. Lehmann, "The Mobilization of God's Pious Children," 195.

95. Lehmann, "The Mobilization of God's Pious Children," 197.

96. Lehmann, "The Mobilization of God's Pious Children," 195.

97. Johnson, "The Location of Christian Missions in Africa," note on pg 177.

98. Pirouet, "The Legacy of Johann Ludwig Krapf," 69.

99. Beaver, *Ecumenical Beginnings in Protestant World Mission*, 72.

100. Krapf, *Travels, Researches, and Missionary Labors*, 210. There was a natural association between missionary societies and the abolitionist efforts in several locations of Africa. Both were developed out of the experience of engaging people of other locations and cultures and the desire that this engagement would reflect Christian convictions. Sanneh charts the way these two efforts worked in coordination in his *Abolitionists Abroad*. The message of Christianity was but one tool that abolitionists efforts employed. Other solutions included developing new forms of economic opportunity and creating settlements of those who were emancipated or those so-called recaptives who had been intercepted on their way across the Atlantic. Likewise, "missionaries believed that only

rationale was that, "if more attention were given to the formation of a chain of such missions through Africa, the fall of slavery and of the slave-trade with America and Arabia would be quickly and thoroughly effected."[101] With these stated reasons in mind, it should not be overlooked that Krapf was also an explorer and his journals were filled with geographic descriptions of inland lakes and snow-covered mountains. Pirouet notes that, "British geographers who had never been near Africa argued fiercely about their findings, and these writings whetted the appetites of geographers and travelers and encouraged exploration of the interior."[102] It seems possible that his desire to press inward was built on multiple motivations.

Krapf was never able to see much realization of his strategy and instead by 1863 he was drawn into achieving Spittler's design of the Apostle's Road.[103] He states that, "thus the African continental mission chain will be started from the north instead of from east to west, as I had originally contemplated."[104] Yet he was optimistic that this was the beginning of greater things. From the furthest station of the Apostle's Road in Abyssinia, "other stations will be hereafter established toward the south, east, and west of Africa, as it shall please Providence to show the way."[105] This was indeed the case.

Soon others, likewise focused particularly on the interior, carried the linear expansion model forward. Johnson states that, "many missionaries who remained bound to the coast expressed ideas of strategic linear expansion."[106] She lists several attempts at chain stations: John Leighton Wilson in Gabon created three stations headed toward Zanzibar, George Grenfell sought to link several stations in the Congo to stations in Uganda,

---

the safety valve of civilization could control the flow of Christian ideas and values and safeguard the religion from syncretism," Sanneh, *Disciples of All Nations*, 210.

101. Krapf, *Travels, Researches, and Missionary Labors*, 210.

102. Pirouet, "The Legacy of Johann Ludwig Krapf," 71.

103. While Fielder suggests that Krapf was influenced by Spittler in his formation of the chain concept, it seems possible that he came to the plan independently and then adjusted, Fielder, *The Story of Faith Missions*, 73. Krapf makes regular geographic commentary that uses the language of "chains," such as "chain of lakes." Krapf, *Travels, Researches, and Missionary Labors*, xxxi and "chain of mountains," 138 and 316. One could say he thought in terms of chains.

104. Krapf, *Travels, Researches, and Missionary Labors*, n 133.

105. Krapf, *Travels, Researches, and Missionary Labors*, n 133.

106. Johnson, "The Location of Christian Missions in Africa," 177.

and William Taylor had five stations between Luanda and Malanga.[107] One could add to this the efforts of Peter C. Scott of African Inland Mission, who hoped to establish stations from Mombasa to Lake Chad.

Fielder states that "the chain idea" was one of the "strong motivating visions for the early faith missions."[108] So as not to be in competition with the older missionary organizations in the coastal areas, faith missions distinguished themselves by including the world *Inland* or *Interior* in the name of their organizations: China Inland Mission, Africa Inland Mission, Congo Inland Mission, Sudan Interior Mission.[109]

Competition also played an important role in the development of strategic linear expansion. While Spittler's and Krapf's approaches classified territory and sought to influence places, the growing emphasis on competition demonstrated increased enforcement. A chain of stations was designed to pass through the whole of West Africa to stop the southern advance of Islam. Fielder states that "a barrier against the advance of Islam . . . was one of the basic ideas of the Sudan missions."[110] Similarly, Walls tells how some "begged for missionary reinforcements to stem a tide of Islamic advance they expected (an expectation not always justified by the event.)"[111] The objective "was to 'occupy,' that is to get there first."[112] Protestants were additionally concerned about the Catholic advance but "since the Catholics entered Africa from various points, a barrier was not possible."[113] Instead, "one could try to 'be ahead of them' or 'not leave an area to the Catholics alone.'"[114] There was also competition between different Protestant organizations. In the Congo, Johnson describes how Protestant missionaries rushed "neck to neck" to reach the interior body of water now known as Pool Malebo.[115]

Missionaries thought strategically about the placement of mission stations in relation to other religious bodies. There was a rush to setup mission stations and to establish a religious presence in a place before others. The

107. Johnson, "The Location of Christian Missions in Africa," 177.
108. Fielder, *The Story of Faith Missions*, 78.
109. Fielder, *The Story of Faith Missions*, 126.
110. Fielder, *The Story of Faith Missions*, 78.
111. Walls, *The Cross-Cultural Process in Christian History*, 154.
112. Walls, *The Cross-Cultural Process in Christian History*, 154.
113. Fielder, *The Story of Faith Missions*, 78.
114. Fielder, *The Story of Faith Missions*, 78.
115. Johnson, "The Location of Christian Missions in Africa," 175.

chain of stations approach demonstrates a view of territory as empty of that which is religiously meaningful and therefore in need of being filled before others attempt to do so. It took the form of religious or denominational competition over land and it was built on "the conviction that 'time [was] more essential than concentration.'"[116] The emerging competitive spirit demonstrated that even as a secondary territoriality, the perceived need of enforcement was present–perhaps increasing.

With the pressure to outpace Islam, one could imagine that Muslim teachers followed a similar strategy. This was not the case. Christian missionary effort emphasized organizational tools, physical structures, and material things. Sanneh comments that "while the missionaries labor at these material things, Muslims advance by their own spiritual power."[117] He quotes missionary William Maude's comparison of his own practice to that of Islamic teachers in The Gambia around 1910.

> The Mohammedan teacher is everywhere. He needs no society behind him, no funds to sustain him. He goes forth as the first Christians went with his staff and his wallet, and wherever he goes he is at home! . . . The Christian teacher goes as a stranger among foreigners and must be supported from without . . . Even the native ministers and European missionaries show not only lack of special training but want of sympathy and local knowledge . . . a certain aloofness and assumption of superiority [leads them to think] "I belong to a superior race. I condescend to come among you but should never think of living with you or even eating with you."[118]

The missionary's conclusion to this observation is that missionaries must become more neighborly. Around this time, the Christian ministry of William Wade Harris, provided just such a model.

William Wade Harris

Harris's itinerant and spontaneous ministry was a striking contrast to the stationary approach of European missionaries. Yet Harris "almost single-handedly, in a matter of months, revolutionized the religious life of almost the entire southern Ivory Coast."[119] Harris's ministry was not well contained to national borders. Traveling from Liberia to the jurisdiction of the French

116. Johnson, "The Location of Christian Missions in Africa," 177.

117. Sanneh, *Disciples of All Nations*, 228.

118. Sanneh, *Disciples of All Nations*, 201–2.

119. Walker, *Religious Revolution in the Ivory Coast*, 12.

in Côte d'Ivoire to the English in the Gold Coast and Sierra Leone, he seemed to disregard the colonial delimitations as if they were a meaningless intrusion by an external agent. His experience as a member of the Grebo people may have influenced this thinking. The dividing line that separated Liberia and Côte d'Ivoire was the Cavalla River that ran right through the middle of the social territory of the Grebo people.[120] Sanneh's account of Harris states, "he made Christianity a religion of the open road, a religion without borders, and left introspective Catholic and Protestant missions equally in his debt."[121] 'A religion without borders,' is an appropriate description both geographically and denominationally.

The movement that Harris's ministry inspired did result in the formation of a church that bears his name, but that was not his intent. His ministry also encouraged membership to both Catholic and Protestant churches. According to Sanneh, Harris did not view converts as "denominational prizes" that expanded one particular group's numbers.[122] He was working outside of the denominational and ecclesiastical structure but did not set himself up as in competition to them. He was not sent by any group and not territorially delimited.[123] Sanneh states that, "in his hands, Christianity was loosened from its Western frame and given primal range."[124] Harris shows that Christianity could have a new local beginning that "did not need to be tied to overseas sponsorship."[125]

Harris is also a reminder that "modern African Christianity is not only the result of movements among Africans, but it has been principally sustained by Africans and is to a surprising extent the result of African initiatives."[126] Despite the significant influence of his ministry, colonial administrators saw him as a threat and many missionaries treated him with ambivalence. Sanneh states that "missionary jealousy stands to explain a good deal" of this response.[127] They believed too strongly in the superiority of their own culture and military might and yet the massive movement of Africans to the Christian faith was not by their initiative. As late as 1961, the

120. Walker, *Religious Revolution in the Ivory Coast*, 10.

121. Sanneh, *Disciples of All Nations*, 201.

122. Sanneh, *Disciples of All Nations*, 207.

123. Allen, *The Ministry of Expansion*, 93.

124. Sanneh, *Disciples of All Nations*, 214.

125. Sanneh, *Disciples of All Nations*, 205.

126. Walls, *Missionary Movement in Christian History*, 86.

127. Sanneh, *Disciples of All Nations*, 207.

ministry of Harris was still thought of "under the rubric of non-Christian religions."[128] Sanneh summarizes the situation as follows: "by their aloof self-contentment, missionaries took on the attributes of remote agents with little sensitivity to local people and, by doing so, placed the Gospel beyond reach, threatening to make it irrelevant. Harris and his transnational movement averted such a negative outcome for Christianity."[129] In the hands of "unofficial agents" like Harris, Africans spread the Christian faith. Sanneh states, "furnished with the Scriptures in the vernacular, Christianity assumed a frontier imperative and commenced its inexorable march across the continent, intersecting the path of colonial advance with a magnetic appeal to African empowerment."[130] In contrast, Sanneh writes of European missionaries as "leaden-footed," another term for their tendency toward being stationary.

Mission Stations and Chains of Stations

Mission stations provide an example of organizing space on a smaller territorial scale. Territory was classified and the spaces were organized according to principles and styles similar to the missionaries' home. Territoriality was used to structure the space according to what goes here and there and what was not allowed. However, as the idea of chain of stations developed, one can see the relationship between different scales. Where building a mission station could be used as a strategy to divide and spiritually conquer a larger area of land. Territoriality could be used to create a barrier of influence against Islam, to discourage other religious expressions from occupying an area, or as a competitive advantage over another mission organization to reach a location.

If Sack is right, that territoriality creates more territoriality, then the expression of this strategy on various scales provides an example. Understanding territoriality at one scale may illuminate territoriality at another scale and the possible connections between these expressions. The shift from mission stations to strategic linear expansion illustrates how missionaries connected small- and large-scale evangelistic designs for Africa, employing territoriality to pursue their aims.

As Christianity's territorial footprint grew on the continent of Africa, the mission station strategy revealed its own limitations by weighing down

128. Sanneh, *Disciples of All Nations*, 197.

129. Sanneh, *Disciples of All Nations*, 213.

130. Sanneh, *Disciples of All Nations*, 143.

societies and inhibiting movement. Missionaries from Europe or the US may have needed mission stations, but ministers like William Wade Harris did not. He could take the more neighborly approach and was not bound by organizational ties or restricted by arbitrary national borders. He initiated what Venn foresaw, a church rising self-supporting, self-governing, and self-propagating.

EXAMPLE: COMITY AGREEMENTS

Comity is one of the clearest examples of how Christians continued to be territorial beyond Christendom. Territory was classified, this was communicated, and steps were taken to achieve outcomes that were measured territorially, and there were instances of enforcement. While Walls and Sanneh do not directly mention comity, this is consistent with the fact that they did not intentionally pursue a line of argumentation regarding continued territorial behavior. Walls makes only a passing reference to the word, and Sanneh leaves it unaddressed.[131] They were instead interested in highlighting the ways that territorial behavior had decreased as Christendom diminished. Without contradicting that narrative, a more complete picture of Christian use of territoriality should consider the example of missionary comity agreements.

Writing in 1962, R. Pierce Beaver's *Ecumenical Beginnings in Protestant World Mission: A History of Comity* argues for the continuation and strengthening of comity agreements at a time when most had already abandoned the practice. While he may not have persuaded many, his work is a helpful starting point for understanding the dynamics associated with comity.

What Is Comity?

Within the realm of Christian and missionary activity, Beaver describes comity as "denominationalism by geography."[132] A similar definition is used by Johnson, who defines comity as "the peaceful areal delimitation of fields."[133] Comity agreements granted territorial rights over a geographic area to denominations or mission organizations. This was not a granting of primary territorial rights, but instead the goal was to create non-competing,

131. Walls, *The Cross-Cultural Process in Christian History*, 51.

132. Beaver, *Ecumenical Beginnings in Protestant World Mission*, 298.

133. Beaver, *Ecumenical Beginnings in Protestant World Mission*, 182.

cooperative secondary territorialities. Comity became a strategic arrangement of the idea expressed by Carey–that there was "room enough for us all."[134]

The term *comity* came into use in the late 1600s, and its meaning was closely associated with respecting international territorial sovereignty.[135] However, Byun understands Protestant comity agreements as modeled on prior Roman Catholic territorial divisions such as the *Inter Caetera*. He argues that "the right of entrustment presupposes the right of pre-occupation and non-interference, thus overcoming rivalry, conflicts and duplication of limited resources of all missionary societies."[136] Protestantism expressed these notions with the use of the term *comity*.

Agreements were set up so that different organizations were not serving in the same place, and so that empty places would be filled. In this way, territoriality was used as a mold to define, fill, and hold a space as empty–as if it were abstract emptiable space. There were four foundational rules that applied to the practice:

1. "That missionary societies should not claim a territory for the purpose of evangelism that they are incapable of occupying."
2. "That the significant cities are considered neutral or common ground territory."
3. "That aside from these cities, no other territory should be classified as neutral."
4. "That societies respect other societies claims of territory and communicate with them if they enter that territory."[137]

The expectations, derived from Anderson and Venn, were that the occupation and custodial responsibility would be short-lived. Furthermore, comity was not intended as protection against those who were unwilling or incapable of fulfilling their responsibility. Beaver explains that, "any mission that failed to fulfill this obligation was bound both to incur the censure of its neighbors and the desire of others to share its field."[138]

134. Walls, *Missionary Movement in Christian History*, 247.

135. Yntema, *The Comity Doctrine with an Introduction*.

136. Byun, "The Influence of Roman Catholic Mission on Comity Agreements," 181.

137. Beaver, *Ecumenical Beginnings in Protestant World Mission*, 54–55.

138. Beaver, *Ecumenical Beginnings in Protestant World Mission*, 282.

According to Beaver, "the practice of comity first appears clearly in the missionary literature in the decade of the 1830s" though the idea of comity predates it.[139] This first recorded example occurred when Wesleyan missionaries and those of the London Missionary Society (hereafter LMS) made an agreement in the South Pacific to contain their work to specific islands and to respect each other's territory. The Wesleyans would have Fiji and the LMS would have Samoa. Beaver provides an optimistic summary, stating that, "four men in a friendly conference on a South Pacific island had contributed decisively to the formation of a pattern that was coming to prevail over wide areas."[140] Beaver does not further discuss the outcomes of this first recorded comity agreement, but, as will be made clearer, their case was indicative of several emerging patterns within the practice of comity.

Many comity agreements grew out of informal networks of relationship among different mission organizations. Friendships and collaborations between missionaries developed based on shared commitments and experience. In light of their commonality, they could gather to study, pray, and find fellowship, thereby creating missionary associations that included multiple denominations within a given location. Awareness of other denominations engaging in mission activities raised questions about cooperation. Was there a way to express unity in Christ while respecting deeply held denominational distinctives? According to Beaver, "the idea of local or regional comity was an early fruit of the intimate fellowship and constant consultation enjoyed by the representatives of the several societies who almost simultaneously took up residence in the great port cities and national or provincial capitals."[141] A broader vision of comity was also being developed by the leadership of several mission societies. The world could be divided in such a way as to "avoid trespassing on each other's work."[142]

The Basis and Extent of the Practice

Calls for a global comity structure were first issued in 1836 by Rufus Anderson. The organized coordination of missionary efforts, he argued, would "speed the total evangelization of the whole world."[143] With effective cooperation, all the empty spaces of the world could be filled by missionaries.

139. Beaver, *Ecumenical Beginnings in Protestant World Mission*, 44.

140. Beaver, *Ecumenical Beginnings in Protestant World Mission*, 45.

141. Beaver, *Ecumenical Beginnings in Protestant World Mission*, 42–43.

142. Beaver, *Ecumenical Beginnings in Protestant World Mission*, 43.

143. Beaver, *Ecumenical Beginnings in Protestant World Mission*, 51.

Some Christian bodies that were more exclusive in their theology, polity, or practices chose not to participate in the agreements. However, from Beaver's perspective, "the practice of comity had long been an almost universal characteristic of the societies and boards which comprise the mainstream of the Protestant foreign missionary enterprise."[144] As the title of Beaver's work suggests, comity formed an important part of the foundation of the ecumenical movement.

Beginning with the voluntary society, missionary activity tended to focus on the beliefs held in common. The foundation of comity agreements was built on this mutual respect among Protestant organizations. They recognized "that God was no discriminator among them, and that the Holy Spirit effected the same fruits through the labors of each and every mission."[145] Their shared vision was articulated as "proclaiming the gospel to every last man on the globe and of fostering a native church in every part of the earth."[146] As a result, they could rejoice in the success of their fellow worker.[147] If a neighboring missionary could be trusted to hold the same central commitment at the heart of their ministry, why should questions of baptism or polity divide the greater unity that is found in Jesus? With so much work to be done, territories could be divided and "responsibilities for evangelistic occupation" could be split between denominations or organizations with similar commitments.[148]

The Goal of a National Church

The development of an independent national church was an important goal that comity could help to achieve. In Beaver's words, "territorial comity was intended first of all to assure responsible evangelistic occupation everywhere and then to be a preliminary step toward a united, independent church in every land."[149] Venn and Anderson's convictions regarding the self-supporting, self-governing, and self-propagating church were becoming more widely accepted as best practice. Beaver summarizes the early intentions as the hope of forming one church enriched by a variety

144. Beaver, *Ecumenical Beginnings in Protestant World Mission*, 272.

145. Beaver, *Ecumenical Beginnings in Protestant World Mission*, 26–27.

146. Beaver, *Ecumenical Beginnings in Protestant World Mission*, 322.

147. Beaver, *Ecumenical Beginnings in Protestant World Mission*, 30.

148. Beaver, *Ecumenical Beginnings in Protestant World Mission*, 322.

149. Beaver, *Ecumenical Beginnings in Protestant World Mission*, 325.

of traditions while being thoroughly "indigenous."[150] The task was not considered complete until a single, spontaneously expanding national church emerged.[151] The planning and expectation of a national church resembled the post-Reformation notion of religious territoriality: it rested on assumptions of domicile—a molded territory, well defined and substantially homogenous.

Reasons for Comity

Distributing Resources Equitably

There were multiple reasons for establishing comity agreements, some more pressing than others. The most urgent concern was the shortage of both missionaries and funds. No single missionary organization possessed the resources necessary to cover the whole world. At the same time, missionary activity was expanding rapidly, raising the possibility that different groups might inadvertently interfere with one another's work. There remained a deep optimism that the knowledge of God would one day flow over the earth, but not an overabundance of missionaries volunteering for service. Something more centralized and coordinated was deemed necessary to promote efficiency and make the best use of limited resources.

In 1885, A.T. Pierson presented a paper entitled "The Problem of Missions and Its Solution." Dana Robert states that "Pierson advocated global organization and a world council of missions to mobilize the resources of Protestantism, to map out the world field, and to distribute resources equitably."[152] The means for achieving this goal lay in assigning responsibility for specific territory to specific denominations.[153] Pierson was affirming the necessity of and the increased practice of comity. Mission activity had developed an ad hoc form of territoriality which was producing an inequality. Some territory was getting more missionaries, more money, and more attention than others. Pierson's hope was that a more organized system would reduce this inequality and distribute resources in a more geographically equitable way. Comity was to "prevent any waste of material through two or more societies occupying the same field or any portion of the same

150. Beaver, *Ecumenical Beginnings in Protestant World Mission*, 275.

151. Beaver, *Ecumenical Beginnings in Protestant World Mission*, 299.

152. Robert, *Occupy Until I Come*, 142.

153. Robert, *Occupy Until I Come*, 130.

field."[154] Promoting comity became a means of faithfully stewarding resources while pursuing ambitious evangelistic goals.

Limiting Confusion

One of the rationales given for comity agreements was the conviction that too many different Christian denominations or mission organizations would muddle the message. If multiple groups were converging in one area, all presenting the gospel with their its particularity on display, was it not possible that this could create confusion among those hearing the message?[155] Consequently, "one great purpose of delimitation of territory was the isolation of denominational differences in order to prevent confusing and distracting the native Christians."[156] The territorial subdivisions were not intended as denominational fiefdoms, though. Delimitation did not imply that missionaries should focus their attention on the particularities of their polity, worship practices, or doctrine. European denominations were not to increase their own brand of Christianity, but to bring the gospel and allow Christianity to rise up in a way thoroughly influenced by the culture and the people of the place. There was an evangelistic obligation that needed to be fulfilled as a first-order priority.

The greater goal that all missionaries were to hold in common was the desire to free the people they served to develop their own "self-supporting institutions of the gospel."[157] Yet this conviction may, in fact, reflect the preference for a "single code of sacred custom" which Walls refers to. It may have made sense from a Western perspective well versed in Christendom and less familiar with pluralism—but in many places, pluralism was not rare. The assumption that multiple voices would create confusion may reveal more about the missionaries' own preferences and the distorting caricatures they held of others.

154. Beaver, *Ecumenical Beginnings in Protestant World Mission*, 35.

155. Beaver, *Ecumenical Beginnings in Protestant World Mission*, 17.

156. Beaver, *Ecumenical Beginnings in Protestant World Mission*, 39.

157. Beaver, *Ecumenical Beginnings in Protestant World Mission*, 31.

Demonstrating Unity

The concern for confusion was part of a larger argument for the necessity of presenting Protestant Christianity as unified. The general consensus was that while Christian unity may be an ideal worth pursuing in places like Europe or the United States, it was considered "vital on the mission field" where disunity would be "a sin and a scandal."[158] In Beaver's estimation, such division would result in "a totally chaotic multiplicity of overlapping and competing agencies."[159] Without a unified approach, it seemed likely that local governments would interpret the divisions among Christian organizations as a threat to their own domestic harmony.[160]

A spirit of unity had characterized earlier Protestant missionary activity. Missionaries could rejoice in each other's successes and find commonality in their shared burden for mission. Comity took this a step further: missionaries coordinated their efforts, dividing territory among themselves to spiritually occupy the land. Through the delimited boundaries of comity agreements, a form of Christian unity was expressed—one that was expected to give way to a "true unity" that would unfold to eventually replace comity.[161] Delimiting territory also provided denominations with a measure of security, clarity in their task, and greater trust between organizations through the decision-making process.

The argument for comity based on Christian unity was also buttressed by theological and biblical rationale. Beaver cites Bishop Jacob Newcastle of the 1897 Nottingham Church Congress, whose conviction regarding comity rested on the foundation of fundamental doctrines: "Admission by baptism into one society, however divided that society may be, and the holding of one faith in the Father, the Son, and the Holy Ghost, seems to me the doctrinal basis of missionary 'comity.'"[162] Comity was also understood as a manifestation of the love of Christ and an expression of Christ's prayer "that all of them may be one, Father, just as you are in me and I am in you. May they also be in us so that the world may believe that you have sent

158. Beaver, *Ecumenical Beginnings in Protestant World Mission*, 34.

159. Beaver, *Ecumenical Beginnings in Protestant World Mission*, 34.

160. Beaver, *Ecumenical Beginnings in Protestant World Mission*, 326.

161. Beaver, *Ecumenical Beginnings in Protestant World Mission*, 280.

162. Beaver, *Ecumenical Beginnings in Protestant World Mission*, 30–31.

me."[163] While comity was only one means of expressing these theological convictions, the arguments were nonetheless compelling.

Comity promised to achieve greater equality, clarity, and unity, yet the implementation of the practice rarely lived up to its ideals. Its eventual breakdown seemed, in retrospect, almost inevitable.

Comity Breaks Down

In the "History and Facts" section of the California Southern Baptist Convention website, the following statement is made regarding the denomination's early efforts in California: "Not much happened in Baptist life for several decades until Southern Baptist work in California began anew on May 10, 1936, when 16 members constituted the First Baptist Church in Shafter."[164] No reason is given for the period during which "not much happened." However, other articles and convention statements reveal that the Southern Baptists had entered into a comity agreement with the Northern Baptists to restrict their territorial expansion.[165] The church in Shafter was, in fact, a breach of this agreement.

The comity breach in Shafter occurred for reasons similar to many other comity breaches—people moved. In this case, a few families from Southern Baptist churches relocated to California and desired to worship in ways that were comfortable and familiar to them. It was not necessarily an intentional effort by the Southern Baptists to expand beyond their recognized territory; rather, it was a somewhat spontaneous development resulting from human migration. The dynamics of denominational expansion within the United States reflected a broader pattern already taking shape around the world.

Consider Bradley Hill's description of evangelism along the Ubangi-Mongala border, a four-hundred-mile-long ecclesiastical boundary that separates various mission organizations in northwestern Zaire, now known as the Democratic Republic of the Congo. He presents a dynamic resembling guerrilla warfare, in which missionaries cautiously crossed comity borders, fearful of repercussions but seeking to rescue religious refugees. Hill writes, "Migrations across comity borders create an ecclesiastical 'refugee problem—the migrants are not of the host community, nor are

163. Beaver, *Ecumenical Beginnings in Protestant World Mission*, 323.

164. "History and Facts," *California Southern Baptist Convention.*

165. Nettles, "Southern Baptists: Regional to National Transition."

their ministers allowed the right of 'hot pursuit' into alien territory."[166] The movement of people created situations that comity agreements were not designed to manage. Violations of the comity agreements occurred, and retaliation followed, calling into question the whole basis of the agreement and frustrating the groups still holding to the principles.

The Problems of Comity

The tendency of humans to move was not well accounted for in comity's formula for world evangelism. It was built instead on the assumption that, aside from missionaries, people tended to remain rooted in their locations. This conceptual tethering of people to place presumed that those of the same ethnicity, culture, and language were contained in a specific area, and there they would stay. Proponents of comity may have acknowledged occasional exceptions, but they concluded that such cases were too few to challenge the principle itself. Indeed, iterations of a similar logic existed long after comity had mostly fallen out of practice.[167] Yet the impact of human migration was underestimated, and as a result, the very foundations of the principle began to crumble. Comity ultimately broke down as missionary and denominational leaders struggled to respond to population growth, increased urbanization, migration, and colonial expansion.

Some of what may have appeared to be the movements of people was actually the result of poorly placed boundary lines subdividing territory. Comity applied a territorial definition of social relationships to places that had far more complex and difficult-to-map social definitions of territory. In general, many of the classifications made by comity agreements revealed how little the decision-makers understood the realities on the ground. The lines of demarcation separating different mission territories were often arbitrary, based on latitude and longitude.[168]

Problems arose when these boundaries proved ill-suited to regions later recognized for their greater social and cultural complexity. For example, missionaries might agree to confine their work to specific islands, but if socioeconomic patterns of contact continually brought those islands within each other's sphere, the delimitation would be exposed as an external rubric

166. Hill, "Rethinking Comity," 175.

167. See McGavran, *Understanding Church Growth.*

168. Burton and Kilgour, *Missionary Survey of the Pacific Islands.*

designed primarily for the missionaries' own purposes and restrictive only to them.[169]

The greatest frustrations arose when comity subdivisions, though initially reasonable, became unsustainable as circumstances changed. Consider how comity agreements classified cities. When two or more mission organizations operated within the same country, the port city or capital needed to be "open ground."[170] Cities were viewed as too large for any single organization and contained resources that were needed by everyone. This system functioned well at first, but problems emerged as populations shifted. Large cities expanded, "erupting over ever-wider areas" encroaching on what had previously been non-neutral territory.[171] At the same time, new urban centers developed in regions once considered rural and already assigned to specific mission organizations.[172]

The Effect of People Moving

The mission *field* was changing, while the boundary lines of comity agreements were working from old maps. This created a number of problems. First, the mission organization assigned to a particular area often lacked the capacity to address the spiritual needs of those migrating into "its" territory. Migrants might speak a different language or belong to a different cultural group. Though they were inside the missionary's designated territory, they were outside missionary's linguistic and cultural knowledge base.

Secondly, there were cases in which a missionary was ministering to a family who later migrated to one of these new cities. Would the missionary have the right to "follow-up" if a discipleship relationship had already been formed? This question was especially pressing given the legitimate concern that those who migrated might remain on the margins of the mission organization responsible for that new territory. Would the evangelistic seed that had been planted be lost in the journey if the relationship were abandoned?

Thirdly, shifting populations often meant that no single mission organization was adequately serving the growing needs of those in the cities. Comity had established a Protestant priority for the countryside, and the

169. Garrett, "The Conflict between the London Missionary Society and the Wesleyan Methodists."

170. Beaver, *Ecumenical Beginnings in Protestant World Mission*, 282.

171. Beaver, *Ecumenical Beginnings in Protestant World Mission*, 289.

172. Beaver, *Ecumenical Beginnings in Protestant World Mission*, 282.

city was consequently neglected. Beaver describes how "in some countries in Africa the missions were reluctant to get into city work, and the fact that a city was in the sphere of another society seemed to excuse them."[173] In this way, comity restrained missionaries even when they recognized unmet needs and possessed the capacity to respond. They were discouraged from doing so out of deference to their territorial container. Consequently, as populations became increasingly mobile, many Protestant missionary societies continued to adhere rigidly to territorial definitions based on outdated information.

The population shift toward cities raised questions about whether comity was facilitating effective evangelism or standing in its way. These developments "raised grave problems of comity," calling its very foundation into question.[174] Comity depended on the trust that if a person under one's care moved to another territory, they would continue to receive spiritual oversight. Yet as circumstances changed, some organizations "claimed the right . . . to 'follow' their people with pastoral ministry into the territory of another mission."[175] This practice of follow-up revealed the tenuous nature of trust between organizations. In response, adjustments to comity were considered.

There may have been ways to preserve the spirit of unity without relying on territorial delimitation, but these adjustments were, in Beaver's view, insufficient. He argued that follow-up practices reflected a form of controlling tutelage by missionaries, which he associated with a "colonial mind."[176] The transition of authority to nationals had become a process of certifying that they had reached the missionary's own standards of maturity.[177] Such observations align with Sanneh's portrayal of missionary tendencies. He notes that "having tasted power at a safe distance from the home board," some missionaries were reluctant to hand over control.[178]

In the city, rather than relaxing the delimitations of territory, Beaver argued that the situation required an even more coordinated and centralized program.

173. Beaver, *Ecumenical Beginnings in Protestant World Mission*, 282–83.

174. Beaver, *Ecumenical Beginnings in Protestant World Mission*, 288, 291.

175. Beaver, *Ecumenical Beginnings in Protestant World Mission*, 273.

176. Beaver, *Ecumenical Beginnings in Protestant World Mission*, 275.

177. Beaver, *Ecumenical Beginnings in Protestant World Mission*, 299.

178. Sanneh, *Disciples of All Nations*, 158.

> These can never be solved by denominational piecemeal efforts which involve wasteful duplication and deny essential Christian unity and mock the message that all preach about the reconciliation which God has granted men in Christ. Not one of the great cities of Asia or Africa has a plan, either long-range or short-term, for total Christian witness and ministry, and in not one of these cities do the local agencies have the resources in men and money to implement such a plan were it made, in face of the population explosion and industrialization of society.[179]

This quotation expresses concern for what could be described as the mismatch and spillover effects of territoriality. The solution, Beaver argues, is for even more territoriality, not less. Increasing territoriality would ostensibly allow for greater centralization and more efficient long-term planning. This reasoning aligns with Sack's observation that the problems created by territoriality are often addressed through the creation of additional territoriality.

Other Movements of Other People

Comity agreements were disrupted by the movements of people to whom missionaries had been assigned. Yet shifting political dynamics and the arrival of missionaries from other organizations also brought a variety of people and concerns to the field. In many countries, one of the most significant political changes affecting comity arose from colonial expansion.

As outlined at the beginning of this chapter, missionary societies, organizations, and denominations represent examples of secondary territoriality. These entities operated as guests under the authority of a primary territoriality. When European powers sought to dominate other parts of the world, they altered the power arrangements in which missionaries functioned. This required missionaries to adjust to new primary territorialities and to navigate an influx of administrative agents and colonial officials.

In British colonies, the Church of England organized and subdivided land according to the diocese model familiar to them. "A diocese was normally coextensive with a large administrative unit, perhaps the whole country, and its responsibility was for the pastoral care of the British officials, commercial community, and probably for the families of the military,

179. Beaver, *Ecumenical Beginnings in Protestant World Mission*, 290–91.

as well as for the mission churches."[180] Missionary efforts may have become marginalized as meeting the spiritual needs of the European colonists took priority. Anglican missionaries also held a form of home-turf advantage over other missionary organizations, as their territorial position could be defended by their compatriot military apparatus.[181] The security and enforcement provided by European powers shaped how missionaries were perceived by the local population. It also undermined their claim that the ultimate goal was a national church characterized by self-governance and decreasing missionary control. It must have been difficult to trust missionaries who spoke of self-governance as soldiers from their own country were marching over the hill.

More Missionaries

An increase in missionaries who were not bound by comity agreements also affected the perceived usefulness of comity itself. There had always been mission organizations that disregarded such arrangements, but as long as most denominations and societies remained compliant, a few outliers caused little concern. Over time, however, the number of supposed outliers grew, and those not participating became numerous enough to make even long-standing supporters of comity question its value when convenient. Some organizations would "claim the protection of comity agreements" when others interfered in their territory, yet excuse their own acts of territorial infringement. This dynamic effectively redefined land previously considered *filled* as once again *empty*.

Situations arose in which missionary expansion into other territories was described as a spontaneous movement of the Spirit. In some locations, missionaries labored with reportedly "no response in a generation," whereas in other areas there was a significant but unmet response because "the workers were too few."[182] Responding to these underserved yet spiritually receptive communities was often framed as obedience to the leading of the Holy Spirit. Such spontaneous expansion stood in contrast to the "monopolistic claim" of organizations operating under comity.[183] Why should some be restrained by territorial limits when so many others were not?

180. Beaver, *Ecumenical Beginnings in Protestant World Mission*, 275.

181. Hovland, *Mission Station Christianity.*

182. Beaver, *Ecumenical Beginnings in Protestant World Mission*, 303.

183. Beaver, *Ecumenical Beginnings in Protestant World Mission*, 308.

Many came to view comity as a plan best suited for the pioneering stage of mission. It proved difficult to maintain, and cross-boundary work seemed inevitable. The effort required to preserve the system no longer appeared justified, particularly when so many organizations chose not to comply.

One of the stated purposes of comity agreements was to restrain the competitive spirit between mission organizations. The ultimate goal of comity was the establishment of a national church, an objective that naturally emphasized the temporary nature of the missionary presence in any given location. In theory, this mitigated competition because missionaries were merely filling a short-term gap until the national church emerged. However, when the national church ideal was abandoned, the missionary presence in a place often became indefinite. Johnson notes that "with increased accessibility, the idea of preempting and invading fields in the interior revived competition . . . in spite of the advocation of comity."[184] Missionaries were also aware of differing stipendiary amounts approved by other societies,[185] and Sanneh observes that new approaches to fundraising "fostered an environment of unhealthy competition."[186] Comity did not succeed in eliminating competitiveness among organizations. In the field, debates persisted over whether an organization was *truly occupying* a space and who held legitimate claim to a given territory.

The Reassertion and Dissolution of Comity

For all of these reasons, those still committed to comity sought ways to withdraw from their agreements without creating ill will. Such concerns, however, seemed hollow to Beaver. He would not be shaken from his initial conviction that "too many agents . . . simply drown out each other's voices."[187] If too many Christian organizations operated in one location, he argued, the message would be lost amid a confusing dissonance. It was better, in his view, for them to be dispersed and remain within their assigned areas.

Beaver held that those who sought to abandon comity were motivated by ambitious expansionism. He regarded appeals to spontaneity as disingenuous, masking a desire for "stature and prestige through expansion."[188]

184. Johnson, "The Location of Christian Missions in Africa," 182.

185. Walls, *Crossing Cultural Frontiers*, 104.

186. Sanneh, *Disciples of All Nations*, 227.

187. Beaver, *Ecumenical Beginnings in Protestant World Mission*, 321.

188. Beaver, *Ecumenical Beginnings in Protestant World Mission*, 306.

Arguments invoking "evangelistic responsibility, spontaneous expansion, the harvest, and the need of follow-up," he claimed, merely concealed imperialist ambitions.[189.] Freed from the territorial constraints of comity, these denominations would pursue geographic growth at the expense of unity. Without delimited boundaries, competition would only intensify, and efforts to cultivate national networks and a truly indigenous church would falter. "Confessionalism blended with the colonial outlook; the expectation of the imminent united, national, indigenous church with a different kind of life faded; and the missionaries indoctrinated the native pastors and the laity with loyalty to the denominational heritage."[190] In his view, spontaneity had become an excuse to "justify an undisciplined or scanty spread of a church body which ought to face its more immediate surroundings with the truth of the gospel."[191] Faithfulness to one's assigned territory was more important than how the inhabitants responded.

In Beaver's view, organizations that refused to cooperate with others were not to be emulated but reasoned with, so that they might understand the value of comity. The unwillingness of some missions to participate did not, in his judgment, invalidate the need to express Christian unity. Nor did the persistence of territorial ambition among missionaries diminish comity's restraining influence. To Beaver, if the older agencies had become immobile, the newer ones were reckless. At best, they ignored churches already established and failed to "see the missionary enterprise in its totality."[192] Moreover, he argued that these newer organizations were indifferent to the ideal of forming national churches and unaware of "the political, cultural, social, and economic circumstances," pursuing instead only verbal proclamation.[193] The second wave of missions was missionary centric, individual convert focused, and, in contradiction to the long-standing principles of comity, were willing to proselytize "among Christians who are the products of other missions."[194]

Tiedemann's review of Christian mission organizations in China corroborates aspects of Beaver's argument. His analysis shows that efforts toward Christian unification often resulted instead in heightened division

189. Beaver, *Ecumenical Beginnings in Protestant World Mission*, 307.

190. Beaver, *Ecumenical Beginnings in Protestant World Mission*, 274–75.

191. Beaver, *Ecumenical Beginnings in Protestant World Mission*, 304.

192. Beaver, *Ecumenical Beginnings in Protestant World Mission*, 294.

193. Beaver, *Ecumenical Beginnings in Protestant World Mission*, 294.

194. Beaver, *Ecumenical Beginnings in Protestant World Mission*, 294.

and competition, which ultimately hindered witness. As Tiedemann observes, "when foreign missionary operations ended in China in the middle of the twentieth century, the Protestant movement was far more divided than it had been at the beginning of that century."[195] It remains difficult to determine with certainty whether comity contributed to this fragmentation or functioned as a restraining force against it.

Another challenge facing the system of comity was the growing need for stronger mechanisms of enforcement. The territoriality of comity agreements rested on goodwill, trust, and gentle persuasion as their principal form of enforcement. Over time, however, these proved inadequate, and the system began to fail "for lack of teeth."[196] Without stronger means of enforcement necessary to ensure compliance among participating organizations, comity was becoming the source of friction not the antidote to it. The 1910 Edinburgh Conference addressed the problem of overlapping mission work, but its proposed solutions did not question whether comity itself might be an insufficient solution to the issues. Instead, the conference called for missionaries to transfer to other organizations if they wished to serve in another territory, for greater clarity of standards, and for stricter disciplinary measures.[197] Once again, the weakness of territoriality was addressed by increasing or clarifying the system of territoriality. This continued until it was clear that most were no longer interested in upholding the system.

It is worth returning to the first recorded comity agreement of 1830, where, as Beaver observes, "four men in a friendly conference on a South Pacific island had contributed decisively to the formation of a pattern that was coming to prevail over wide areas."[198] As it turned out, that pattern included not only the establishment of agreements but also their rather disappointing dissolution. The LMS and Wesleyan comity agreement, which assigned Fiji to the Wesleyans and Samoa to the LMS, was troubled from the outset and completely dissolved by 1857. John Garrett notes that the decision between the LMS and the Wesleyans was made without consulting all the Wesleyan missionaries then serving in Tonga.[199] The boundary

195. Tiedemann, "Comity Agreements and Sheep Stealers," 7.

196. Beaver, *Ecumenical Beginnings in Protestant World Mission*, 309.

197. Beaver, *Ecumenical Beginnings in Protestant World Mission*, 324.

198. Beaver, *Ecumenical Beginnings in Protestant World Mission*, 45.

199. Garrett, "The Conflict between the London Missionary Society and the Wesleyan Methodists," 68.

lines had been drawn by missionaries newly arrived in the region, unaware of the social and economic networks that regularly connected the islands of Tonga and Samoa through trade, marriage, and cultural exchange. The mutual influence was such that Wesleyan Christians in Tonga had already shared their faith and established a church in Samoa prior to European missionary efforts.

By the time the LMS–Wesleyan agreement was ratified in England, Samoan Christians were already requesting Wesleyan teachers from Tonga.[200] The resulting arrangement only intensified political tensions in the region, fostered ill will between missionaries, and frustrated the people of Samoa. That such agreements were so short lived foreshadowed the eventual irrelevance of comity agreements as a whole.

Comity functioned as a territorial strategy designed to achieve certain missiological goals. The outcomes of this approach closely parallel Sack's theory of territoriality, illustrating patterns of classification, enforcement, emptiable and fillable territorial containers, inequality, centralization, and secession (manifested here as noncompliance). As such, comity serves as a compelling example of the persistence of territoriality beyond Christendom.

Beaver was advocating for a system that had largely fallen out of practice. While some may view comity agreements as little more than a fascinating relic of missionary territoriality, Byun contends that understanding comity "poses critical lessons and challenges to today's mission field."[201] His concern is that "many Korean missionaries are repeating the mishaps of Western missionary practices such as denominationalism, wasteful duplication, and competition, creating an atmosphere of discourteous rivalry." He stops short of calling for a renewal of comity, but believes the history of such practice "gives us an admonition of encroaching on the territory of others, which may cause conflict in the mission field today" and "reminds us of the notion of mutual respect and ecumenical unity among the missions as fellow co-workers of God's mission."[202] While Byun is right to call attention to these concerns, any contemporary effort to classify or enforce territorial designation must be approached cautiously, with careful attention to the theory of territoriality and the unintended consequences such strategies may produce.

200. Garrett, "The Conflict between the London Missionary Society and the Wesleyan Methodists," 69.

201. Byun, "The Influence of Roman Catholic Mission on Comity Agreements," 181.

202. Byun, "The Influence of Roman Catholic Mission on Comity Agreements," 182.

It is also worth noting that in some conversations, particularly from ecumenical corners, certain assumptions shape perspectives on the question, "Who is being territorial?" The charge is usually directed toward those who enter another group's space, those who implicitly treat the space as empty until they fill it. Yet this defensive posture overlooks the territorial assumptions embedded in the claims of those already present. It presumes that being first to a location grants ecclesiastical rights of possession and that the space has been sufficiently "filled." These assumptions are just as territorial as the one who's ministry may encroach on another. Theologically these perspectives should be reexamined with the foundational perspective that it is God who fills heaven and earth (Jer 23:24).

The logic of territoriality evident in comity agreements also appears in the decisions made by the leadership of the 1910 World Missionary Conference in Edinburgh.

EXAMPLE: 1910 EDINBURGH MISSIONARY CONFERENCE CLASSIFICATIONS

The conference's initial objective was to "discuss how the Gospel could be proclaimed to the whole world."[203] However, its leaders ultimately chose to divide the world into Christian and non-Christian regions. An important distinction was made, "in reality it is not a Commission on Carrying the Gospel to All the World but a Commission on Carrying the Gospel to the Non-Christian World."[204] These were not abstract or purely conceptual distinctions; they were territorial designations established through maps and demographic statistics.[205] This large-scale, area-based approach to defining Christianity presumably helped quantify the missionary task. According to Walls, the conference leadership "started from the idea of Christendom, of Christianity as territorially based."[206]

The use of the term *Christendom* is not merely an anachronistic label imposed by Walls; it was the language of the conference leadership itself. Brian Stanley notes that "the central question facing the commission was how 'to define Christendom.'"[207] This marked a shift from a time when defining Christendom was based primarily on the principle of *cuius regio,*

203. Stanely, *Defining the Boundaries of Christendom*, 171.

204. Stanely, *Defining the Boundaries of Christendom*, 172.

205. Stanely, *Defining the Boundaries of Christendom*, 172.

206. Walls, "The Significance of Christianity in Africa," 1.

207. Stanely, "Defining the Boundaries of Christendom," 171.

eius religio, "whose realm, their religion."[208] The conference planners were not looking to the monarchy of the respective countries to determine their status as a Christian nation. Instead, they relied on nonpolitical entities that classified regions according to populations and statistical data. Accordingly, the classifications made by the conference leadership had no official standing outside the conference. No country altered its self-understanding based on these designations, and even disagreements among conference attendees were unlikely to be resolved by such designations. Despite the continued use of the term *Christendom* by conference leadership, Christendom had ended. Only the territorial mentality and subsequent territoriality, reminiscent of Christendom, remained.

The classifications established by the conference, along with the controversies they generated, illustrate yet another way territoriality continues to change with different organizations and shifting contexts of power. Compared to the territorial structures of Christendom, the territoriality created by the 1910 conference leadership was more restrained in scale, proportion, and force. Nevertheless, the key elements of territoriality—classification, communication, and enforcement—can still be discerned in Stanley's account of the pre-conference debates over these designations. Of the effects of territoriality related to the conference decisions, the issue of inequality and inaccurate classification were particularly evident.

Evidence of Territoriality

The three markers of territoriality, while subtle, are all present in the designations made by the conference leadership. Classification began when the organizers determined that the conference's focus would not be on mission to the entire world indiscriminately but specifically to the non-Christian places of the world. It would be, in their words, "mission from 'Christendom' to 'heathendom.'"[209] As Stanley observes, "there was no dispute that the two worlds could be differentiated on a territorial basis: the issue was where to draw the boundary."[210] All were in agreement that Europe was Christian territory. The challenge came when considering Christian communities who lived outside Europe. What was to be made of Protestant missionaries serving among communities of Assyrian Christians, Catholics, or the Eastern Orthodox? What about places where Christianity was relatively nominal?

208. Sanneh, *Encountering the West*, 189.

209. Stanely, "Defining the Boundaries of Christendom," 171.

210. Stanely, "Defining the Boundaries of Christendom," 171.

If places like Egypt, Syria, and Turkey were more Muslim than Christian, how were they to be categorized?[211] The subcommittee on statistics did not want vague guidelines; they wanted to determine the exact percentage of Christians required for a place to be called Christian.

What followed was a highly negotiated, political process of boundary-making and classification that took place largely behind closed doors. Decisions were made by men in New York and London who assessed the Christian-ness of locations far removed from their own personal experience. The process was convoluted, producing judgments that were often inconsistent. For some locations, missionaries would be counted, but not their converts. The final classifications were agreed upon, at least in part, to prevent the potential withdrawal of Anglican representatives from the conference. In this instance of territoriality, the pressure exerted by the Anglicans served as a form of enforcement. Their threats of withdrawal were intended to ensure that the demarcation—the classification—aligned with Anglican and Anglo-Catholic preferences. Their intent to influence likely extended beyond this, however. Their conviction was that no missionary should operate in places where other Christians were already at work. Perhaps this was based on their interpretation of biblical texts or from a desire to uphold the spirit of comity. It is also possible that they feared that the more nimble, enthusiastic additions to the missionary landscape may negatively influence their own denominational numbers. Such interpretations may seem cynical, but as Beaver states, a wave of new missionary activity was willing to proselytize "among Christians who are the products of other missions."[212] The Anglicans sought to discourage this, and the conference classifications were one way of making their influence felt.

To keep the unity, the conference leadership would comply with their territoriality. Walls describes the results. "The fully missionized areas were, for practical purposes, Europe, North America, Australia, and New Zealand (Latin America was passed over in silence to avoid splitting the conference on the issue of whether Latin America was really Christian). The rest of the world, including the whole of Africa (save for a small section of South Africa), was deemed not yet fully missionized."[213] The form of territoriality that emerged from the conference both validated and encouraged missionary efforts directed toward so-called *non-Christian places.*

211. Stanely, "Defining the Boundaries of Christendom," 173.

212. Beaver, *Ecumenical Beginnings in Protestant World Mission*, 295.

213. Walls, *The Cross-Cultural Process in Christian History*, 117.

Competition with other Christians was to be avoided, regardless of the depth of Christian commitment within a given location. The decision of the conference leadership was a territoriality designed to influence the choices and approaches of those engaged in missionary activity. This was a particular concern for U.S. missionary organizations, which were acutely aware that such categorizations could either endorse or discredit their work in certain locations.[214]

Inaccurate Classification and Territorial Inequality

The classifications established by the conference leadership were based on faulty assumptions that so-called *fully missionized* lands would remain permanently Christian. Pietistic and evangelical movements within the churches had already begun to challenge this notion. A Methodist hymn written by Charles Wesley employs the understood territorial classifications to expose the hypocrisy of Christendom: "The world, the CHRISTIAN world convince of damning unbelief."[215] The "radicals of Christendom," as Walls describes them, recognized the emptiness of nominal Christian commitment.[216] Yet nominalism eroded even further with the savagery of the so-called Christian nations during the World Wars. Sanneh observes that this period marked "the beginning of a massive loss of confidence, an internal corrosive doubt about the power of the gospel to change the world or the lives of those who controlled the world."[217] Few would have doubted that Germany was as fully missionized as any place missionaries were attempting to evangelize; yet the atrocities committed by this *Christian nation* brought the designation into question.[218]

The notion that there were "fully missionized lands that would continue to form the base for the evangelization of those not yet missionized" came under serious doubt after World War II.[219] The supposed center of Christianity, which had once supplied the energy, resources, and enthusiasm for world evangelization, now faced a crisis of confidence, largely unaware of the monumental developments taking place at what it had considered the periphery. The classification of *Christian land* proved to be a

214. Stanely, *Defining the Boundaries of Christendom*, 173.

215. Soule, *A Collection of Hymns for Public, Social, and Domestic Worship*, 71.

216. Walls, *Crossing Cultural Frontiers*, 51.

217. Sanneh, *Encountering the West*, 195.

218. Sanneh, *Encountering the West*, 195.

219. Walls, *The Cross-Cultural Process in Christian History*, 63.

fleeting designation at best. Such places do not exist in any geographical, political, or spiritual reality, if indeed they ever truly did.

The conference leadership also operated from a view of land as a series of containers corresponding to countries. In theory, dividing the world into Christian and non-Christian places appeared straightforward, but in practice it was far more complex. Some religions fail to be contained well within their borders, and some containers hold more than one religion. This approach inevitably produced issues of mismatch and spillover, as seen in the cases of Egypt, Syria, and Turkey mentioned above. The awkward compromises that followed both reflected and deepened existing inequalities.

The decision made by the conference leadership "restricted the mission of the church and, by implication, the mission of God to certain geographically demarcated portions of humanity."[220] As a result, "Edinburgh 1910 implicitly declared Protestant proselytism of Roman Catholics and, rather less clearly, of Orthodox and Oriental Christians to be no valid part of Christian mission."[221] Stanley concludes that, "the deleterious consequences of that restriction are still being played out."[222]

Walls identifies the classifications regarding Africa as among the most egregious examples of inequality. The rich history of Christianity in Africa predates that of the Europe, and by 1910 even Protestant missionary efforts on the continent were more than a century old. The Anglicans had already elected a bishop of Africa. Yet not only were African countries excluded from the conception and designation of *Christian nations*, the conference itself was devoid of African representation.[223] The conference was attentive to "confessional comprehensiveness" but far less concerned with "ethnic, cultural, and geographical comprehensiveness."[224] How far the leadership fell short of their own ideals. As Hans P. Andersen noted in a letter to John R. Mott, although the scope of the conference was limited to the non-Christian world, "the title 'World Missionary Conference' does not have reference to the field but to the participants."[225] That participation consisted

220. Stanely, "Defining the Boundaries of Christendom," 176.

221. Stanely, "Defining the Boundaries of Christendom," 176.

222. Stanely, "Defining the Boundaries of Christendom," 176.

223. Walls, *The Cross-Cultural Process in Christian History*, 32.

224. Walls, *The Cross-Cultural Process in Christian History*, 57.

225. Stanely, *Defining the Boundaries of Christendom*, 173. Andersen to John R. Mott, April 6, 1909, box 2, folder 26, Mott Papers, Yale Divinity School Library, New Haven, Conn.

of only "a symbolic handful of Indian, Chinese, and Japanese Christians," reflecting the leadership's limited expectations for these regions.[226] The voice of Africans was absent. The inaccuracy of their expectations has become increasingly apparent with the passage of time.

The Motivating Rationale

Why was it necessary to divide the world into Christian and non-Christian locations? Sanneh describes how the "leaders at Edinburgh spoke grandiloquently of the need for a 'comprehensive plan for world occupation,' an echo of the late nineteenth-century American Student Volunteer Movement's slogan, 'the evangelization of the world in this generation.'"[227] The designations were intended to represent the geographic spread of the gospel in how far it had progressed and in how far it had to go. These classifications were meant to clarify the task at hand, but they also implicitly created a kind of large-scale, collective comity agreement. And, as with earlier comity agreements, not everyone was invited to the decision-making table.

The territoriality that emerged reflected the perspectives and values of the Anglo-American leadership. By contrast, "today initiatives for mission may begin almost anywhere in the world and be directed to almost anywhere in the world."[228] For some, *Christendom to heathendom* has given way to *from everywhere to everywhere*, no longer territorially limited to specific locations. Though this remains far from the consensus view.

The large-scale international bifurcation between Christian and non-Christian countries had echoes of Christendom, yet it also revealed how much the situation had changed. The territoriality that was applied sought to focus missionary work in particular locations while delegitimizing other forms. The effects exposed the inaccuracies of the classifications, the inequalities they reinforced, and the mismatch and spillover inherent in viewing land as a set of containers.

The study of territoriality enables one to recognize, and perhaps even anticipate, the ongoing and changing manifestations of such spatial behavior. In light of this, the question naturally arises: what forms of territorial structure continue to shape mission practice today?

226. Walls, *The Cross-Cultural Process in Christian History*, 32.

227. Sanneh, *Disciples of All Nations*, 272.

228. Walls, *Crossing Cultural Frontiers*, 264.

CONTEMPORARY TERRITORIAL STRUCTURES

When Walls describes the voluntary societies associated with mission organization, he presents them as an innovation set against the backdrop of prior models. He then poses a question that is equally fitting for the present conversation: What comes next? What patterns emerge after those already examined? How are territorial structures, from which territoriality can arise, currently being made manifest?

Formulating comprehensive answers to these questions would require a deeper investigation beyond the scope of this study. It is, however, helpful to at least point in the direction of potential new patterns from which territoriality may emerge. Doing so is not without challenges. As noted in the preliminary matters of chapter one, there is a persistent tendency to privilege other ways of understanding reality over the geographical. Consequently, as specific forms of territorial behavior fade, we can fail to recognize new patterns emerging on the horizon.

This inclination can give one the impression that the world has become less territorial, when in fact territoriality is simply taking shape through different structural forms. The following section offers one example of a changing territorial structure. This example hints at some of the complex dynamics involved with interpreting shifts in territorial behavior.

The Precision Revolution

New patterns of territoriality are often rooted in technological innovation. Prior to the rise of GPS technology, people relied on paper maps to navigate. But changes to the geographic tools that mediate one's encounter with the world often pass unnoticed. Transitions between mapping systems may seem minor, but each carries distinct assumptions about how space is perceived and organized. Movement from one approach to another may go unnoticed even as different structures and tools have the capacity to shape how one views the world. In *After the Map*, William Rankin describes the paradigmatic movement "from paper to electronic signals, from the logic of representation to the logic of the grid, [and] from a focus on contiguous areas of space to a framework of points."[229] Few reflect on these changes

229. Rankin, *After the Map*, 295. The conclusion of the first World War had military leadership of both sides looking for a more precise technology than the maps that were available to them. They were also looking for a more universal cartographic approach. Grids had often been used as a map-making tool, as the underlying mathematical structure. This logic was expanded, and the structure was abstractly applied directly to earth

when using a phone to navigate from one place to another, yet their implications are significant.

The presuppositions underlying GPS technology also coincide with innovations that enable exacting strategic engagement with the world. Drone technology and stealth aircraft used by military forces have contributed to what has been called a "precision revolution."[230] Along these lines, Daniel Immerwahr observes that after World War II powerful countries such as the United States began to favor controlling strategic points on a map rather than attempting to claim large amounts of territory. Describing this strategy of "pointillism," he writes that "the US mastery of logistics would diminish the value of colonies and inaugurate a new pattern of global power, based less on claiming large swaths of land and more on controlling small points."[231] This new form of territoriality allowed dominance through a network of smaller strategic locations, and without the direct responsibility or accountability of larger scale colonial rule. Immerwahr, drawing on the work of retired Russian military general Vladimir Slipchenko, describes this shift in reference to warfare. "The very spatial categories of war were changing. In the future . . . area-based military concepts such as front, rear, and flank would be irrelevant. There would be only 'targets and non-targets' . . . 'there will be no need to occupy enemy territory.' Controlling territory would not matter because war was no longer about area, it was about points."[232] A prioritization on points rather than area marks a substantial change in the shape of spatial power.

There are various ways this change has been interpreted. For example, the use of drones and targeted raids can "enable intervention across international boundaries and coordination in unfamiliar locales."[233] Such tactics may appear to functionally subvert the importance of nation-state territoriality, leading some to conclude that "territory has declined in importance as airborne weaponry has entered arsenals."[234] Rankin, however, considers such conclusions too simplistic. Rather than signaling the decline of territoriality, he sees its layered intensification. As he explains, "this new spatiality of knowledge and power was not a retreat from territory; instead,

in a way "that unified the entire western front into a single mathematical space" (125).

230. Rip and Hasik, *The Precision Revolution*.

231. Immerwahr, *How to Hide an Empire*, 216.

232. Immerwahr, *How to Hide an Empire*, 379.

233. Rankin, *After the Map*, 124.

234. Klinghoffer, *The Power of Projections*, 127.

it was an intensification and multiplication of territory beyond the cleanly delimited borders of the territorial state."[235] In other words, territoriality has not disappeared, it merely appears different and is more likely intensifying. Rankin's belief in territorial intensification aligns with Sack's understanding as well. As Europeans engaged the world outside of Christendom, Sack notes that they cleared space to "form territories to organize and fill it at all geographical levels and with an intensity that was impossible to match in the Old World."[236] He adds that this "use of space did not occur at once. It is in fact still emerging and intensifying."[237] Territoriality may at times appear less as an all-powerful national territoriality delimited and neatly contained within its own borders. Yet, as the COVID-19 global pandemic has made clear, the power of national territoriality has not disappeared—it can reassert itself when circumstances demand. Over and above this primary governmental territoriality lies an increasing proliferation of secondary territorialities. These territorialities are overlapping, unevenly distributed, often decentralized, and always subject to change. The result is a world in which territoriality itself is becoming increasingly complex, diversified, and layered.

Parallels in Mission

The shift from maps and area to GPS grids and *pointillism* is one innovation in a long history of how humans conceive of and influence territory. Territory, and the use of territoriality, is a constant; only its expressions and effects vary. As humans have created new territorial structures and ways of expressing territoriality, Christians, in their missionary endeavors, have often mirrored these changes. Their engagement has been influenced by their place and made evident in how they relate to land and space and developed missionary strategy. Just as linear tactics characterized the trench warfare of the First World War, nineteenth-century Christians adopted a linear strategy through their chains of mission stations. Similarly, as European powers divided land amongst themselves and occupied these places in the Americas, Africa, and Asia, Christian missionary organizations established comity agreements to divide non-Christian territories and "spiritually" occupy them. Likewise, just as latitude was used to categorize and partition vast areas of unknown land, such as the Korean peninsula, a similar logic

235. Rankin, *After the Map*, 295.

236. Sack, *Human Territoriality*, 131.

237. Sack, *Human Territoriality*, 131.

underlies the creation of the 10/40 Window. In light of these parallels, are there recent examples of mission activity that may reflect the influence of the precision revolution or pointillism?

Consider the language of "points" used by Leonard Bartlotti in an article in the *International Journal of Frontier Missiology*. He proposes that effective work among some "unreached people" involves "determining a set of practical, geographically and contextually relevant 'engagement' or access points, which serve as strategic centers of influence among a people group."[238] To Bartlotti, this approach solves problems of access that he had himself experienced and that were echoed by other Christian workers. When particular territories cannot be occupied, he advocates identifying strategic points of engagement for missionary presence.

Another example of the turn toward pointillism appears in a missionary resource map produced by the Joshua Project (see Figure 6.1).[239] Several observations can be made about this map. First, this image is the screenshot from an interactive map on the Joshua Project website. The default setting displays most of Africa and Asia, along with portions of Europe. Earlier versions of this map left out places such as North and South America, Australia and parts of Oceana. In more recent versions, these places can be found at the margins when the user zooms out. This emphasis in the default setting may reflect the limitations of representing a spherical world on a flat map, or it may indicate the continued influence of the 10/40 Window on contemporary missionary planning materials.

238. Barlotti, "On Strategies of Closure," 138.

239. Joshua Project "Frontier Peoples."

Figure 6.1 "Frontier Peoples" Joshua Project 2025

The *people groups* are represented as small circles or points that vary in size according to population. National borders are present, but rendered in much lighter shades. The interactive map on the Joshua Project website contrasts brightly colored circles with countries shown in light gray. Where other missionary maps that emphasize national boundaries may have conveyed "constraint rather than fluidity," the pointillism of this map suggests fluidity without constraint.[240] Yet, in practice, access to each point remains subject to authorization by state entities.

In many areas, the circles on the map overlap, and in India they overlap significantly, encouraging deeper investigation through zooming in for more details. The map thus illustrates a shift toward precision thinking. Rather than conceiving of the missionary task in terms of large, classified areas—such as regions or nations—it is now represented through points.

Bartlotti's advocacy of engagement points for so-called unreached peoples and the Joshua Project's depiction of "Frontier People Groups" are two examples of the pointillism that Immerwahr and Rankin describe. While *people group* thinking is sometimes contrasted with geographical conceptions of mission, these examples show how *people group* thinking continues to intersect with geographical conceptualization in the service of missionary goals.[241] Rather than viewing the contrast as one between the sociological (i.e., people groups) and the geographical, it may be more

240. Klinghoffer, *The Power of Projections*, 128.

241. Lee and Park, "Beyond People Group Thinking," 213.

accurate to understand it as a shift in territorial structures, specifically from area-based approaches to pointillism. These approaches should be examined to consider what effects of territoriality may be present and how one's place may have influenced their development. Such an examination would likely show that contemporary territorial structures in mission are not so different from the classifications and territorial logics that have long characterized Christian faith and mission.

CONCLUSION

In a relatively short span of time, Christianity moved from a unified Christendom to a constellation of distinct Christian nations and, eventually, to a religious environment characterized by voluntary associations. Various societies, denominations, and mission organizations developed territorial strategies to accomplish their goals. A few of these have been highlighted in this chapter to illustrate the continuity and adaptation of territoriality within mission practice. From mission stations that cluster together or formed chains, to assigning and delimiting area by collaborative agreements under a system of comity, to large-scale international divisions between Christian and non-Christian space, and finally to a contemporary focus on points—territoriality continues to shape mission activity.

Throughout most of Christian and mission history, evidence of territoriality can be found. It has existed prior to Christendom and has persisted beyond Christendom. Its manifestations have varied, taking different forms, producing different effects, and operating through differing mechanisms of enforcement. With this broader understanding of territoriality, one can conclude that the end of Christendom is not the end of territoriality.

7

Conclusion

THE ARGUMENT

WE SET OUT TO answer the question: To what extent are Walls and Sanneh correct in their assertion that the end of Christendom signifies the end of territoriality? To address this question, Sack's theory of territoriality and his geographic awareness paradigm have provided the primary analytical framework. He defines territoriality as "*the attempt by an individual or group to affect, influence, or control people, phenomena, and relationships by delimiting and asserting control over a geographic area.*"[1] This understanding has been applied to show that territoriality existed both before and after Christendom.

Territoriality was presented as a common human behavior. Humans classify space and influence what enters or exits it. It occurs on multiple scales, through multiple means, and for multiple purposes. While its particular expressions may vary, with different beginnings and endings, and new forms continually emerging, the existence of territoriality is a consistent part of how humans relate to physical space. The theory of territoriality was also presented with attention to the causes and effects that characteristically flow from it, as well as the perspectives, shaped by one's place, that feed into it.

This theory was explored in light of Christian history. If territoriality existed prior to Christendom and continues beyond it, then the end of Christendom cannot serve as the basis for concluding that Christianity is

1. Sack, *Human Territoriality*, 19.

no longer territorial. This underscores the continued relevance of understanding territoriality for Christian faith and mission.

Reframing Walls's and Sanneh's Claims of Non-territoriality

At first glance, the evidence suggests that Walls's and Sanneh's claims that Christianity is no longer territorial are inaccurate. While this is a reasonable conclusion, there is another way of framing their statements that better accounts for the broader scope of their work.

If Walls's and Sanneh's statements are understood to mean that *Christianity is no longer territorial in the way it once was*, this can be affirmed. There has indeed been change. Christianity is no longer synonymous with territorial Christendom, no longer a contiguous landmass confined to a corner of the world map. There has also been a shift from a Christianity fundamentally tied to governmental (primary) territoriality to one that operates as a form of secondary territoriality. In many places, Christianity exists within a broader marketplace of ideas, within pluralistic societies of varying degrees, and in a continuously negotiated relationship with the primary territoriality. These characteristics, different from and associated with the dismantling of Christendom, need to be taken seriously, something that Walls and Sanneh are keen to do.

It has been established that Christendom and territoriality are closely linked in Walls's and Sanneh's writing. Christendom stands as a kind of epitome of territoriality. This is the reason behind Walls's and Sanneh's statements of non-territoriality. Yet Christendom is neither the only nor the earliest example of territoriality in Christian history, nor is it the last.

Sack's definition of territoriality offers a way to understand Christianity's relationship to territoriality that does not require Christendom as the constant reference point. Evaluating instances of territoriality should therefore take into account both the discontinuity with past manifestations as well as the continuity. In light of this, historians of Christianity and missiologists should ask not only *how has Christianity ceased to be territorial as it once was?* but also *how has Christianity continued to be territorial, as it once was, or in ways different than before?*

The thrust of Walls's and Sanneh's argument for non-territoriality explicitly emphasizes the first question–the discontinuity between what was and what is. But they do not engage this as a matter of historical fact. Rather, they challenge their reader, in ways similar to the writer of Hebrews, to recognize that the old way has passed. It is futile to try to resurrect that old territorial system. Christendom, and the contemporary forms explicitly hoping to revive it, are a dead end, and never the wonderous blessing once imagined.

To write in this way also implies the second question. It implies the potential for continuity of territoriality, even if not directly addressed. They write as though Christianity stands at a crossroads, a critical moment where Christians must decide what kind of future they hope to create. Viewed in this light, Walls's and Sanneh's assertions that "Christianity is no longer territorial," along with many of their broader reflections, reveal an aspirational vision of what Christianity *can* become. In this sense, their statements could be understood as expressing that Christianity *need not be* territorial, at least, not in the ways it once was.

The problem with asserting that "Christianity is no longer territorial," even with the above qualifications, is that such a claim effectively closes the door on further territorial analysis. In light of the evidence presented here, that door needs to be reopened.

The Combination of Sack, Walls and Sanneh

When Walls and Sanneh write about the history of Christian mission, they are not merely describing geographical realities. They invite readers to be attentive to the theological and faith dimensions in history. Sack does not share this aim. Had Walls and Sanneh employed Sack's theory, they could have explored more fully both the continuity and discontinuity of the various forms that territoriality has taken. When Sack's framework is brought into the conversation with theirs, much of Walls's and Sanneh's work proves valuable for cultivating a distinctively Christian wisdom concerning territoriality. This is particularly helpful since Sack's ethical dimensions remain underdeveloped.

Walls and Sanneh tend to write with larger geographic territories in view. While they provide principles that can inform a wide range of territorial scales, Sack's work makes the variety of possible spatial interactions more explicit. In these ways, the three thinkers complement one another. Taken together, their insights invite those engaged in Christian mission to discern both the theological and spatial dimensions of their practice with greater attentiveness and care.

Because humans must, by necessity, order their spatial world, territoriality will likely always find expression within the church and the practice of mission. Recognizing this enduring dynamic invites a further question:

how might mission thinking benefit from a deeper understanding of geography, territoriality, and place?

THE SIGNIFICANCE OF GEOGRAPHY

If the discipline of geography has been overlooked in missiological discussions, this study seeks to addressing that oversight. While some have claimed that mission has moved beyond geography, this is not the case. What is true is that missiology has too seldom employed the tools that geography has to offer. This neglect has limited the discipline's ability to recognize how geographical ideas shaped the history of mission and how they continue to inform the ways mission is represented and articulated today.

In light of this study's contribution, there are several ways the significance of geography can be more fully embraced within missiology. First, missiologists should resist the false dichotomy between viewing the world as entirely borderless and assuming that the boundaries of nation-states are fully capable of containment. Instead, one should gravitate toward more complex renderings of the situation, acknowledging the tendencies of both fixity and fluidity and the continual reconfiguration of territorial structures.

Second, missiologists and mission practitioners should attend carefully to their use of maps and their classifications of space. Churches, schools, and mission organizations face the ongoing challenge of communicating their engagement with the world effectively. Yet, they must also consider how to convey that God, and the mission of God, are larger than any single institution. The use of labels such as *reached* and *unreached*, *Christian* or *non-Christian* can be both dismissive and disabling: dismissive to those Christians who do not see themselves represented in such categories, and disabling to those who may be lulled into a false sense of permanence.

Third, missiologists should exercise care in their use of the term *culture* and consider whether their usage presupposes or neglects place. While topics such as migration, diaspora, and cultural hybridity are common in missiological discourse, they are often discussed without sufficient attention to spatial dynamics or engagement with geographical theory. Culture must be understood in relation to place—both in its connection to place and in its distinction from it.

In particular, those who write about territorial behavior as an extension of Christendom, including missiologists and historians, should critically examine their use of Christendom as a framework for interpreting territoriality.

Beyond Christendom As a Rubric

More recent evidence of territoriality is often attributed to the lingering effects or continued influence of Christendom and its mentality. In their analyses of the 1910 conference, both Stanley and Walls interpret the classifications through this lens. Stanley contends that the classifications reflect a "territorial Christendom" mentality,[2] while Walls observes that the Conference "started from the idea of Christendom, of Christianity as territorially based."[3]

One implication of this study is that such evidence is better understood as representing new and distinct forms of territoriality, forms that may be unique but are not wholly disconnected from earlier manifestations. While some may interpret these expressions as the continuation of a Christendom mindset. There is a more helpful way to frame them: as shifting territorial patterns that need not depend on Christendom for their explanatory power. Reframing the conversation in this way enables one to identify and evaluate territoriality without constant reference to its high-water mark in the era of Christendom.

Christendom has been a useful—or at least a well-used—category for organizing ideas. There may still be a place for it, but when considering instances of territoriality, the Christendom rubric is often applied too quickly. For instance, when Sanneh discusses the rise of "home fellowship groups" in response to the megachurch movement, he reflects: "I am unclear as to whether the perceived failure of the churches is one of size and scale or of kind and style: have the churches become too big . . . in a vain gambit to retrieve an illusory Christendom, leaving the faithful to grope after small-scale private assurance."[4] Large churches may indeed share certain characteristics with *Christendom*, and drawing on these comparisons can be valuable. Yet there are often better tools for spatial analysis than framing such phenomena as attempts to recreate *Christendom*. Continuing to interpret new territorial strategies through this rubric risks undercutting the very argument that *Christendom* has ended.

Churches take different territorial expressions, each with its own inherent challenges. The theory of territoriality helps to clarify these dynamics and reveals the nuances that the *Christendom* framework can obscure.

2. Stanley, "Defining the Boundaries of Christendom," 176.

3. Walls, "The Significance of Christianity in Africa," 1.

4. Sanneh, *Encountering the West*, 220.

Alternatively, one can too quickly assume the absence of territoriality in an effort to emphasize the contrast between current arrangements and the past. When Walls describes the emergence of new Christian communities taking root outside of Europe and European colonies, he makes the claim that they "did not embody the territorial Christendom principle."[5] Certainly, these newer territorial structures could not match Christendom in terms of population proportion or capacity for enforcement. These new communities did not conceive of themselves as controlling a primary territoriality, nor did they seek to conquer land and require all that are within that territory to convert to Christianity. Walls is right to emphasize this discontinuity—the magnitude of change from Christendom is significant—but it is equally important to recognize the continuity.

It is true that these new Christian communities outside Europe did not embody the same territorial Christendom principle, but that does not mean they were without territorial dimensions. Churches around the world have developed geographically dispersed and hierarchically structured organizations based on territorial subdivisions. For example, the Anglican Church has brought the parish system to several countries in East Africa. Many contemporary practices and modes of territorial organization share clear similarities with earlier models. The concept of territoriality enables these continuities to be explored without constant reference to Christendom.

After such an extended period under the Christendom model, it is understandable that new expressions of territoriality would raise questions as to whether they represent yet another form of Christendom. The term *territoriality* itself is unfamiliar to many, and broader tendency to move away from geographical concepts makes its presence even harder to discern. Territoriality is not easily recognized when it is subtle rather than overt, persuasive rather than forceful, or when it operates on a scale smaller than large-scale land acquisition. Without the clarity that geographical language and theory provide, such instances often remain obscure. When they are noticed, the more familiar framework of Christendom can seem the easier interpretive choice.

At the same time, the term Christendom can overcomplicate the very issues it seeks to explain. The fact that Christendom can be used to describe multiple features, and the fact that there is no uniformly agreed upon definition among scholars, creates significant ambiguity.[6] Greater analyti-

5. Walls, *Crossing Cultural Frontiers*, 186.

6. In some cases, authors have used the vague understanding of Christendom to

cal possibilities emerge when new territorial innovations are understood as expressions of territoriality rather than as mere shadows of past configurations. It is time to move beyond Christendom not just historically but theoretically, as a framework for interpreting territorial behavior. The theory of territoriality offers a more precise and productive rubric.

The major contribution of this study lies in clarifying the value of geography as a discipline for the study of missiology. Within that broader field, it has focused on one central concept—*territoriality*. What conclusions, then, can be drawn from this inquiry?

THE SIGNIFICANCE OF TERRITORIALITY

The church engages in territoriality whenever it locks its doors at night, or determines who may stand at the front of the church, or decides whether to have a church building at all. Those involved in mission likewise employ territoriality in shaping strategy, logistics, and the distribution of resources. Territoriality is evident when mission is confined to specific geographic areas or when broad evangelistic plans are created for bringing the gospel to an entire region of the world.

Since territoriality persists, how should this awareness inform the work of missiologists and mission practitioners? This question can be approached from two angles. The first considers the challenge of viewing religion through territorial containers. This is generally an issue that emerges on a larger scale and involves the ways religious identity becomes tied to spatial classifications. The second angle focuses on practical guidance for assessing territoriality within organizations themselves.

The Challenge of Territorial Containers of Religion

The findings of this work suggest the need for critical examination of the limitations inherent in religious containers. Territoriality produces such containers that mold behavior and shape perspectives. The history

address cultural change under the label *post-Christendom*. Bolger defines post-Christendom as "that period in the West where the practice of religion is no longer a cultural expectation but is more of an individual choice," Bolger, *The Gospel After Christendom*, xxiv–xxv. Bolger's definition demonstrates how some use Christendom and Post-Christendom as a kind of metaphor for cultural change. The ubiquity of Christendom, and the vague sense that change has occurred, allows the authors to use the metaphorical approach and to then focus their attention more on current trends that interest them (See Muggeridge, *The End of Christendom*; Smith, *Mission After Christendom*; Bolger, *The Gospel After Christendom*).

of territorial organization has conditioned many to view human life as confined within discreet geographic units. Most, if not all, of these containers have implicit or explicit religious designations as well. While there are both opportunities and consequences in conceiving of territory as a set of containers, this discussion focuses specifically on the association between religion and territorial containment.

The way territory becomes a container for religious affiliation is the effect of territoriality to which Sanneh is most attentive. Although Sanneh never defines it explicitly, his use of the term territoriality aligns closely with Sack's description of the container effect. For Sanneh, Christendom serves as the clearest example of Christian territoriality, leading him to conclude that the end of one entails the end of the other. Yet territoriality can be expressed in many forms and the creation of geographic containers, religious or otherwise, is only one such expression. While the end of Christendom brought significant changes, thinking in terms of religious containers has persisted, much as it did before Christendom itself.

The designation of space as religious, or as belonging to a particular faith, is a pattern present in the Old Testament. The New Testament, however, presents a different model. In the early centuries of Christianity, the development of territoriality was minimal, expressed primarily through responsibility for local congregations. Christianity was never confined to a single national container but spread geographically, adapting to new contexts. Walls observes that Christian centers have shifted throughout history: "Christian faith has fixed itself at different periods in different heartlands, waning in one as it has come to birth in another,"[7] yet it has had "no permanent geographical or cultural center."[8] Christianity has taken root in many places, but it has never been bound to any one perpetually.

At particular moments in history, the church assumed the form of a highly territorialized institution, deeply intertwined with primary territorial authority. This was evident both in its hierarchical structures and in the conception of the European landmass as a container for Christianity. This feature of Christendom represents perhaps the most recognizable and significant expression of Christian territoriality in terms of force, scale, and proportion. Early Protestant Reformers initiated changes to this dynamic, yet left many pieces of territoriality in place, including the religious container model. Subsequent movements within Europe—among them later

7. Walls, *Missionary Movement in Christian History*, 256.

8. Walls, *Crossing Cultural Frontiers*, 217.

reforming groups—helped bring an end to this distinctive form of Christian territoriality known as Christendom. Both Walls and Sanneh suggest that the loss of Christendom has, on the one hand, reawakened the church's earliest impulses, but it has also left some floundering without the perceived security of territorial support.[9]

In place of Christendom arose a more voluntary, privatized, and individual model of faith. The state became "the carrier of the doctrine of birth and soil" while Christianity was "driven from the public square and made personal and subjective."[10] In this sense, Sanneh describes Christianity as having become "deterritorialized."[11] He contends that "Westerners have in the main given up identifying land and territory with faith."[12] This is perhaps true with respect to their own self-understanding. The separation of church and state, which Sanneh refers to as "non-territoriality," has convinced many Westerners of their capacity for religious pluralism.[13] Yet upholding that conviction becomes more complex when other religions and their approaches to territoriality are considered.

The concept of geographical religious containers extends beyond Christianity. Sanneh describes how, for other religions "their equivalent of 'Christendom' is to some degree in place, as Hindus (in India), Buddhists (in Tibet, Sri Lanka or Thailand), Kodo or Jinja Shinto (in Japan), Jews (in Israel), Confucians (in China) and Muslims (in the Arab world)."[14] Adherents of these faiths are, of course, found outside these geographic containers. Yet their practices often redirect them toward these regions as religious centers. Such practices reinforce the primacy of those places within their respective traditions.

Islam serves as a particularly significant example of these dynamics for Sanneh. Muslims may be found in nearly every country of the world, but the practice of pilgrimage (*hajj*) and prayer create a consistent directional orientation toward Mecca. Together with Medina and Jerusalem, the symbolic role of these places underscores a prioritization of one particular region of the world. This emphasis is further reinforced by the centrality of the Arabic language, which traces its origins to the same region. Walls

9. Sanneh, *Encountering the West*, 227.
10. Sanneh, *Encountering the West*, 189.
11. Sanneh, *Encountering the West*, 211.
12. Sanneh, *Encountering the West*, 215.
13. Sanneh, *Encountering the West*, 185.
14. Sanneh, *Encountering the West*, 213.

states that Islam has gained adherence far from its origin, but "with relatively few (though admittedly important) exceptions, the areas and peoples that accepted Islam have remained Islamic ever since."[15] The progressive expansion of Islam has not diminished the importance of its geographical origins. Islam can take root in many contexts, but it remains bound to the fixity embodied by Mecca—a kind of permanence that Christianity cannot claim.

The religions listed above are not immune to the transformations that dismantled Christendom. Sanneh does not regard Islam's particular approach to territoriality as inherently unchangeable. Christianity began from a position of secondary territoriality, transitioned into a more all-encompassing primary territoriality, and later returned to a secondary position. Islam, by contrast, has long maintained primary territorial demands in its geographic centers. Yet those Muslims living beyond these centers have found a variety of ways to embody their faith without the reinforcement of a primary territoriality. Sanneh believes that Islam could "embrace privatization on moral and ethical grounds," adding that doing so "would show how faith can thrive without being armed at the same time."[16] With this optimism duly noted, it remains the case that, "territorial orthodoxy rings far truer to the experience of . . . Muslims, Buddhists and Hindus than it does to that of Europeans and Americans."[17] This leaves Christians in a distinctive position—many have abandoned the notion of a Christian territorial container even as other faith traditions have yet to do so.

The Consequence of Religious Containers

The assumption that land can function as a religious container obscures the diversity and complexity of faith found in every corner of the world. While such assumptions are often unhelpful, the more serious consequence of religious territoriality occurs when these containers become exclusion zones, where religions employ increasingly coercive measures of enforcement to maintain the perceived homogeneity of their territorial boundaries. This danger is especially acute when the scale of the territory encompasses a country or region, and when religious leaders either collaborate with, or themselves constitute the agents of the primary territoriality. In such cases,

15. Walls, *The Cross-Cultural Process in Christian History*, 29.

16. Sanneh, *Summoned from the Margin*, 188.

17. Sanneh, *Encountering the West*, 213.

religious minorities often experience religious territoriality as a mechanism of oppression. When used to enforce conformity or marginalize dissent, territoriality fosters environments of intolerance, persecution, and, ultimately, exile or martyrdom. In 2019, for example, changes to India's citizenship laws targeted its sizable Muslim population, revealing a Hindu nationalist agenda. Religious minorities in so-called Muslim countries or even in predominantly Muslim regions have faced similar forms of exclusion. Efforts to reassert Christian territoriality are likewise increasingly visible throughout parts of Europe and North America. Moreover, Christians have at times reinforced—rather than resisted—the very notion of religious territorial containers.[18]

The acts of exclusion created by religious territorial containers are among the primary reasons many Christians have abandoned the practice. Sanneh concludes that "territoriality carried too severe a handicap to be advantageous to religion, and that its abandonment by Christians . . . has proved beneficial to the cause of Christian renewal and witness."[19]

Nevertheless, there remains voices within Christianity that wish to "retreat into a nostalgic Christendom and strive for territoriality" even without the demographic dominance or the capacity for sustained enforcement.[20] Such efforts resemble the Crusaders' reclamation of Jerusalem, only to relinquish it soon after. Following brief temporal gains, they left the already-marginalized Christians of the region to face the repercussions.

Is it truly in the best interest of Christians to employ malevolent forms of territoriality in order to protect themselves, particularly when doing so compromises their witness in the public square? As Sanneh asks, "can we as believers witness to faith without the coercive recourse implicit in religious territoriality?"[21] Instead, Christians should choose to uphold the voluntary society and embody a winsome presence in public life. They should use their limited power not to secure their own safety, but to defend the rights

18. A detail from Sanneh's own life shows the tendency of some Christians to willingly maintain the religious classifications of others. Desirous of being baptized, Sanneh discloses how he approached a Christian bishop who surprisingly would not accept his conversion out of fear that doing so would create problems. Sanneh reflects on the moment stating, "the irony was inescapable: the bishop's unwillingness to acknowledge me was because of his implicit acceptance of Islam's eminent domain." Sanneh, *Summoned from the Margin*, 253.

19. Sanneh, *Encountering the West*, 227.

20. Sanneh, *Encountering the West*, 228.

21. Sanneh, *Encountering the West*, 222–23.

of religious minorities. While Christians need not dictate to adherents of other religions, they should lead by example, resisting territorial exclusion and expressing their disapproval when such tactics are employed against others.

Other Problems with Religious Containers

While the oppression of religious minorities is the most consequential issue associated with the containerizing effect of territoriality, there are other challenges it can create. Some Christians have rightly rejected oppressive kinds of religious territoriality as mentioned above, but their language reflects a continuation of similar ideas. It is quite possible that this is for the sake of efficiency. Making space into containers allows one to avoid enumerating the complexity that is found in the space. Instead, one can speak in general broad strokes and at times doing so is necessary and helpful. But at other times, it may be beneficial to move beyond this tendency and to wade at least a little deeper into the complexity.

The 1910 missionary conference classified countries as *Christian* or *non-Christian*. And yet, as Walls points out, some of the locations once considered *Christian* are today "the prime mission fields of the world."[22] The labels used by the 1910 conference planners seem to ignore the history of Christian recession and the fragility of such classifications. If faith is a matter of individual choice, rather than a function of where one lives, there will be those who choose not to be Christian. For a place labeled *Christian* this provides a false sense of security that the place will remain permanently Christian. The land classified as *non-Christian* also can ignore the presence of vibrant communities of Christians within these places.[23] These labels also are complicated by the way people do not always stay in the containers they are assigned. As comity demonstrated, people move and their movements render labels inaccurate. The efficiency of these claims is undeniable, but this does not reduce the influence of the dismissiveness. As Christians attempt to make sense of the breadth of diversity of the body of Christ around the world, they should seek to understand the limitations of such sweeping classifications.

Unintentionally, territorial containers can also be used in ways that diminish the significance of a particular community's contribution. Walls

22. Walls, *The Missionary Movement in Christian History*, 237.

23. Rynkiewich, "Corporate Metaphors and Strategic Thinking," 217.

speaks of the way that "African theologians and pastoral practitioners wrestle with the issues that arise from the interaction of the Christian gospel with African culture, [but] their insights may have much relevance outside Africa."[24] While the fruit of this labor may serve the needs of that location first, they also have applicability beyond Africa. If the insights have been placed in geographical containers that mitigate a broader interaction, other Christians lose the opportunity to hear wisdom from the whole body of Christ. Placing the work of these scholars under geographic labels, or ignoring their scholarship because of these labels, trivializes their contribution.

Specific labels can also give the impression that a particular expression does not have analogous counterparts in other locations. Such geographical labels undermine the idea that certain practices and perspectives are more common as opposed to uniquely "exotic." For example, Walls explains how beliefs and practices said to be "associated with 'African traditional religion' also occur outside of Africa."[25] He goes on to describes locations in the South Pacific, China, South America, and in the Arctic which share elements of commonality that the language often obscures. "The fact is that much of what in Africa is called 'African traditional religion' is not uniquely African."[26] When a geographic label is attached to a phenomenon or idea, there is often a corresponding tendency to draw boundaries around it—as if to say, "this happens over there," and by extension, "not over here." Reflecting on one's use of language can reveal how such labels create containers that trivialize, dismiss, or obscure complex realities. Christians should therefore be attentive to how their own language may contribute to this dynamic.

Sanneh urges that "we should place ourselves in the dynamic context of world Christianity whose presuppositions are so vastly different from those of our Christendom with its exclusivist territorial scruples."[27] What, then, is this place? World Christianity is "worldwide in scope" and has "worldwide roots" shaped in part by a "post-colonial, post-nationalist era" which helped to form "its culturally diverse polycentric character."[28] It stands without territorial support, embodying a seemingly boundless faith that is too big to be contained behind the borders of one country. Sanneh

24. Walls, *Crossing Cultural Frontiers*, 143.

25. Walls, *Crossing Cultural Frontiers*, 143.

26. Walls, *Crossing Cultural Frontiers*, 143.

27. Sanneh, *Encountering the West*, 222.

28. Sanneh, *Summoned from the Margin*, 237.

understands this opportunity as a contrast to past territorial arrangements "not the diocesan model of Roman vintage, but communities of faith characterized by an inclusiveness of idioms and practices that has little resemblance to the organized and regulated boundaries of the diocesan Western prototype."[29] Yet while this form may differ from the "organized and regulated boundaries" of earlier eras, new organizing principles have undoubtedly emerged to shape and mold the spatial behavior of Christians. There is no longer one unifying institutional center; rather, there are many, making the contemporary spatial organization of Christianity more complex than ever before.

Christians should not continue to see the world in terms of homogenous territorial blocks of faith, even if others do. Nor should mission be understood as an activity from a collection of Christian nations directed to a contrasting group of non-Christian nations. Mission is better understood as from everywhere to everywhere. Rather than marking gains on a map, as if they are now permanent Christian containers, new churches should be thought of as "positions through which the influence of Jesus Christ may come to bear on people and communities" for a period of time.[30]

As noted at the outset, Sanneh believed that the issue of religious territoriality required critical reflection. This study contributes to that ongoing reflection, particularly concerning the religious containers Sanneh had in mind. At the same time, Sack's theory of territoriality offers additional value by providing concrete tools for assessing territorial dynamics within organizations.

Evaluating an Organization's Use of Territoriality

Aside from some specific and limited situations, I don't seek to commend territoriality as a strategy to be employed, mostly because it is already being utilized. What is necessary is for missiologists and mission practitioners to be attentive to how territoriality is at work, where it may be present, and what effects it produces or has produced. Those engaged in mission practice must think critically about how they spatially organize themselves. One of the contributions of this study is to help missiologists and mission practitioners identify instances of territoriality, recognize the effects that flow from it and the perspectives that feed into it.

29. Sanneh, *Summoned from the Margin*, 238.

30. Walls, *The Cross-Cultural Process in Christian History*, 13.

Many leaders of schools, churches, denominations, and mission organizations inherit territorial structures that often mirror their hierarchical arrangements. These territorial structures warrant careful evaluation. The following framework is offered to facilitate that process.

First, take stock of how the organization is spatially ordered.

1. Are there distinct physical places that belong to the organization—such as campuses, offices, properties, or other locations? Are members of the organization distributed across different places? If so, where are they located, and how do these sites relate to one another?
2. Is the hierarchy of the organization connected to its spatial distribution? In what ways?
3. Given the organization's spatial structure, is it possible to discern why it developed in this particular way? How did this structure once serve—or how does it continue to serve—the organization's goals?

Second, evaluate whether the existing territorial structure continues to meet the needs of the organization. After assessing the organization's geographical distribution, hierarchy, and historical rationale, the next step is to determine whether its current territorial structure remains effective. The following questions may guide this evaluation:

1. Has the level of bureaucracy increased? Has it become cumbersome and inefficient, or has it brought clarity and structure to the organization in helpful ways?
2. Are there inequalities in access to knowledge, responsibility, or resources across different locations? Do the organization's internal divisions privilege some while disadvantaging others? Are key decisions regularly made at a distance from where they are implemented?
3. Has the organization itself become an excuse for inaction—for instance, through sentiments such as, "We just don't do that here"?
4. Can the organization respond to new challenges and opportunities with agility?
5. Is the organization vulnerable to secession or fragmentation? If so, does this vulnerability relate to any of the issues noted above?

In addition to organizational assessment, one should also reflect on how Scripture might shape principles of territoriality. This study has highlighted several passages that bear on the topic and noted the relatively low territorial structure of the early church. While these references do not constitute an exhaustive list of ways Scripture can inform territorial practice, they offer a meaningful starting point. Christian organizations should reflect on the examples and teachings of Scripture and consider how these insights align with—or challenge—their own territorial behaviors.

Finally, if changes are deemed necessary, the proposed adjustments should themselves be carefully evaluated.

1. What specific changes are being proposed, and how can members of the organization anticipate and minimize any negative effects of territoriality? Should existing classifications be expanded or contracted? Should subdivisions be created or merged?
2. Do the proposed changes risk reinforcing a center–periphery dynamic that stratifies the organization and increases inequality?
3. Do the proposed changes genuinely address the underlying problem, or do they merely shift it to a lower level without questioning deeper assumptions?
4. Do the proposed changes introduce new vulnerabilities? Have additional bureaucratic layers increased impersonality or inefficiency?
5. Do the proposed changes help to mitigate the tendency toward increasing territoriality?

It is particularly instructive to emphasize the question of how to *mitigate the tendency toward increasing territoriality.* As noted earlier, I do not seek to commend territoriality as a strategy, except in specific and limited circumstances. One such circumstance involves fostering organizational restraint. In this sense, territoriality can serve as a means of focusing an organization's attention on a particular, clearly defined area. This should never be undertaken with the intent of exclusion or a sense of exclusive ownership over an area. Nor should it presume that one's organization occupies the entirety of that territory or does so permanently. Territorial classifications, when used in this way, should remain open to reevaluation and adjustment. The purpose of employing territoriality in this restrained form is to establish reasonable limits on an organization's scope of activity.

At times, self-restraint is especially necessary when new opportunities arise. One should seek to keep their organization to the determined classified limits unless the expansion opportunity has been thoroughly weighed along with consideration of the motivations by those making the decision, and the capacity of the organization to expand the territory in an equitable way. Territoriality often expands with a momentum of its own, and leaders may be tempted to pursue growth without critically examining how it might produce greater hierarchy, mismatch and spillover, inequality, or other unintended effects. Instead, leaders should engage in honest reflection on whether such expansion stems from a desire for self-promotion or institutional aggrandizement. Before extending beyond established boundaries, organizations should consider how expansion could generate unequal access to resources, increased bureaucracy, inefficiency, or rigidity—any of which might jeopardize the organization's mission. It should not be assumed that every expansion of ministry is in the best interest of the organization.

Nondenominational megachurches provide a helpful example of several of the concepts discussed here. In the United States, the development of these organizations happened in part as a reaction against the denominational system. William Swatos argues that "the essence of denominational religiosity is localism," yet by the latter half of the nineteenth century, many denominations in the United States had expanded their bureaucratic apparatus. "Denominations developed national staffs, headquarters, programs . . . far beyond the reach of local constituents."[31] This bureaucratic expansion brought with it increased centralization and impersonalization. Although such structures may have been well suited to their original context, changing circumstances exposed and amplified their inefficiencies and inequalities, creating conditions ripe for secession. Many came to view denominationalism as problematic because it removed decision-making and financial resources from local congregations. In response, some turned to nondenominational churches that promised "local control and autonomy from an invading corporate structure."[32]

Many of these new nondenominational churches expanded rapidly, adding services, programs, campuses, and corresponding hierarchies of staff. As these organizations grew, standards became formalized and relationships became increasingly impersonal. Staff roles were often filled, not with theologically or ministerially trained clergy, but by specialists in marketing, media, facilities management, and human resources. Centralization inherently concentrates knowledge and responsibility in the hands of a few

31. Swatos, "Beyond Denominationalism," 223.

32. Swatos, "Beyond Denominationalism," 225.

at the top of the hierarchy, yet in this model such concentration is further reinforced by spiritual authority. It is therefore unsurprising that this authority can become difficult to question, with significant consequences for both perceived transparency and actual accountability.

These large nondenominational churches have, in effect, become a new form of denominationalism. Rather than the dispersed territorial footprint characteristic of traditional denominations, they have established clusters of churches organized around main and satellite campuses. These represent new territorial patterns—though not entirely new—that create a reconfigured center-and-periphery dynamic. Territoriality begets territoriality, and the earlier advantages of seceding from established systems are lost as the bureaucracy once resisted is simply reorganized under a different form.

Had denominational churches reflected more carefully on how to balance local and national dynamics, they might have retained more of their members. Had the large non-denominational churches evaluated their territorial structure along the way, perhaps they could have prevented some of the inevitable bureaucratic increases and other negative aspects of territoriality. The framework presented here offers at least a starting point for assessing how territoriality operates within an organization. What is most important is that leaders critically examine their territorial structures and spatial arrangements. One should expect that territoriality will continue, though its expressions will continually change. Evaluating the dynamics of territoriality ought to be part of the best practices for Christian organizations.

As discussed in chapter 2, territoriality arises from one's perspective, which itself is shaped by one's place. This, too, requires critical reflection. In this way, the study contributes not only to understanding territoriality but also to recognizing the enduring significance of place.

THE SIGNIFICANCE OF PLACE

The classifications underlying any form of territoriality arise from the perspective of individuals who are embodied in particular places. Every thought ever conceived has emerged within a place. Sack's *geographic awareness paradigm* provides a useful framework for conceptualizing how place functions as a formative force in shaping one's perspective. To understand one's perspective, therefore, requires careful attention to the significance of place.

This study contributes by offering a reflexive tool for exploring one's self-understanding without diminishing or reducing any particular element of one's life. Sack's *geographic awareness paradigm* provides a means of examining one's historical geography—encompassing the natural, the social, and the mental elements that assemble in one's place over time. The purpose of this paradigm is not to assign fixed characteristics to any particular place, but rather to invite questions about one's place and to engage the complexity it presents. The paradigm enables this complexity to be examined, fostering self-awareness of the many intersecting forces that shape one's life.

By contrast, exploring one's experience through another analytical lens, such as culture, can fail to account for the diverse ways that culture is lived and experienced across different places. The study of place, however, is flexible enough to accommodate individualized experiences, hybridity, and mobility, while still attending to the significance of collective social influence. As demonstrated by Benson, Sack's paradigm can illuminate the experiences of those shaped by multiple places. This tool helps individuals discern how their places have influenced them and shaped the ways they engage the world.

Beyond serving as a tool for personal reflection, the paradigm underscores the importance of actually going to places. Place functions as a formative force that profoundly shapes individuals and expands their awareness of the world. Commitment to the practice of going to places becomes even more vital in an age when technology enables connection across vast amounts of space. Such tools should support, not replace, the "person-embodied, context-dependent, spatially sticky . . . direct physical interaction" that occurs only within a place.[33] One cannot extract a singlee-ature or element of a place and assume that interaction with it in isolation carries the same value as embodied presence within the place itself.

Because place exerts a shaping force on how one views the world, the act of going is valuable even when travel is costly, tiring, or challenging. This is not to suggest that simply going is sufficient to broaden one's worldview. Some enter new places primarily intent on influencing them rather than being influenced by them, thereby limiting engagement with the social and mental dimensions of those places. Yet for many, encountering a new place provokes questions. In seeking answers to these questions, they formulate new perspectives and expand their mental maps. Such experiences enlarge

33. Morgan, "The Exaggerated Death of Geography," 12.

one's personal sense of place, weaving new contexts into the tapestry of one's historical geography.

Sack's paradigm is intended not only to deepen one's understanding of a particular place but also to expand one's awareness of the world. This can create a tension similar to that found between Christianity as a world-wide faith and Christianity as lived in a particular place. This theme has appeared throughout this study and was developed more fully in chapter 3. How does one's faith influence their relationship to a particular place, and how can this be harmonized with a sense of belonging to a world-wide body of believers? The findings of this study suggest that integrating Sack's geographical insights with the theological principles advanced by Walls and Sanneh can help to harmonize the tension between one's particular place and the larger world.

Particular and Rooted

Jesus came to a particular place, not to the world in general. Christianity reflects this same pattern, it exists in particular places, in various scales of local expression. Sanneh speaks of the necessity of "localizing Christianity," noting that without such localization "Christianity becomes nothing but a fragile, elusive abstraction, salt without its saltness." There is no "essence of Christianity" that can be extracted to avoid consideration of the particular expressions.[34] Walls echoes this notion when he writes that Christianity "cannot be separated from life in a particular place, at a particular time, within a particular culture-because that is the only sort of life there is."[35] The many particular expressions of Christianity are possible because the faith can be made at home in any place. This capacity for translatability gives rise to what Walls calls the "indigenizing principle," which brings the gospel to bear on the particulars of one's place.[36] Walls further explains that "Christ must rule in the minds of his people, which means extending his dominion over those corporate structures of thought that constitute a culture."[37] Through this sanctifying activity, Christ and his teachings become at home in a location, binding together a community of faith in a shared identity. In such instances, Christianity does not appear foreign but becomes deeply integrated into the patterns of thought and life so as

34. Sanneh, *Encountering the West*, 129.
35. Walls, *The Missionary movement in Christian history*, 46.
36. Walls, *Missionary Movement in Christian History*, 9.
37. Walls, *Missionary Movement in Christian History*, 25.

to belong. This integration suggests that a place, with its particular social, mental, and physical forces, can shape how one understands Scripture, participates in Christian practices, and conceptualizes mission. At the same time, the presence of Christians in a place can have a reflexive influence: they can be a blessing to that place, and their absence can be a loss of blessing.

When Christianity can be said to be at home in a particular place, at whatever meaningful scale this may occur, certain limitations and an accompanying impulse to protect often emerge. From at least the time of Paul's letters, Christians were identified by the places they inhabited.

Early leaders were chosen within and for these locations, emphasizing the importance of leadership rooted in place. In a relatively short period of time, a diocesan model of jurisdiction developed in which priests assumed responsibility for a defined territorial area. There were understood limits to what providing spiritual care could feasibly entail. After the Protestant Reformation, such territorial models were questioned, sometimes discarded, but sometimes maintained.

There is value in settling deep into the challenges and the opportunity that comes from shepherding disciples within a particular place. Likewise, there is value in the kind of gospel guardianship embodied by Christians who seek the peace of the city (Jer 29:7) and earnestly pray for the inhabitants. Such focus directed at a particular place can generate an impulse to protect. The roots of territoriality in the church grew from this impulse. One of the chief responsibilities of early church leadership was to guard the faith against false teaching and to administer discipline. In Sack's terms, these activities reflected a "custodial" responsibility. The recognition of limitation and the impulse to protect formed part of the rationale for territoriality.

Over time, Christianity made its home among the people who lived in Europe. There was an alignment of culture, place, and religion which produced what Sanneh calls "collective national affirmations."[38] The faith was shared and practiced communally, and the world was interpreted through a distinctly Christian lens. As previously noted, the very ground of Christendom represented "natural privilege" for Christians.[39] Eventually, however, this system broke down as "religion ceased to be synonymous with territorial security and social standing."[40] Faith became a personal and

38. Sanneh, *Encountering the West*, 214.

39. Sanneh, *Encountering the West*, 214.

40. Sanneh, *Encountering the West*, 214.

increasingly private matter. These shifts continued to evoke an impulse to protect, though now from a disempowered position no longer supported by the enforcement mechanisms of a primary territoriality.

From the position of secondary territoriality, expressions of the impulse to protect take different forms. For some, concern for the spiritual condition of a place may be expressed through a longing for revival, a commitment to prayer, or renewed evangelistic efforts.

It may also appear in the desire for Christians to be perceived rightly within a place and in the call to live ethically, particularly in matters where Scripture and the place are in broad agreement. In recognition of one's limitations, such an impulse of protection looks like personal, or organizational commitment to direct one's energy toward being a blessing to a particular place. In such cases, territoriality may be used to classify the limitations of one's intended ministerial impact. It does not presume that the place is empty of meaningful spiritual activity, nor that one's ministry or organization adequately or permanently fills that void. Instead, it discourages competition, encourages collaboration among those with shared aims, and acknowledges the likelihood that ministry influence may spillover beyond its designated area.

For others, the impulse to protect may become intertwined with nationalist or autochthonous ideology. Sanneh identifies this as a particular threat for those who had not yet grown accustomed to their more diminished position of power after Christendom, that is, within a secondary territoriality. While the first approach perceives the threat to a place as internal, concerning the spiritual condition of its inhabitants, the latter regards the threat as external. The place is changing as a result of those coming from the outside, the foreigner in their midst who does not hold their particular mix of cultural and religious expression.

Sack identified a subtle shift in the early Christian church, where letters spoke of Christians being *in* a place and then subsequently *of* a place.[41] The former suggests a kind of punctiliar impermanence—a passing presence—while the latter conveys a more rooted reality. Autochthonous tendencies take this a step further. Instead of understanding oneself as belonging to a place, the protective impulse comes to view the place as belonging to oneself. What begins as custodial stewardship can thus become the perspectival foundation for malevolent territoriality. Nationalist and autochthonous ideologies often construct a myth of originality grounded

41. Sack, *Human Territoriality*, 105.

in nebulous or unverifiable criteria of belonging.[42] The desire to protect gradually transforms into a drive to control, defend, and enforce by whatever means necessary. These are the roots of a form of Christian territoriality that is unable to tolerate the presence of those who differ from them. This may include those of a different faith, or those who claim the same faith but whose convictions, practices, and reading of Scripture is not familiar. Such differences are perceived not as opportunities for understanding but as threats to the integrity of the place.

Such expressions of Christian territoriality operate almost seamlessly when Christianity aligns with primary or political territoriality and the greater proportion of the population. However, as Christians have moved into secondary positions, with smaller proportions of the population, their attempts at asserting dominance over a place appear more desperate. Christians can "make the Church so much a place to feel at home that no one else can live there or we can use the sense of Christian identity to legitimate some group's economic and social interests."[43] In such circumstances, Christianity risks becoming a pawn in political disputes and serving aims that diverge from the gospel itself. When territorial strategies are used to enforce conformity within a place, they are often perceived—especially by those one hopes to influence or bless—as coercive or even malevolent distortions of the good news of Jesus Christ.

Territoriality that arises from a desire to serve a particular expression of Christianity in a place can be exhibited in a concerted effort toward being a blessing to a place. Recognizing one's ministerial limits and cultivating deep love and concern for a specific location or people is both appropriate and commendable. Yet an intense focus on one place, when coupled with an impulse toward protection, can easily merge with agendas that fail the scrutiny of Scripture. Power is an alluring temptation, and the exertion of control over others can become a means to an end. Such attempts at control are a domineering grasp for an elusive permanence that can backfire.

Universal and Boundless

If the indigenizing principle is associated with the rooted and particular expressions of Christianity, its counterbalance lies in Walls's pilgrim principle, which emphasizes the universal and boundless character of the faith.

42. Geschiere, *The Perils of Belonging*.

43. Walls, *Missionary Movement in Christian History*, 54.

The pilgrim principle is evident whenever Christianity transcends borders and when it is repeatedly translated into new places. No place stands as permanently excluded, or inherently beyond the reach of God. Nor does Christianity belong exclusively to any one place. While the faith can make its home in any context, the pilgrim principle represents the yearning that arises when Christians recognize that they are "not fully at home in this world."[44] As Walls notes, "that society never existed, in East or West, ancient time or modern, which could absorb the word of Christ painlessly into its system."[45] And yet, the pilgrim principle affirms that the diversity of particular expressions, taken together, reveal a coherent unity within Christianity.

The promise to Abraham that he and his descendants would be a blessing to all nations provides a far-reaching vision of God's salvific activity that extends beyond the particularity of one family or nation (Gen 12:3). In the New Testament, Christianity propels the worship of the Messiah beyond the boundaries of culture and the borders of the nation-state, drawing people from every background. The result, as Walls observes, was the formation of "a people of God transcending time and space."[46] As noted in chapter 4, this de-spatialized faith stood in contrast to the fixity of Judaism, contributing to its universal appeal. The book of Acts portrays the early Christian movement as one that steadily crossed boundaries, taking on ever more universal dimensions.

Over time, the leadership of the church also gave expression to this universal dimension. While clergy were chosen in particular locations, each community appointed territorial representatives to serve in wider ecclesial bodies. Councils determined what was considered orthodox and established rules of discipline across all churches. These developments marked the beginning of a more centralized hierarchy that enabled coordination and enforced shared standards on a broader scale. In the Western church, this process culminated in increasing hierarchy centered on the papacy in Rome. Although the Protestant Reformation challenged this centralization, smaller forms of it persisted, continuing to express a vision of universality within the church. Mission societies and their subsequent comity agreements exemplify later efforts to sustain a cohesive and coordinated vision

44. Walls, *Missionary Movement in Christian History*, 54.

45. Walls, *Missionary Movement in Christian History*, 8.

46. Walls, *Missionary Movement in Christian History*, 24.

of the church and its activity. Such endeavors reflect the universal impulse of the Christian faith embodied in the pilgrim principle.

In contrast to the rootedness of the indigenizing principle, the pilgrim principle carries an element of detachment from the land. This detachment is foreshadowed in the Old Testament through themes of dislocation, exile, captivity, and migration. These motifs reemerged in the first and second centuries when Christians increasingly identified as exiles and sojourners whose true citizenship was elsewhere. Such self-understanding distinguished Christianity from many other religions, for Christians were not bound to a single sacred geography. Their worship was not confined to a particular temple, city, or river but could be offered freely and fully in any place on earth.

In some other religions, a certain place can serve as a reification of the faith. Because the loss of these holy places could be a destabilizing force, territoriality is often employed to protect them. While Christians have, at times, defended their places of worship, they have not done so because it was required of them in Scripture or by the founders of their faith. Christianity can be rooted in a place, yet it is never permanently bound to one. As Walls observes,

> A place that had been a Christian heartland, a shining center of Christian devotion and activity, ceased to have this function; the light burned down or burned out, and the candlestick was taken out of its place. But in none of these cases did this decline mean the disappearance of the Christian faith or the end of the Christian witness—rather the reverse. By the time the Jerusalem church was scattered to the winds, the gospel had taken hold in the Hellenistic world of the eastern Mediterranean.[47]

Certain sites may hold deep cultural or historical significance, but the continuity of Christianity does not depend on their preservation. This helps explain why Dr. Ghada Talhammi, mentioned in the introduction, could describe Christians in the so-called Holy Land as "not very territorial." Christians certainly have used, or misused, territoriality to press their advantage. But the believers she encountered did not perceive territorial control as essential to the practice of their faith. This stood in contrast to other religious groups vying for control over contested sacred spaces, casting the Christians of that region in a comparatively favorable light.

47. Walls, *The Cross-Cultural Process in Christian History*, 66.

Missionary activity, which could be understood as an expression of the pilgrim principle, has a more complex territorial history. From the beginning, it required Christians who were willing to uproot themselves, and often their families, to go and live in foreign lands. Such movement represented a form of self-imposed exile, undertaken by those who believed deeply that God's salvific plan was for all the people of the world. In the early development of missionary societies, these endeavors were frequently ridiculed by Christians whose vision of faith remained geographically fixed. Sanneh recounts how early missionaries were dismissed as "little detachments of maniacs, benefiting us much more by their absence, than the Hindus by their beliefs."[48] Despite such derision, missionaries and their societies persisted, convinced of the universal applicability and the boundless truth of the Christian message.

Missionaries were separated from their place of origin, yet that place had profoundly shaped their understanding of Christianity. It was easier to remove the Christian from their place, than it was to remove the influence of the place on the Christian. And this affected the kind of Christianity they carried with them. They could not represent God apart from the tools of their own culture, yet a transcendent God "may not be identified with some cultural manifestation to the exclusion of others, so that partial cultural representation does not become the comprehensive criterion of God."[49] To do so would make access to God dependent on a single cultural framework.

Sanneh describes how in some cases, "converts were torn from their roots in their own society to wilt in an alien missionary environment."[50] Christianity, in such cases, uprooted converts from their homes and rendered them cultural defectors. In other places, as Christianity began to take root, new teaching disrupted established understandings of hierarchy and ancestry, challenging social orders deeply bound to the land.[51] The picture that Sanneh and Walls present is one in which missionaries sometimes promoted a kind of detachment that was less about the boundless, universal truth of the gospel and more about the domineering particularity of the missionary's own cultural expression. This amounted to a demand for universal conformity. Statements about conquering land, whether spiritual or otherwise, could easily be perceived as expressions of malevolent

48. Sanneh, *Disciples of All Nations*, 125.

49. Sanneh, *Encountering the West*, 133.

50. Sanneh, *Disciples of All Nations*, 223.

51. Walls, *Missionary Movement in Christian History*, 131.

territoriality. For some, the close association of missionary organizations with colonial powers only reinforced the perception that Christianity threatened their ancestral connection to the land.

The territoriality that developed was the result of missionaries who had imagined that their particular Christian expression had universal relevance. Their brand of Christianity was uprooted but nonetheless remained bound to locations far away. They attempted to consign new expressions to perpetual marginality. Walls maintains that such local expressions of Christianity are not only inevitable but beneficial, "provided that we remember that they *are* local."[52] Christianity is not the "private possession" of any one group or location.[53] Unfortunately, when particular groups seek to dominate others, their ambitions undermine Christianity's universal character and diminish the potential for authentic expressions to arise from a place.

Christianity can also prompt instances of detachment from land that do not originate with missionaries. Walls explains how in some cases "traditional spirits of the land" urge the people to "no longer worship them but worship *Nhiliac*, God, instead."[54] Regarding the Urapmin of Papua New Guinea, Joel Robbins observes that Pentecostalism offered a transnational religious identity that opened new avenues of commerce unavailable to those bound to the land. Kahler states that Christianity "provided a symbolic alternative to deities rooted in their locale."[55] In a global economy that rewards mobility, the fact that Christianity does not confine believers to particular sacred sites can be perceived as a benefit. The cross-cultural mobility this faith permits has fostered global networks of relationships grounded in a shared belief and widened vision of the world.

Seeing Near and Far

In Walls's perspective, the indigenizing and pilgrim principles work together in complementary ways. "It is not possible to have too much of the localizing and indigenizing principle which makes the faith thoroughly at home, nor too much of that universalizing principle which is in constant tension with it, and which links the local community with its "domestic" expression of faith in the same Christ of Christians of other times and places. It is

52. Walls, *The Missionary Movement in Christian History*, 235.

53. Walls, *The Missionary movement in Christian history*, 255.

54. Walls, *Crossing Cultural Frontiers*, 89.

55. Kahler, *Territoriality and Conflict in an Era of Globalization*, 8.

possible only to have too little of either."[56] The indigenizing principle "tends to localize the vision of the Church" while the pilgrim principle tends to "universalize it."[57] Just as the ability to see near and far is necessary for clear vision, neither principle can be sacrificed in favor of the other.

The tension is well illustrated in the command found in Deut 26. In this passage, a time is anticipated when the people of Israel will bring forth produce from the soil. Farming evokes notions of intimacy with the land, and the metaphor of rootedness arises naturally from such activity. It suggests permanence, of cycles of recurring seasons and a long relationship with a place. The offering of the first fruits stands in contrast to the confession that begins "my father was a wandering Aramean" and ends with the recognition of the foreigner living among them. These declarations remind the worshiper that their forefather was "a nomadic herdsman, who owned no land himself."[58]

Their current experience of rootedness followed a time of diaspora and migration. Furthermore, as the foreigner among them could attest, permanence was never guaranteed. They, or their children, might one day be uprooted from the land and return to the experience of Jacob. Such statements, in the time of rootedness are preparation for what could be, a reminder of their fragile relationship with the land and the truth that all such gifts come from the Lord.

The principles are also embodied in what Walls describes as the paradox of Christianity, "the twofold affirmation of the utter Jewishness of Jesus and of the boundless universality of the Divine Son."[59] They are similarly reflected in the already-not yet tension of eschatological hope. The history of Christianity could be viewed as a "series of cultural specifics" that, through their "coherence and interdependence" nonetheless still "belong together."[60] Through these examples, Walls establishes a theological foundation for understanding how the two principles function together.

The question remains: how do Christians, who are necessarily rooted in a particular place, engage the broader world of Christianity? And can this be done in a way that preserves the value of their particular expression without elevating it above others? Walls's indigenous and pilgrim principles

56. Walls, *Missionary Movement in Christian History*, 30.

57. Walls, *Missionary Movement in Christian History*, 54.

58. Walls, *Crossing Cultural Frontiers*, 56.

59. Walls, *Missionary Movement in Christian History*, xvi.

60. Walls, *Missionary Movement in Christian History*, xvi.

help clarify several perspectival commitments that should be recognized before practicing territoriality. The answer to this "how" question is primarily cognitive, shaped by the notions Christians must acknowledge and the implications that follow.

First, one must recognize that their own expression of Christianity is only one among many. Christians can meaningfully speak of "a church across the world, across the continents, across cultures, [and] across languages."[61] The geography of Christianity is no longer, if it ever was, cloistered in one container of religious territoriality, but spread out across the world. "The spatial dimension of the body of Christ" Walls observes, has returned to a configuration more akin to that of the earliest centuries.[62]

Though this may seem self-evident, there are reasons it bears repeating. Sanneh reminds readers that mental maps (i.e., perspectives), often lag behind changing reality. It is for this reason he claims, "the case today for an alteration in our mental maps . . . has never been more urgent and necessary."[63] Too easily, the near-sighted Christian focuses only on their particular place, holding at best a vague or blurry sense of the wider world without fully grappling with its opportunities or implications. What is needed, Walls argues, is "a world Christian consciousness" that perceives contemporaneous Christian expressions with growing clarity and cohesion.[64]

Second, one must recognize that their particular expression of Christianity should not be elevated to the status of norm-setting Christianity. If one can develop "a world Christian consciousness," can they also engage that world without the temptation to dominate, subdue, or chart it? For some, having a world Christian consciousness can lead to a desire for universal cohesion by demanding conformity of the other particular expressions. Can Christians instead place themselves in the mutual context of world Christianity, rather than above it? More specifically, can Western Christians, as Walls writes, "find a joyful place in a predominately non-Western church."[65]

Some Christian communities regard themselves as defenders of orthodoxy without fully recognizing how their own particular expression has

61. Walls, *Crossing Cultural Frontiers*, 16.

62. Walls, *The Cross-Cultural Process in Christian History*, 75.

63. Sanneh, *Disciples of All Nations*, 96.

64. Walls, *Crossing Cultural Frontiers*, 16.

65. Walls, *The Missionary Movement in Christian History*, 196.

become the standard by which others are judged. In response, some local expressions of the faith may resist the demand for conformity, while others may surrender, accepting their submission as the cost of global participation. Such compliance upholds the elevated status of the domineering particular and smoothers indigeneity.

If Christians take Christ's headship over the church seriously, there is no need for any particular expression to dominate. In the opening chapters of Revelation, Jesus is portrayed as actively involved in disciplining the various churches through the Holy Spirit (Rev 1–3). The image that emerges is not of a passive spectator, but of a present and active Lord. As Walls explains, "the New Testament is clear that God can dispense even with self-important Christian communities, and that God depends on no single instrument."[66] The misplaced ambition to create unified cohesion through ever increasing hierarchical centralization should find its satisfaction in the knowledge that the head of the church is Christ (Col 1:18). The universal vision of God's salvific work should motivate one's worship and invite participation, but not their attempts at control.

Within the context of mission activity, it is worth asking whether traces of a similar norm-setting Christianity remain, where one particular group formulates universal plans and proclamations. A sense of ownership is evident in the desire to complete the "unfinished task," however this might be articulated today. The intentions may be laudable, yet one must still question whether any single expression of Christianity should devise global evangelistic strategies in isolation. Are missiologists and mission practitioners still sitting in rooms with maps, far from the places of impact, in ways uncomfortably reminiscent of how the dividing line of North and South Korea was drawn? Before the map is unrolled and a new territoriality is established, Christians who are geographically and culturally closer to the context should be consulted, and their perspectives and their wisdom incorporated. Better still, they should be invited to take the lead.

Third, one must recognize the value of other expressions of Christianity as mutual partners, belonging together, offering insight, and sharing in the experience of Christian fragility. As Walls describes, the story of Christian expansion is not one of unceasing gains. Not so one could "mark up gains on the map of the world, or chart progress towards the final goal."[67] There is a fragility and impermanence inherent in a boundless faith.

66. Walls, *The Cross-Cultural Process in Christian History*, 13.

67. Walls, *The Cross-Cultural Process in Christian History*, 26.

Drawing on Heb 13:14, Walls frequently returns to the reminder that, "for here we do not have an enduring city, but we are looking for the city that is to come."[68]

There is no Christian territory that can claim to be permanently Christian, no place where one could truly say, "Christians have always lived here and always will." If such a place exists, it is the exception rather than the rule. No single community of Christianity can claim permanence, "until the new Jerusalem comes down out of heaven at the last day."[69] No matter how deeply rooted Christianity may be in a location, Christians are waiting for something more permanent, more perfect.

That is the experience of Christians in some places, yet Christianity as a whole has never ceased. Where the faith may fade from significance in one place, it becomes vibrantly rooted in another. Experiencing the fragility of Christianity can be discouraging, but its flourishing elsewhere can serve as a source of reassurance and encouragement. How much richer the witness of the church would be if those who experience the fragility of faith could find belonging and strength in partnership with those in places where Christianity is thriving.

There is great opportunity for edification for those who have ears to hear. As Walls explains regarding Scripture, "the crowning excitement which our own era of Church history has over all others, is the possibility that we may be able to read them together." He continues, "never before . . . has there been so much potentiality for mutual enrichment and self-criticism, as God causes yet more light and truth to break forth from his word."[70] Reading Scripture together offers the chance to imagine viable alternatives to one's own perspective and to resist the impulse to draw "the teeth of the Scriptures so that they will not bite us."[71]

However, this kind of mutual engagement requires more than the narrow frame of a typical short-term mission trip. The act of going should not be abandoned. Allowing a place, with all its various social, mental, and physical influences, to shape one's life can have profound value. Yet it requires the posture of a learner, one who is curious, attentive, and unwavering in their conviction of the dignity of those who differ from themselves.

68. Walls, *Missionary Movement in Christian History*, 8, 25; Walls, *Cross-Cultural Process in Christian History*, 30; Walls, *Crossing Cultural Frontiers*, 74.

69. Walls, *Crossing Cultural Frontiers*, 74.

70. Walls, *The Missionary Movement in Christian History*, 15.

71. Walls, *The Missionary Movement in Christian History*, 15.

As Walls states, "instruments are now needed for *two*-way traffic: for sharing and receiving"[72] This moment, like many throughout Christian history, may indeed call for new territorial arrangements to achieve this goal.

CONCLUDING STATEMENT

Christendom has ended, yet territoriality has a much longer trajectory. It existed prior to Christendom and continues to shape Christian life today. Throughout history, Christians have used territoriality to organize groups of Christians. It should not be surprising that they still do so, even if those collectives take a different shape from the past. Territorial thinking has likewise guided the pursuit of mission, framing goals and shaping strategies. Likewise, it is not surprising when they continue to imagine mission goals in territorial ways and pursue those goals with the use of territoriality. Whether it is a drive toward the interior or an emphasis on the city; a line of mission stations or a targeted pointillist strategy, a comity agreement or layers of *empty space* waiting for investment, territoriality shifts to achieve goals and respond to changing circumstances. Christians and missiologists alike should expect its persistence and draw upon the insights of geography to understand and engage their world more faithfully.

72. Walls, *Missionary Movement in Christian History*, 239.

Bibliography

Agnew, John, Anssi Paasi, and Robert David Sack. "Classics in Human Geography Revisited." *Progress in Human Geography* 24.1 (2000) 91–99.

Allen, Roland. *Roland Allen's The Ministry of Expansion*. Edited by J. D. Payne. Pasadena, CA: William Carey Library, 2017.

Altman, Irwin, and William Haythorn. "The Ecology of Isolated Groups." *Behavioral Science* 12 (1967) 169–82.

American Board of Commissioners for Foreign Missions. *Report of the American Board of Commissioners for Foreign Missions*. Boston: The Board, 1812–1861. 23rd–27th (1832–1836).

Report of the Ecumenical Conference on Foreign Missions. 2 vols. London and New York: Religious Tract Society and American Tract Society, 1900.

Bagge, Sverre. "The Making of a Missionary King: The Medieval Accounts of Olaf Tryggvason and the Conversion of Norway." *Journal of English and Germanic Philology* 105.4 (2006) 473–513.

Banks, Robert J. *Paul's Idea of Community: Spirit and Culture in Early House Churches*. Grand Rapids: Baker Academic, 2020.

Bartlotti, Leonard N. "On Strategies of Closure: Refining Our Strategies for 'Engaging' All Peoples." *International Journal of Frontier Missiology* 27.3 (2010) 133–38.

Bauckham, Richard. *Bible and Mission: Christian Witness in a Postmodern World*. Grand Rapids: Baker Academic, 2003.

Beaver, Robert Pierce. *Ecumenical Beginnings in Protestant World Mission: A History of Comity*. London: Nelson, 1962.

Benson, John S. *Missionary Families Find a Sense of Place and Identity: Two Generations on Two Continents*. Lanham, MD: Lexington, 2015.

Berend, Nora. *At the Gate of Christendom: Jews, Muslims, and "Pagans" in Medieval Hungary, c. 1000–c. 1300*. Cambridge: Cambridge University Press, 2001.

Berger, Peter L. *The Sacred Canopy: Elements of a Sociological Theory of Religion*. New York, NY: Open Road Media, 1967.

Bernabé Ubieta, Carmen. "'Neither *Xenoi* nor *Paroikoi, Sympolitai* and *Oikeioi tou Theou*' (Eph 2:19): Pauline Christian Communities: Defining a New Territoriality." In *Social Scientific Models for Interpreting the Bible: Essays by the Context Group in Honor of Bruce J. Malina*, edited by John J. Pilch, 260–80. Biblical Interpretation Series 53. Leiden: Brill, 2001.

Black, Eric. "The Korean Crisis, 'The Sirens of Titan' and Col. Bonesteel's Line on a Map." *MinnPost*, November 24, 2010. https://www.minnpost.com/eric-black-ink/2010/11/korea-crisis-sirens-titan-and-col-bonesteels-line-map.

Bolger, Ryan K., ed. *The Gospel After Christendom: New Voices, New Cultures, New Expressions.* Grand Rapids: Baker Academic, 2012.

Bowden, Henry Warner. "Human Territoriality: Its Theory and History." *Church History* 56.4 (1987) 557.

Braudel, Fernand. *The Mediterranean and the Mediterranean World in the Age of Philip II.* London: Collins, 1972.

Brown, Peter. *The Rise of Western Christendom: Triumph and Diversity, AD 200–1000.* Cambridge, MA: Blackwell, 2013.

Burke, Peter. *Cultural Hybridity.* Cambridge, UK: Wiley, 2009.

Burton, John Wear, and R. Kilgour. *Missionary Survey of the Pacific Islands.* London: World Dominion, 1930.

Byun, Chang-Uk. "The Influence of Roman Catholic Mission on Comity Agreements: Development of Territorial Division in Christian Mission History." *Korean Presbyterian Journal of Theology* 52.4 (2020) 159–86.

Calvin, John. *Tracts and Treatises of John Calvin.* 3 vols. 1844. Reprint, Eugene, OR: Wipf & Stock, 2002.

Casey, Edward S. "Between Geography and Philosophy: What Does It Mean to Be in the Place-World?" *Annals of the Association of American Geographers* 91.4 (2001) 683–93.

Carroll, Warren Hasty. *The Founding of Christendom.* Front Royal, VA: Christendom College, 1985.

"Charles H. Bonesteel 3d, Army General Who Lead U.N. Command in Korea." *New York Times*, October 14, 1977. https://www.nytimes.com/1977/10/14/archives/charles-h-bonesteel-3d-army-general-who-lead-un-command-in-korea.html

Clark, John, and Marcus Peter Johnson. *The Incarnation of God: The Mystery of the Gospel as the Foundation of Evangelical Theology.* Wheaton, IL: Crossway, 2015.

Decret, François. *Early Christianity in North Africa.* Cambridge, UK: Lutterworth, 2009.

Derrick, Matthew. "Containing the Umma?: Islam and the Territorial Question." *Interdisciplinary Journal of Research on Religion* 9 (2013) 1–30.

de Korte, Hannah, and David Onnekink. "Maps Matter: The 10/40 Window and Missionary Geography." *Exchange* 49 (2020) 110–44.

DeRogatis, Amy. *Moral Geography: Maps, Missionaries, and the American Frontier.* New York: Columbia University Press, 2003.

Dicken, Peter. "Geographers and Globalization: (Yet) Another Missed Boat?" *Transactions of the Institute of British Geographers* 29.1 (2004) 5–26.

Dreher, Rod. *The Benedict Option: A Strategy for Christians in a Post-Christian Nation.* New York: Sentinel, 2017.

El-Awaisi, Abd al-Fattah M. *Introducing Islamic Jerusalem.* Dundee, UK: Al-Maktoum Institute, 2005.

Elden, Stuart. *The Birth of Territory.* Chicago: University of Chicago Press, 2013.

Elliott-Binns, L. E. *The Beginnings of Western Christendom.* 1948. Reprint, Eugene, OR: Wipf & Stock, 2019.

Elvin, Mark. "A Working Definition of 'Modernity'?" *Past & Present* 113 (1986) 209–13.

Fiedler, Klaus. *The Story of Faith Missions.* Oxford: Regnum International, 1994.

Foucault, Michel. *Power/Knowledge: Selected Interviews and Other Writings, 1972–1977.* New York: Pantheon, 1980.

Frost, Robert. *North of Boston.* New York: Holt, 1914.

Fry, Michael. "National Geographic, Korea, and the 38th Parallel." *National Geographic,* August 4, 2013. https://www.nationalgeographic.com/news/2013/8/130805-korean-war-dmz-armistice-38-parallel-geography.

Garrett, John. "The Conflict between the London Missionary Society and the Wesleyan Methodists in 19th Century Samoa." *Journal of Pacific History* 9 (1974) 65–80.

Geschiere, Peter. *The Perils of Belonging: Autochthony, Citizenship, and Exclusion in Africa and Europe.* Chicago: University of Chicago Press, 2009.

Glick, Thomas F. "In Search of Geography." *Isis* 74.1 (1983) 92–97.

Greenlee, David. Review of *Missionary Families Find a Sense of Place and Identity: Two Generations on Two Continents,* by John S. Benson. *Mission Studies* 34.2 (2017) 271–72.

Greenslade, S. L. "The Unit of Pastoral Care in the Early Church." In *Studies in Church History,* Vol. 2: *Papers Read at the Second Winter and Summer Meetings of the Ecclesiastical History Society,* edited by G. J. Cuming, 102–18. Cambridge: Cambridge University Press, 1965.

Hanciles, Jehu. *Beyond Christendom: Globalization, African Migration, and the Transformation of the West.* Maryknoll, NY: Orbis, 2008.

Hefele, Karl Joseph von. *A History of the Christian Councils, from the Original Documents.* 2nd ed., rev. Edinburgh: T. & T. Clark, 1872.

Held, David, Jonathan Perraton, Anthony G. McGrew, and David Goldblatt. *Global Transformations: Politics, Economics and Culture.* Stanford: Stanford University Press, 1999.

Hill, Bradley N. "Rethinking Comity: Conflict or Confluence Along the Ubangi–Mongala Border?" *Missiology: An International Review* 13.2 (1985).

"History and Facts." *California Southern Baptist Convention.* Accessed December 13, 2020. http://csbc.com/about/history-and-facts.

Hof, Elenora. "Re-imagining World Christianity: Challenging Territorial Essentialism." *Journal of the European Society of Women in Theological Research* 22 (2014) 173–86.

Hovland, Ingie. *Mission Station Christianity: Norwegian Missionaries in Colonial Natal and Zululand, Southern Africa 1850–1890.* Studies in Christian Mission 44. Leiden: Brill, 2013.

Immerwahr, Daniel. *How to Hide an Empire: A History of the Greater United States.* New York: Farrar, Straus & Giroux, 2019.

Inge, John. *A Christian Theology of Place.* 2003. Reprint, New York: Routledge, 2016.

Jenkins, Philip. *The Next Christendom: The Coming of Global Christianity.* Oxford: Oxford University Press, 2007.

Johnson, Dominic D. P., and Monica Duffy Toft. "Grounds for War: The Evolution of Territorial Conflict." *International Security* 38.3 (2013) 7–38.

Johnson, Hildegard Binder. "The Location of Christian Missions in Africa." *Geographical Review* 57.2 (1967) 168–202.

Jones, Reece. "Whose Homeland? Territoriality and Religious Nationalism in Pre-Partition Bengal." *South Asia Research* 26.2 (2006) 115–31.

"Frontier Peoples." Joshua Project, 2025. https://joshuaproject.net/frontier/1.

Kahler, Miles. "Territoriality and Conflict in an Era of Globalization." In *Territoriality and Conflict in an Era of Globalization*, edited by Miles Kahler and Barbara F. Walter, 1–24. Cambridge: Cambridge University Press, 2006.

Kenzer, Martin S. "Geographical Reviews: *Homo Geographicus* by Robert Sack." *Geographical Review* 88.1 (1998) 166.

Klinghoffer, Arthur Jay. *The Power of Projections: How Maps Reflect Global Politics and History*. Westport, CT: Praeger, 2006.

Koelsch, William A. "Wallace Atwood's 'Great Geographical Institute.'" *Annals of the Association of American Geographers* 70.4 (1980) 567–82.

Kraidy, Marwan M. *Hybridity, or the Cultural Logic of Globalization*. London: Pearson Education, 2005.

Krapf, Johann Ludwig. *Travels, Researches, and Missionary Labors, During an Eighteen Years' Residence in Eastern Africa*. London: Trübner, 1860.

Kreider, Alan. *The Change of Conversion and the Origin of Christendom*. Christian Mission and Modern Culture. 1999. Reprint, Eugene, OR: Wipf & Stock, 2007.

Kunstler, James Howard. *The Geography of Nowhere*. New York: Free Press, 1993.

Landon, Edward Henry. *A Manual of Councils of the Holy Catholick Church: Comprising the Substance of the Most Remarkable and Important Canons Alphabetically Arranged*. London: Rivington, 1846.

Langmead, Ross. "What Is Missiology?" *Missiology* 42.1 (2014) 67–79.

Lechner, Silviya. "Sovereignty and Territoriality: An Essay in Medieval Political Theory." Paper presented at the SGIR Pan-European Conference on International Relations, Turin, September 12–15, 2007.

Lee, Peter, and James Sung-Hwan Park. "Beyond People Group Thinking: A Critical Reevaluation of Unreached People Groups." *Missiology* 46.3 (2018) 212–25.

Lefebvre, Henri. *The Production of Space*. Translated by Donald Nicholson-Smith. Democracy and Urban Landscapes. Oxford: Blackwell, 1991.

Lehmann, Hartmut. "The Mobilization of God's Pious Children in the Era of the French Revolution and Beyond." *Pietismus und Neuzeit* 34 (2008) 189–98.

Leithart, Peter J. *Defending Constantine: The Twilight of an Empire and the Dawn of Christendom*. Downers Grove, IL: IVP Academic, 2010.

Lewis, Martin W., and Kären Wigen. *The Myth of Continents: A Critique of Metageography*. Berkeley: University of California Press, 1997.

Light, Paul. *Thickening Government: Federal Hierarchy and the Diffusion of Accountability*. Washington, DC: Brookings Institution, 2011.

L'Huillier, Peter. *The Church of the Ancient Councils: The Disciplinary Work of the First Four Ecumenical Councils*. New York: St. Vladimir's Seminary, 1926.

Luther, Martin. *Martin Luther's 95 Theses: With the Pertinent Documents from the History of the Reformation*. Edited by Kurt Aland. St. Louis, MO: Concordia, 2004.

Lyons, Terrence. "Diasporas and Homeland Conflict." In *Territoriality and Conflict in an Era of Globalization*, edited by Miles Kahler and Barbara F. Walter, 111–29. Cambridge: Cambridge University Press, 2006.

Magda, Ksenija. *Paul's Territoriality and Mission Strategy: Searching for the Geographical Awareness Paradigm Behind Romans*. Wissenschaftliche Untersuchungen zum Neuen Testament 2/266. Tübingen: Mohr Siebeck, 2009.

Malina, Bruce J. "'Apocalyptic' and Territoriality." In *Early Christianity in Context: Monuments and Documents*, 369–80. Jerusalem: Franciscan Printing, 1993.

McClay, Wilfred M. "Introduction." In *Why Place Matters: Geography, Identity, and Civic Life in Modern America*, edited by Wilfred M. McClay and Ted V. McAllister. New York: Encounter, 2014.

McGavran, Donald A. *Understanding Church Growth*. Grand Rapids: Eerdmans, 1970.

Merton, Robert King. *Social Theory and Social Structure*. Glencoe, IL: Free Press, 1949.

Michels, Robert. *Political Parties*. Translated by Eden and Cedar Paul. Glencoe, IL: Free Press, 1968.

Millett, Benignus. "Dioceses in Ireland Up to the 15th Century." *Seanchas Ardmhacha: Journal of the Armagh Diocesan Historical Society* 12.1 (1986) 1–42.

Morgan, Kevin. "The Exaggerated Death of Geography: Learning, Proximity and Territorial Innovation Systems." *Journal of Economic Geography* 4 (2004) 3–21.

Muggeridge, Malcolm. *The End of Christendom*. Grand Rapids: Eerdmans, 1980.

Nagy, Dorottya. "Where Is China in World Christianity?" *Diversities* 12.1 (2010) 70–83.

Nettles, Tom J. "Southern Baptists: Regional to National Transition." *Baptist History and Heritage* 16.1 (1981) 13–23.

Newbigin, Lesslie. *Foolishness to the Greeks: The Gospel and Western Culture*. Grand Rapids: Eerdmans, 1986.

Oberdorfer, Don, and Robert Carlin. *The Two Koreas: A Contemporary History*. New York: Basic Books, 2013.

O'Brien, Richard. *Global Financial Integration: The End of Geography*. London: Pinter, 1992.

Oden, Thomas C. *Early Libyan Christianity: Uncovering a North African Tradition*. Downers Grove, IL: InterVarsity, 2011.

O'Donovan, Oliver. "The Loss of a Sense of Place." *Irish Theological Quarterly* 55.1 (1989) 39–58.

Park, James Sung-Hwan. "Chosen to Fulfill the Great Commission? Biblical and Theological Reflections on the Back to Jerusalem Vision of Chinese Churches." *Missiology: An International Review* 43.2 (2015) 163–74.

Penrose, Jan. "Nations, States and Homelands: Territory and Territoriality in Nationalist Thought." *Nations and Nationalism* 8 (2002) 277–97.

Percival, Henry. *The Seven Ecumenical Councils of the Undivided Church: Their Canons and Dogmatic Decrees, Together with the Canons of All the Local Synods Which Have Received Ecumenical Acceptance*. New York: Scribner, Parker, 1900.

Peters, George W. *A Biblical Theology of Missions*. Chicago: Moody, 1984.

Pirenne, Henri. *Mohammed and Charlemagne*. New York: Taylor & Francis, 1939.

Pirouet, M. Louise. "The Legacy of Johann Ludwig Krapf." *International Bulletin of Missionary Research* 23.2 (1999) 69–74.

Prickett, Barbara B. Island Base. *A History of the Methodist Church in the Gambia, 1821–1969*. Bo, Sierra Leone: Bunumbu, 1971.

Radford, David. *Religious Identity and Social Change: Explaining Christian Conversion in a Muslim World*. London: Taylor & Francis, 2015.

Raffestin, Claude. "Space, Territory, and Territoriality." *Environment and Planning D: Society and Space* 30.1 (2012) 121–41.

Rankin, William. *After the Map: Cartography, Navigation, and the Transformation of Territory in the Twentieth Century*. Chicago: University of Chicago Press, 2016.

Reynolds, Susan. "Human Territoriality." Review of *Human Territoriality*, by Robert Sack. *American Historical Review* 94.1 (1989) 103.

Rip, Michael Russell, and James M. Hasik. *The Precision Revolution: GPS and the Future of Aerial Warfare*. Annapolis, MD: Naval Institute, 2002.

Robert, Dana L. *Occupy Until I Come: A. T. Pierson and the Evangelization of the World*. Grand Rapids: Eerdmans, 2003.

Rosenau, James N. *Along the Domestic-Foreign Frontier: Exploring Governance in a Turbulent World*. Cambridge: Cambridge University Press, 1997.

Roudometof, Victor. "Greek Orthodoxy, Territoriality, and Globality: Religious Responses and Institutional Disputes." *Sociology of Religion* 69.1 (2008) 67–91.

Ruggie, John Gerard. "Territoriality and Beyond: Problematizing Modernity in International Relations." *International Organization* 47.1 (1993) 139.

Rusk, Dean. *As I Saw It: A Secretary of State's Memoirs*. London: Tauris, 1991.

Rynkiewich, Michael A. "Corporate Metaphors and Strategic Thinking: 'The 10/40 Window' in the American Evangelical Worldview." *Missiology: An International Review* 35.2 (2007).

Sack, Robert. *Human Territoriality: Its Theory and History*. Cambridge Studies in Historical Geography 7. Cambridge: Cambridge University Press, 1986.

———. *Homo Geographicus: A Framework for Action, Awareness, and Moral Concern*. Baltimore: Johns Hopkins University Press, 1997.

Sacks, Benjamin. "What Happened to the American Geography Department?" *Geography Directions*, April 8, 2015. https://blog.geographydirections.com/2015/04/08/what-happened-to-the-american-geography-department/

Sanneh, Lamin O. *Abolitionists Abroad: American Blacks and the Making of Modern West Africa*. Cambridge: Harvard University Press, 2001.

———. *Disciples of All Nations: Pillars of World Christianity*. Oxford: Oxford University Press, 2008.

———. *Encountering the West: Christianity and the Global Cultural Process*. Maryknoll, NY: Orbis, 1993.

———. *Summoned from the Margin: Homecoming of an African*. Grand Rapids: Eerdmans, 2012.

Schlienz, Christoph Friedrich. *The Pilgrim Missionary Institution of St. Chrischona, near Basle, in Switzerland*. London: Shaw, 1850.

Schnabel, James F. *United States Army in the Korean War: Policy and Direction—The First Year*. Washington, DC: Center of Military History, United States Army, 1972.

Schreiter, Robert J. *The New Catholicity: Theology between the Global and the Local*. Maryknoll, NY: Orbis, 1997.

Scott, James M. *Paul and the Nations: The Old Testament and Jewish Background of Paul's Mission to the Nations with Special Reference to the Destination of Galatians*. Wissenschaftliche Untersuchungen zum Neuen Testament 84. Tübingen: Mohr Siebeck, 1995.

Shenk, Wilbert R. "Rufus Anderson and Henry Venn: A Special Relationship?" *International Bulletin of Missionary Research* 5.4 (1981) 168–72.

———. *Henry Venn: Missionary Statesman*. 1983. Reprint, Eugene, OR: Wipf & Stock, 1983.

———. "The Contribution of Henry Venn to Mission Thought." *Anvil* 2.1 (1985) 25–42.

Shilhav, Yosseph. "Jewish Territoriality Between Land and State." *National Identities* 9.1 (2007) 1–25.

Shults, F. LeRon. *Reforming Theological Anthropology: After the Philosophical Turn to Relationality*. Grand Rapids: Eerdmans, 2003.

Smietana, Bob. "High-Tech Circuit Riders: Satellite Churches Are Discovering a New Way to Grow the Body of Christ." *Christianity Today* 49.9 (2005) 60–63.

Smith, David M. "Book Review Article: *Homo Geographicus* by Robert Sack." *Progress in Human Geography* 22.4 (1998) 607–10.

Smith, David. *Mission After Christendom*. London: Darton, Longman & Todd, 2003.

Smith, Neil. "Academic War over the Field of Geography: The Elimination of Geography at Harvard, 1947–1951." *Annals of the Association of American Geographers* 77.2 (1987) 155–72.

Smythe, John. *The Works of John Smythe*. Edited by W. Whitley. Cambridge: Cambridge University Press, 1915.

Soja, Edward W. *Postmodern Geographies: The Reassertion of Space in Critical Social Theory*. London: Verso, 2010.

Soule, Joshua. *A Collection of Hymns for Public, Social, and Domestic Worship*. New York: John Early, 1847.

Spring, Joseph. "Geographic vs. Geographical." *GeoBuzz*, January 21, 2010. https://geobuzz.wordpress.com/2010/01/21/geographic-vs-geographical.

Stanley, Brian. "Defining the Boundaries of Christendom: The Two Worlds of the World Missionary Conference, 1910." *International Bulletin of Missionary Research* 30.4 (2006) 171–76.

Swatos, William H., Jr. "Beyond Denominationalism: Community and Culture in American Religion." *Journal for the Scientific Study of Religion* 20.3 (1981) 217–27.

Terry, John Mark, and Robert L. Gallagher. *Encountering the History of Missions: From the Early Church to Today*. Grand Rapids: Baker Academic, 2017.

Tiedemann, R. G. "Comity Agreements and Sheep Stealers: The Elusive Search for Christian Unity among Protestants in China." *International Bulletin of Missionary Research* 36.1 (2012) 3–8.

Trivedi, Bijal P. "Survey Reveals Geographic Illiteracy." *National Geographic*, November 20, 2002. https://www.nationalgeographic.com/news/2002/11/geography-survey-illiteracy.

Tuan, Yi-Fu. "Discrepancies Between Environmental Attitude and Behavior: Examples from Europe and China." *Canadian Geographer* 12 (1968) 176–91.

Turner, Frederick Jackson. *The Significance of the Frontier in American History*. New York: Ungar, 1963.

Walls, Andrew F. *Crossing Cultural Frontiers: Studies in the History of World Christianity*. Maryknoll, NY: Orbis, 2017.

———. *The Cross-Cultural Process in Christian History: Studies in the Transmission and Appropriation of Faith*. Maryknoll, NY: Orbis, 2002.

———. *The Missionary Movement in Christian History: Studies in the Transmission of Faith*. Maryknoll, NY: Orbis, 1996.

———. "The Significance of Christianity in Africa." Paper presented at St. Colm's Education Centre and College, 1989.

———. "Ecumenical Missiology in Anabaptist Perspective." *Mission Focus: Annual Review* 13 (2005).

Walker, Sheila S. *Religious Revolution in the Ivory Coast: The Prophet Harris and the Harrist Church*. Studies in Religion. Chapel Hill: University of North Carolina Press, 1983.

Weber, Max. *The Theory of Social and Economic Organization*. New York: Free Press, 1947.

Wesley, John. *Works: Journal*. London: Waugh & Mason, 1835.

Yntema, Hessel E. "The Comity Doctrine." *Michigan Law Review* 65.1 (1966) 9–32.

Yoder, John H. "Is There Such a Thing as Being Ready for Another Millennium?" In *The Future of Theology: Essays in Honor of Jürgen Moltmann*, edited by Miroslav Volf, Carmen Krieg, and Thomas Kucharz, 63–72. Grand Rapids: Eerdmans, 1996.